CASES IN EUROPEAN HUMAN RESOURCE MANAGEMENT

Supported by separate analyses and notes for teachers, this fully revised and updated casebook provides a unique resource for both teachers and students on all aspects of human resource management. The cases selected help to highlight 'best practice' in a number of areas, such as appraisal and assessment, and also provide guidance, at a more strategic level, in organizational restructuring and competitive management.

Compiled by two leading authorities in human resource management, the cases reflect consultancy, research and teaching experience across a breadth of different European organizations and industries. The casebook is an ideal teaching vehicle for both MBA students and undergraduate students of management, for those taking Institute of Personnel Management courses, and for managers on short courses.

Andrew Kakabadse is Professor of Management Development at the Cranfield School of Management. He has extensive experience as a consultant, has lectured all over the world, and has published thirteen books and over sixty articles, including the bestselling *Politics of Management, Working in Organizations* and *The Wealth Creators*.

Shaun Tyson is Professor of Human Resource Management, Dean of Faculty of Management and Director of the Human Resource Research Centre at Cranfield School of Management. He has published ten books and over fifty articles and conference papers.

CASES IN EUROPEAN HUMAN RESOURCE MANAGEMENT

Second edition

Edited by Andrew Kakabadse and Shaun Tyson

London and New York

First published in 1987 by William Heinemann Ltd

This edition first published in 1994
by Routledge

11 New Fetter Lane, London EC4P 4EE

Simultaneously published in the USA and Canada
by Routledge
29 West 35th Street, New York, NY 10001

© 1994 Andrew Kakabadse and Shaun Tyson

Typeset in Garamond by J&L Composition Ltd, Filey, North Yorkshire
Printed and bound in Great Britain by
Mackays of Chatham PLC, Chatham, Kent

British Library Cataloguing in Publication Data

A catalogue record for this book is available from the British Library

ISBN 0–415–07414–2

Library of Congress Cataloging in Publication Data
Cases in European human resource management/edited by Andrew Kakabadse and
Shaun Tyson. – 2nd ed.
p. cm.
Rev. ed. of: Cases in human resource management. 1987.
ISBN 0–415–07414–2
1. Personnel management – Case studies.   2. Personnel management–Europe –
Case studies.   I. Kakabadse, Andrew.   II. Tyson, S. (Shaun)   III. Cases in
human resource management.
HF5549 C298 1994
658.3 – dc20
93–18903
CIP

In memory of Patricia Frances Kakabadse, loving wife and mother

CONTENTS

CONTENTS

CONTENTS

FIGURES

FIGURES

TABLES

CONTRIBUTORS

Siobhan Alderson, Research Officer, Cranfield SOM.

John Bank, Lecturer in Industrial Relations, Cranfield SOM.

John Beresford, Senior Lecturer, Civil Service College.

Solveg Bruce-Stupples, Human Resource Manager, Kabi Pharmacia Ltd.

Mairi Bryce, Research Officer, Cranfield SOM.

Paul Dainty, Associate Professor of Management, University of Melbourne, Australia.

Noeleen Doherty, Senior Research Officer, Cranfield SOM.

Vincent Dooley, Chief Training and Development Manager, Bank of Ireland.

Jacqueline Drake, Lecturer in Organizational Behaviour, Cranfield SOM.

Glenys Emam, Senior Adviser of Human Resources, Clerical Medical Investment Group.

Andrew Kakabadse, Professor of Management Development, Cranfield SOM.

Ron Ludlow, Senior Lecturer in Organizational Behaviour, Cranfield SOM.

Peter Norris, Lecturer in Management Development, Cranfield SOM.

Fergus Panton, Management Consultant.

Philippe Poirson, Professeur and Directeur des Resources Humaines, Group ESC Lyon.

Paul Teague, Senior Lecturer in Applied Economics, University of Ulster.

Shaun Tyson, Professor of Human Resource Management, Cranfield SOM.

Paul Willman, Professor of Organizational Behaviour, London Business School.

ACKNOWLEDGEMENTS

We would like to acknowledge the contribution made by the hundreds of managers who have helped to shape these cases by their comments, when the cases have been taught in class. We are grateful for the help of Tony Kippenberger and Jean Bartlett in writing the Grayle Engineering case. We would also like to thank the people depicted here, or whose situations are described. Without them we can truly say there would not have been a book.

The Epicurus Group, Archon Engineering and Thomas Nestor cases are quoted in *Evaluating the Personnel Function* by S. Tyson and A. Fell, published by Hutchinson, 1986. We are grateful for permission to publish them here. Finally, we would like to thank Judith Gray, Ann Davies, Dorothy Rogers and Mairi Bryce for their patience and typing skills.

Shaun Tyson
Andrew Kakabadse

INTRODUCTION

Shaun Tyson

In this book are collected twenty-eight case studies which are designed to expand the reader's knowledge of managing people in organizations. The term 'human resource management' is intended to convey the value of managing people as other scarce resources are managed, so that care and attention may be given to the acquisition, utilization, motivation and development of employees. Managers now recognize how finite the quantities of energy, enthusiasm, and creativity are among their employees, and appreciate how the achievement of organizational objectives is dependent on their employees' abilities. When technology and financial resources are evenly matched between competing organizations the advantage rests with the organization whose employees possess superior experience, knowledge and skill. Hence success or failure in business turns on how human resources are managed. Our chief reason for compiling these case studies was our belief in the importance of this managerial task.

THE CASE FOR CASES

The case study or case history is an ideal vehicle for extending our understanding of organizational behaviour. From the contingency theory of organizations we know that behaviour in organizations is contingent upon a range of factors such as the organization's history, its markets, its preferred management style, the industrial relations traditions which prevail and the many cultural and technological influences which are specific to that particular organization, at that period of time. Case studies may be used to expose the complexities of behaviour, and to provide a context for the study of social action.

Case studies encapsulate experiences, they allow for the singular circumstance, and grant readers the opportunity to select ideas and techniques, and to compare these with their own experience. Although there are different styles of learning, whatever the preferred approach, most managers place a premium on experience in their own development. This seems to be because when we are able to see, feel, and hear, we understand

1

Concrete
experience

Observation and
reflection

Testing new
behaviours

Formation
of concepts
and
generalization

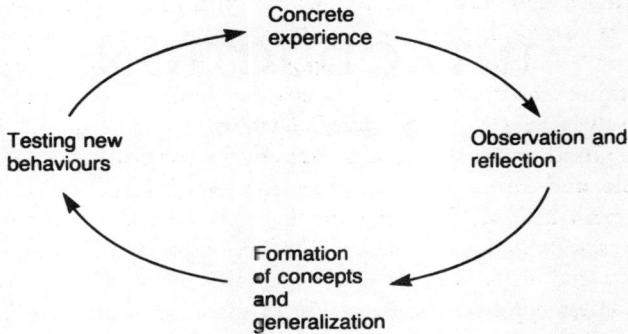

Figure I.1 Kolb's learning cycle

for ourselves. The way learning occurs through experience is described by Kolb.

Stories may be seen as one form of experiential learning, since they encourage us to see in our everyday experience of the world a deeper reality with which we may come into touch, and through our reflection on the message behind the story, we come to learn more about ourselves.

Figure I.1 demonstrates the role of experience in learning, where we generalize from our experience, and experiment with new ideas, as a consequence of what we have learned. The feedback we receive from significant others tells us whether the experimental behaviour was successful, so we may then modify our future behaviours, taking this into account. We may conclude that some generalization from our experience seems to be necessary in order to learn.

The crucial distinction between the case study and other methods is that with the case study method the reader draws specific ideas, or understandings, from a particular context which can then be compared with broader theoretical generalizations. This follows the pattern of our normal method of learning by moving from the particular experience to the broader generalization. Case studies may engage the consciousness of the reader at both the emotional and the intellectual level. In the human resources field an appeal to feelings is entirely appropriate, since the reader's identification with the characters or situations adds an emotional charge to the comparison between the written word and personal experience. This gives a powerful impetus to the learning process: it heightens an awareness of the issues as they were faced by the characters in the case study and from this

2

empathetic experience comes a personal commitment to the acquisition of new learning.

This is not a new device for imparting wisdom and understanding. The case study is a story, and stories have always been used as a way of teaching. Parables are common in most religions, and we know from the New Testament that Christ used stories extensively in his teaching to reveal truths about ourselves. Stories, like *Aesop's Fables* or folk tales usually have a moral to impart. Good and evil, death and renewal are represented symbolically, for example, and the power stories exercise over our minds has even led to the conclusion by Carl Jung that there are universal archetypes to which our subconscious minds respond when these basic human stories are told. Jung argues that myths and fairytales contain motifs which are found in all cultures. 'These typical images and associations are what I call archetypal ideas. The more vivid they are, the more they will be coloured by particularly strong feeling tones. They impress, influence and fascinate us.'

Following these notions, Eric Berne saw stories and fairytales forming an important part of a child's understanding of the world, and hence conditioning its destiny. Whether we accept these psychoanalytic arguments, or the religious view of stories as purveyors of truth about the self, found for example in the insistence within Zen that we should reflect on our experience of life intuitively rather than logically, there is no doubt stories can trigger a response not found in other forms of teaching. Stories turn myths into legends, and offer truths which may be interpreted at several levels of reality.

Organizational realities also may be found on different levels. Stories about organizational heroes help to create the organization's culture, and stories of success and failure are part of the socialization process, as they help to sustain values. The repetition of favoured stories is one way in which organizational continuity is maintained. The tradition on which we draw when using case studies is as old as teaching itself, and is a powerful ingredient in everyday learning from experience.

SELECTING CASES FOR TEACHING PURPOSES

The cases in this book all seek to establish important teaching points about the management of human resources. Teaching notes are published separately which give an outline of how each case could be taught. However, in selecting which case is appropriate, teachers should be open to the possibility of using cases in a number of different ways. The guiding principle on which case study to use is dependent on the teaching purpose. The different purposes for which cases may be used can be seen from the following typology. This typology was developed after many years of teaching cases, and writing them.

A TYPOLOGY OF CASES

Type and description

Areas which are suitable

Organization/environment interaction
Set at organization level, they pose problems of strategy, present broad business problems, and show the interrelationship of different functions.

- Corporate planning.
- Policy issues.
- Organization design.
- Management of change.

Illustrative of behaviour
Cases which illustrate a range of behaviours, or problems to which the student responds, typically by discovering alternative courses of action.

All 'operational' techniques in the areas of personnel management, and interpersonal skills.

Sequential
Core material, supplemented with extra briefs, are used to describe particular problems. Usually set at the organization level, these cases can be operated on a long time scale. The key issues are concerned with the type of information, and how the extra brief supplements or modifies the core material.

The working of policy. Given policy objectives, how can particular problems be solved (e.g. negotiation strategy).

Type and description

Areas which are suitable

Role play
Cases in which the basic information on the situation is supplemented by the students, who act out the roles of the people described. These cases most frequently demonstrate *process*. The focus is on the treatment by the students, rather than on the material itself.

Interpersonal skills areas especially:
discipline ⎫
appraisal ⎬ interviews
selection ⎭
counselling
negotiating
persuasion
conflict resolution
(e.g. third-party interventions)
running meetings
leadership skills

Solution based

Cases for which there is a correct answer, where a particular solution is sought. This may be presented as a forced choice to the students, between alternatives, or in a more open ended way.	Knowledge of techniques, procedures, methods, best practice.

Reader's attitudes

Cases where all that is sought from the student is a reaction to a problem. The focus is then on his/her attitude when faced with the situation described.	Interpersonal skills area. All interviews, and stressful situations.

Clearly it would be possible to classify some cases under several of the headings above, since their subject matter and treatment gives them a versatile use. Teachers may wish to set different questions from those at the end of the case, for example, to ask students to put forward a series of solutions based on an analysis of the different options, or to comment on the skills employed by the participants in the case so far, and to say what they would do, perhaps role playing the characters. Attitudinal questions may be tackled by asking students to say what they feel about a problem or situation.

For those cases described as 'sequential' there are a series of 'add ons' available in the teaching notes which take the reader through a sequence, adding new information following each answer.

THE STRUCTURE OF THE BOOK

Because case studies are such an effective way of bringing experience into the classroom, we have collected these cases especially for students of management, whether on diploma or degree courses, and for practising managers who may be delegates on management training courses. The cases developed here at Cranfield reflect our long tradition of using case studies as a teaching method on our MBA programmes. They are all based on actual events and companies, although in most cases it has been necessary to disguise the names as the material was not in the public domain. These cases have been arranged under three headings:

Managing people effectively

The cases here cover interpersonal perceptions and skills, motivation, inter-personal communication, management style, appraisal, team performances and leadership.

Strategic management

These cases examine the broader issues of how organizations form, change and implement strategies. The cases chosen represent both the more formal, objective planning processes and the change processes, where strategy formation is of a more incremental nature. Change agent roles, interpersonal influences on strategy and management development, communication and change strategies are all illustrated here.

Human resource management

Under this heading we feature cases on employee relations, trade-union structure, joint consultation, and in the substantive policy areas of recruitment, rewards, job design, quality improvement and employee development.

WORKING ON CASE STUDIES

Producing worthwhile answers to case studies is dependent on how the task is dealt with as a process, as much as any knowledge of the content of the case. If working on cases in groups, the process skills practised are similar to those used in a normal management meeting. There is much to be learned by working in groups on case studies, therefore – including the skills of chairing meetings, listening, questioning, checking for understanding and summarizing. These basic communication skills will help in the discussion of the case.

There are also problem solving skills to be deployed. A five-fold framework for problem solving gives structure to the discussion:

1 *Problem definition.* The question here is how do we know there is a problem? It is usually beneficial to spend time on this stage, so that all possible angles are explored.
2 *Analysis.* Here we are concerned with causes. Monocausal explanations of human affairs are seldom adequate. There may be many interlocking causes. It is sometimes useful to consider what is both a necessary and a sufficient condition for something to have happened, but a search for one final cause is not likely to be helpful. There are some simple techniques in analysis, such as listing the strengths, weaknesses, opportunities and threats to an organization (a SWOT analysis). Strengths and weaknesses are usually internal, opportunities and threats, external to the organization.
3 *Generating solutions.* The main danger here is the possibility of becoming attached to a particular solution or offering solutions too soon, before the analysis of the problem is complete. Techniques, such as brain storming, are often a good way of being creative in the generation of solutions. Recording *all* ideas is important, and not evaluating them until the end

against agreed criteria. It is often beneficial to examine the arguments for and against a particular proposal.

4 *Evaluating solutions.* Solutions need to address the problem, and to be workable. Sometimes a range of solutions may be offered, the choice being dependent on how the people in the case might react. In many case studies, there are no 'solutions' as such, and what is sought is the reader's opinion or reaction. If this is the position, then the opinion should be backed by factual evidence from the case.

5 *Presenting/implementing solutions.* When evaluating solutions the question of how would the solution be implemented should be addressed. It may be appropriate to set out a strategy for implementation, and to incorporate this in the answer. Presentation of answers is an important skill to practise: the skills of persuasion, of presentation can all be exercised, either individually or as a group.

CONCLUSION

This is the second edition of our book. By popular demand we are publishing again many of the cases which appeared in *Cases in Human Resource Management*, which was published by Heinemann in 1987.

Since many of the issues drawn out by these cases are timeless, the precise date at which a case is set need not be relevant. Just as plays and novels often address the fundamental questions of human existence and enduring emotions, so many of our cases are centred on what are fundamental questions about human behaviour in organizations. However, we recognize that in some subjects, the social and economic context is critically important. This is acknowledged by the broader European flavour in some of our cases and by case studies which explicitly look at the European institutional context.

We trust our readers will soon see the value of the case history or case study as a vehicle for learning. The adaptability of this method and its strength in bringing practical ideas into the classroom is well established. Hopefully, the benefits of learning in this fashion will encourage readers to write up case histories from their own working experience so that other, succeeding generations may learn in this way.

REFERENCES

Berne, E. (1975) *What do You Say After You Say Hello?* London: Corgi.
Fiedler, F. (1967) *A Theory of Leadership Effectiveness*, New York: McGraw-Hill.
Jung, C. G. (1967) *Collected Works*, vol. 10, Princeton, NJ: Princeton University Press.
Kolb, D. A., Rubin, I., and McIntyre, J. (1974) *Organisational Psychology: an experimental approach*, Englewood Cliffs, NJ: Prentice-Hall.
Tyson, S. (1985) 'The case study as one way of learning', *Banking and Financial Training*, 1 (2).

PART I

MANAGING PEOPLE EFFECTIVELY

Human interaction is a vital area of study in the fields of management and organization analysis. The manner in which human beings relate to each other influences the application and quality of performance by which people do their work. The values, drives, expectations and skills of each person are strong determinants of the commitment people apply to the tasks and activities they undertake. This effect is considerably multiplied when more than one person is involved in the completion of work. The interesting mix of perceptions, motivation and skills leads to outcomes which at times are unexpected and in certain circumstances undesired. It takes considerable understanding and application to attend effectively to the interpersonal behaviour issues of the workplace.

We attempt to provide such breadth and depth of insight and approaches to addressing the people-oriented problems of the workplace. The topics of personal values and needs, motivation, interpersonal perceptions and skills, criteria for performance, effective and ineffective communications, and management style, are encompassed in this section. These are the basic ingredients to address in managing people effectively.

Secure Systems examines the subject of motivation. The drives and expectations of one person are explored, and the reader is asked to provide possible solutions to a commonplace human issue. The theme of motivation is continued in the case of *The Giro Group*, but, taken from an organizational perspective, The Giro Group is portrayed as experiencing changes which have an impact on the levels of motivation of its employees. Identifying the nature of the motivational problems and possible solutions to these problems are the tasks required in the case.

One important influence on the motivation of subordinates is the behaviour of the superior. Such is the underlying issue in the case of *Kleine Plastics (Part 1)*, which describes a situation of managerial succession in a family owned and managed company. The case is sequential and Parts 2, 3 and 4 are to be found in the teaching guide manual.

9

The theme of the relationship between superiors and subordinates is contained in the case of *Herr Mayrhofer*. This case focuses on the issues concerned with conducting effective appraisals, particularly emphasizing the need for being well prepared prior to the appraisal interview. The case of the *Industrial Development Authority* examines the complications of interpersonal behaviour during periods of fundamental organization changes. The threats and opportunities as perceived by each of the key managers in the case, and the manner in which they attempt to address complex issues, highlights the need for a realistic but professional approach to change management.

The terms realistic and professional do not just refer to skills but also to the attitudes and values held by each individual. The case of *D'Arcy and Key* examines how the values, needs, objectives and actions of individuals positively and/or negatively impact on the overall performance of teams. As the team in this case are the 'top team' of the D'Arcy and Key banking organization, individual and team performance is related to overall organisational effectiveness. The case is sequential. Part 2 is to be found in the teaching guide manual.

Values, drives, needs, styles and skills are all elements requiring analysis in the case of *Grayle Engineering*, where the focus is on identifying and evaluating managerial effectiveness. The intermittent and interrupted nature of managerial work is described in a company servicing the needs of one client (Ministry of Defence) who requires high standards of service. The internal coordination and organization issues in Grayle demand that managers perform to high standards in order to provide an adequate service.

1

SECURE SYSTEMS

Ron Ludlow

Bill Johnson looked round his office, which he shared with Leslie Jones, and announced:

'God, this is really crummy, isn't it! How can they expect us to work well in a place like this?'

'You seemed quite happy with it a few months ago, Bill,' replied Leslie. 'In fact, you never seemed to notice the squalor at all!'

The office was 12 feet by 8 feet, had no outside window, two desks which were piled high with files and papers, one filing cabinet which was full to overflowing, two rickety chairs, and a collection of papers in cardboard boxes. It was lit by a single 100 watt overhead light, unshaded, and a small grease-stained rug covered part of the dirty lino floor.

Bill had joined Secure Systems ten months ago. He had come from a major software house and had been excited to join a fast-growing computer security company with an impressive image in the market.

'With the Data Protection Act coming into operation this year, lots of organizations are starting to get very worried about the security of their computer systems, Bill', explained Rod Thomas, the Managing Director, after Bill had had his successful selection interview. 'One particular client, Gremlin Geotronics, does an awful lot of work for the Ministry of Defence, and for them, of course, security is the name of the game. I'd like you to start here by going over Gremlin's systems, making recommendations to their board, and implementing the new high-security systems in line with their requirements.'

This was quite a feather in Bill's cap, his creative genius was being recognized. At his previous job he had shown innovative ability, but the company was quite bureaucratized, and he had felt stifled in that sort of climate. Certainly, he had had a good salary – Secure Systems weren't paying him any more – a pleasant office and good secretarial back-up, but he felt restricted and he had steadily got more frustrated. The chance to move to Secure Systems was just what he had been waiting for.

Over the next eight months he put his heart and soul into the Gremlin project. Most of that time he had worked at Gremlin Geotronics sites

11

anyway, only coming back to his office for a few weeks at a time to revise and consolidate systems designs and to catch up with his mail. He had struck up a friendship with Leslie Jones, a computer analyst who shared his office, and who had a dry, sardonic sense of humour. Leslie made Bill feel slightly uncomfortable at times.

'Bet you never thought you'd have to share a little box like this when you came here, eh, Bill?' Leslie remarked ironically as Bill shifted one box of printouts to get at some papers below it. 'Beats me why you put up with it: after all, I'm only one of the juniors here, not like you. You must be on at least £5,000 a year more than me.'

Bill flustered, 'Well, it's the challenge, Leslie. This project is so fascinating and it's posing all sorts of problems that I like to solve. I think also that some of the new ideas I've got are transferable, in that we'll be able to use them as a basis for work in other companies. Come on, Leslie, it's the work which turns me on, not where I do it!'

After eight months the Gremlin Geotronics project was finished, and Bill Johnson was mostly office based for the next two months. There was no immediate project to follow the Gremlin one, and Bill got locked into a standard office routine, dealing with small jobs as they turned up, and trying to do some development work in his spare time. Leslie's mannerisms and cynical, cutting humour began to get on his nerves. With time on his hands, Bill started to take notice of his surroundings.

QUESTIONS

1 What are Bill Johnson's work needs and values?
2 At what motivational levels is he working:
  (a) Before Secure systems?
  (b) During the first ten months at Secure Systems?
  (c) Now?
3 What possible actions can be taken to improve his motivation now?

2

THE GIRO GROUP

Paul Dainty

The sudden sound of voices in the corridor made Larry jump. He looked at his watch. It was after 8 p.m. and he cursed for having to work late again. But despite the long hours and the pressure, he enjoyed the job, and it was important. He was working on a policy document which was to be considered at the directors' meeting tomorrow. He had been looking at the financing of three heavy engineering factories within the group, and had to make recommendations on their long-term viability. He had come to the conclusion that they were too much of a burden on the company and should be closed. He knew that others would have a say in the decision, and marketing would probably argue against him, but his recommendations were usually accepted.

He recognized one of the voices – Ted Patterson from the personnel department. He had had some real arguments with Ted over the last eighteen months. Ever since his department had been given the major responsibility for finding ways of saving money, he had come in conflict with Ted. 'It was understandable in some ways,' he thought. Many of his cost-cutting suggestions had implications for manpower. After the company had been a model employer for over twenty years, a lot of what the company was doing now probably seemed unpalatable to Ted. Especially as Ted had been with the company for so long, and had been responsible for getting a reasonably good remuneration package for managers, and for getting the idea of management development accepted within the company.

He paused for a moment and thought back to last year when he had argued that the workforce, including managers, should take a cut in pay, and that most developmental activities should cease. Their friendship had been severely strained as a result. 'But it had to be done; these were tough times. Few people in finance, or on the board for that matter, could see the cost effectiveness of the kind of development programmes Ted was advocating. They seemed to be expensive with fairly vague outcomes. Moreover, the overall pay reduction of 5 per cent seemed to have been accepted by managers in most departments. The managing director had gone to a lot of trouble communicating why the cut was necessary, but it seemed to have been worth it.'

Ted put his head round the door. 'Thought you might like to be rescued from your jail. Coming down the pub?'

Larry looked at his watch again 'Why not! But just give me two minutes while I put these files on Marjory's desk.'

As he walked down the corridor he noticed that John Holmes was still working. Although about the same age as Larry, John had been with the company much longer. He was also much less qualified. He had no formal accounting qualifications, although he always talked of getting round to doing something about it. 'That was typical of John,' thought Larry, slightly annoyed. Although he usually seemed to produce his work on time, he seemed to lack real 'go'. He wondered how well John was coping in reality. Tony Sadler's comments about John indicated that he didn't rate him highly either. 'Too quiet,' thought Larry, 'and I've tried to put a bit of life into him, but it hasn't seemed to work.' He thought how he probably knew John least of anybody in his division.

He put the files on Marjory's desk and returned to his office. As he walked in he noticed Ted looking over the report he had just finished.

'You know that recommendation could mean another 800 redundancies. That's nearly a fifth of the workforce.'

'Yes Ted, I know, but the company cannot afford these engineering works.'

'And what about the implications for head office. It could affect some of the people here, especially those who deal with the centralized functions such as personnel, finance and marketing.'

'Yes I'd thought about that – but it could mean that some people might have a bit of a breathing space for a time. That could be a good thing, especially as some seem to have difficulty in coping with the pressure. Sometimes these deadlines we keep having to meet, even get me down.'

'Come on Larry, are you kidding? If your director knows that there are people around with less work to do he will want to do something about it.'

'Hmm. I suppose when I come to think about it, Ted, I'm the same way. I can't really go around paring costs throughout the group, and then ignore the opportunities here.'

'But it won't affect management staff. You know our policy about getting rid of managers, Larry.'

'Yes, I know we have tried to maintain our management structure. Like you, I feel that gives some stability to the company, especially having older men like Tony Sadler around. I know we have a few problems with Tony, but as you know, I think the company needs people with his experience. Even so, as I keep saying, these are tough times.'

John Holmes heard Larry Kearns and Ted Patterson walk down the corridor towards the lift. They broke his concentration and he sat back. He felt good. He had worked hard today and this gave him satisfaction. He was sure his effort was appreciated within the company, and this also made him feel good. He liked to have the day-to-day financial responsibility for the group's engineering factories. It gave him the chance to work quietly, with his own small team of staff.

He knew that the job was not one of the most attractive in head office. It did not have the status of, say, working in the policy-making section, but he liked it. He knew the job and he felt secure doing it. 'Anyway,' he thought, 'once you got into areas like policy making you started getting into arguments.' He disliked that sort of thing, and he wasn't that concerned about getting to the top. He liked to get on with his work rather than be sidetracked with petty disagreements and people playing politics. But there were a few problems lately that were getting him down. He was working longer hours than he did normally and he was having trouble motivating his staff. He had ten people under him and he felt that they were becoming despondent. He put it down to the general feeling of uncertainty within the company. He would have liked to have talked to someone about it, but did not really get much of a chance, and was not really sure who to approach. 'Anyway things would improve when the company was back on its feet,' he thought.

He put his files away and locked his cabinet. As he switched out the light he saw Andrew Low waiting for the lift. He liked Andrew, who was a bright, pleasant man in his late twenties. He, Andrew and Tony Sadler all worked in the same division providing various financial services to the operating companies within the group. Andrew had responsibility for a small number of component firms. The responsibility was not as great as his own, and Andrew was slightly below him in seniority, although both reported to the same boss. Andrew had been with the company about three years now, was well qualified, seemed to run his section well and was ambitious. 'What a contrast he was to Tony,' he thought. Tony was responsible for a group of companies equivalent to his own, and he and Tony had similar status. Tony and Andrew, however, were like chalk and cheese. Tony had been with the company many years. He was an 'old school' type of manager who emphasized his status and had an air of authority, but his section always seemed to be in a shambles. He had heard some of Tony's staff complaining that Tony came in late and never seemed to be there when he was wanted. 'Funny how Larry never seemed to interfere,' he thought.

He caught Andrew up. 'You're working late John.'

'Yes, just a few things to tidy up.'

They got into the lift together. Two girls from the typing pool who had been working late were already in the lift. Andrew caught the end of their conversation.

'Have you heard, they are laying off twenty more clerical staff.'

'No! Who's going this time?'

'I don't know, but you never hear of any managers being made redundant.'

The girls quickly changed the subject as Andrew and John got into the lift. Their comments triggered off something inside Andrew. 'No they hadn't made any managers redundant,' he thought. 'But you never seemed to know where you were. The redundancy rumour probably wasn't true but you never knew what to believe'. All the chopping and changing over the last eighteen months had left him exasperated. He didn't know where he was, and he didn't think those at the top of the company did either.

The lift came to a stop and jolted him back to the present. He heard himself say goodnight to John and was hit by the bitter night chill. He was off to the Harvester's Arms. He usually played table tennis on a Tuesday, but as there was no match tonight he had agreed to go for a drink with one of the other team members.

As he walked into the pub he noticed Arnold seated with two drinks in front of him. Arnold waved.

'Got you one.' Arnold shouted. 'How are you?'

Andrew sat down and unbuttoned his coat. He looked tense. 'I am fed up Arnold. I have been in this job since I joined the company and there does not seem to be any prospect of moving higher. I work like hell but it does not seem to make any difference. And as far as getting any more money goes, well you can forget it.'

'But I thought you were coping all right, and you have never been particularly concerned about money before. Anyway you cannot expect too much in a company that has lost nearly a quarter of the workforce over a year and a half.'

'Perhaps that's the problem. It does not seem to matter how hard I work. Oh, I suppose I can live with the money situation, and the perks aren't too bad, but I resent it when others just seem to plod away and they don't seem bothered. Tony in my division is like that. Oh, I don't mind him that much, but it's the fact that he and others like him are going to be in the job for years. They won't leave because they are settled here and would find it difficult to get a job outside anyway. What do you do when a company is looking to get rid of jobs rather than create them? It's even difficult to get moved to another section. You know, I don't feel I am developing at all.'

'What about Terry Carpenter. He's in your department, isn't he? I heard he was thinking about getting a new job. There would be a vacancy there. Ok, it would not be a promotion for you, but it would be a change.'

'Yes, I would quite like to do his job. The kind of financial analysis he is doing would be interesting and broaden my experience a bit.'

The conversation was broken by a loud voice from behind them. 'Hello Andrew. We don't often see you in here.'

Andrew turned towards the voices. Larry Kearns and Ted Patterson were looking over at him.

'Do you want a drink?'

'Join you in a minute, Larry,' Andrew replied. He was stalling. He noticed Tony was with them, and he wanted to cool down a bit before he went over. Especially as Tony was laughing.

Tony was ribbing Ted about the 'development' programme he had gone on once. The course had not gone as well as expected, and Tony had always used this to excuse himself from going on any other courses. Ted believed that these silly comments of Tony's had an influence on Larry. 'We are the survivors,' he could hear Tony saying, 'What can they teach us on a course that we have not already experienced.'

Ted did not want to get into any more wrangles over development. He became too annoyed when the topic was raised nowadays, and just wanted to let it drop. Tony was a good friend, but he had some set ways and attitudes, and he always seemed to be putting the knife into something or somebody. Both he and Larry had given up trying to change him. Ted felt relief as Andrew joined them and the conversation changed to football and assessments of the latest England squad.

Friday mornings always seemed to bring bad news for Ted. He put the phone down. So the board had accepted Larry's recommendations on the engineering firms. Larry had let him read the report thoroughly, but he had difficulty in fully understanding the financial reasoning of all the proposals. He had half expected what would happen and resigned himself to it. But he still felt he had a duty to maintain the management structure at head office. As some of the changes would affect Larry's department he felt he should go and discuss them with him.

'So what do you think we should do Ted?' Larry asked after they had been discussing the implications for an hour. 'It looks as if John Holmes's section will have to go, but what about John?'

'Well you know how I feel about pushing managers out,' Ted said.

'Yes, but this might be the right time. You know I'm not happy with John. He does not seem to pull his weight. He rarely works late and he has been having problems with his staff for some months. He produces the work all right, but he hardly ever shows any initiative.'

'I think that would be too harsh on him. I accept the section has to be closed down, but what about moving him into Terry Carpenter's job. That will become vacant in a month's time when he leaves us. Ok, so it's a slightly lower status, but he could do that job, and it might give him time to look round for another. We could keep him on the same pay. That would not be a problem.'

'Ok, Ted let's do that. Come back to me tomorrow and we will discuss the details before I approach my director. But I think I will have a word with John as soon as possible.'

Ted turned to leave when he remembered the other issue. 'Oh Larry, what about this move to end the free management lunches and integrate all the dining halls? I'd like to know how the managing director is going to announce that. The managers won't like losing their perks.'

17

'Oh don't worry about that Ted. It will be just done quietly. Pointless making a fuss about something like this. After accepting a pay cut, managers are hardly going to get upset about losing a few free meals.

The next day Andrew met John going down to the dining area. Andrew was annoyed again about the fact that old stagers like Tony were causing problems. His staff had been helping out Tony's staff for the second time that week, and he was sure that it was Tony's inability to cope with the load himself as much as his staff. But he always seemed to find an excuse or bluff his way through. Tony could talk the hind legs of Larry, and that was something. 'In some ways John was just as bad,' he thought. He felt he could do either of their jobs given the chance. But although a bit insipid, John was still probably willing to change, unlike Tony, who was a complacent old mule. However, despite his annoyance with these two, he was feeling a little bit chirpy. He had heard about Terry Carpenter's resignation, and was waiting for the job to be advertised internally. 'At least that's something to look forward to,' he thought.

He looked at John. 'You are looking pleased with yourself, John,' Andrew remarked.

'Yes I am a bit'. John always felt good when he had put in a solid morning's work. But it was the unexpected meeting that he was to have with Larry this afternoon, which had made him feel good. 'Larry must have been told about how I sorted out that tricky personal problem of one of the lads on my section. Ted had heard, and said he was going to mention it to Larry. Nice to have some recognition,' he thought. But John said nothing to Andrew. It did not feel right for him to brag about his little achievements at work.

QUESTIONS

1 Assess what you think are the current motivational problems in the company, and what will they be in the future?
2 What are the management development issues that you can identify:
   (a) For the company.
   (b) For the individuals themselves.

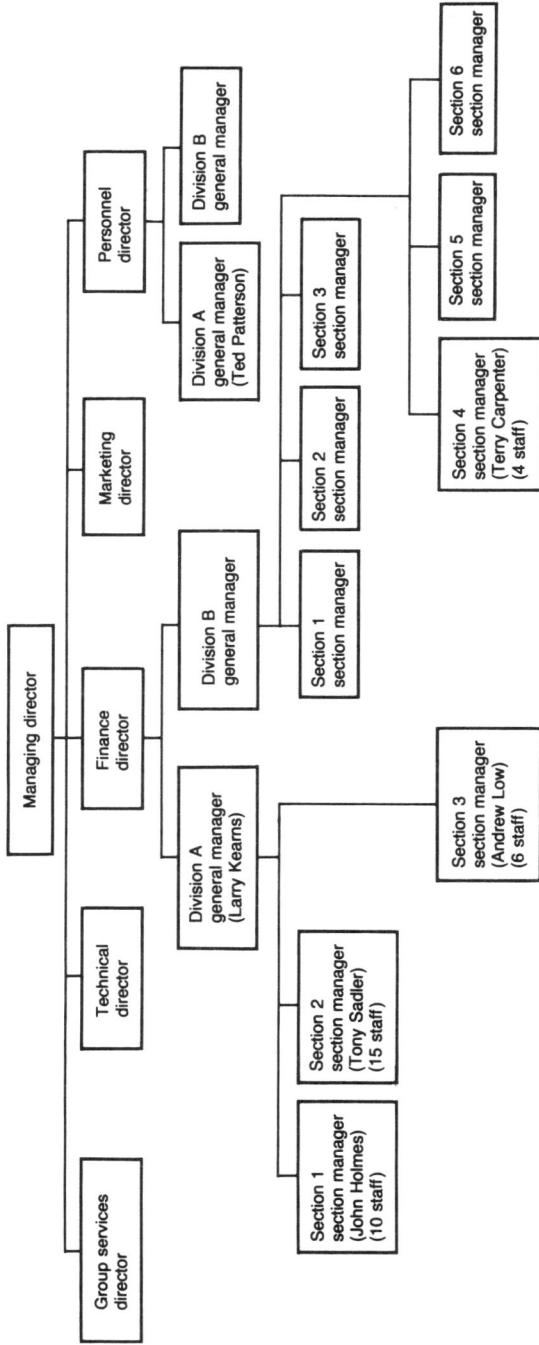

Figure 2.1 Head office organization chart: the Giro Group (parts relevant to the case)

3

KLEINE PLASTICS

Ron Ludlow

PART 1

Kleine Plastics was a small company, which produced a wide range of household plasticware and was based in the East Midlands town of Oxminster. Established in 1960, it was wholly owned by the Kleine family and from the beginning had been managed by Joseph Kleine, a dynamic, yet charismatic, man of 60. Joseph had a reputation for sound technical knowledge combined with the ability to motivate his workforce. He made a tour of inspection of the factory twice a day and in this way he was always aware of what was going on, both on the factory floor and in the offices. He was quick to praise the workers when he felt they had done a good job, and equally quick to remonstrate with them over careless or inefficient work.

In point of fact, Joseph Kleine had few occasions to discipline his staff and he proudly believed that this was because he had chosen a reliable and trustworthy group of managers to support him. The company, which employed some two hundred people, was divided into six departments: design, production, sales, purchasing, warehouse and administration. Each departmental head had a lot of experience and ability in his own field and their average length of service with the company was fifteen years. Joseph felt completely confident that he could delegate work to them and they enjoyed a relative degree of autonomy, knowing they could turn to Joseph for help and advice should they need it.

Over the years, a rapport had developed between Joseph and his managers, based on mutual personal and technical respect. Similarly, a good working atmosphere existed within the departments, each manager having the respect of his staff. Because Joseph believed in plain speaking, he dealt with any disagreement between the managers by sitting down with them and thrashing the problem out on the spot. 'Politics is for Westminster. I'll have none of it at Kleine's,' was one of his favourite sayings.

Kleine Plastics had grown from small beginnings in the early 1960s to a turnover of over half a million pounds by 1970, with most of its products being sold in the East Midlands. However, like many small companies it was hit very hard by the recession in the construction industry in the early 1970s, and looked for markets further afield and commenced exporting in 1974. With the turn-up of the construction industry in the late 1970s, however, the company marched boldly forward due mostly to the dynamism of its founder, Joseph Kleine, and showed steady growth in the early 1980s. Turnover increased from £2 million in 1980 to £7½ million by 1984, with net profit after tax increasing from £90K to £630K in 1984. The year 1985 showed every sign of being yet another profitable one, and Joseph Kleine felt that at last his company was making its mark on the market, both at home and overseas.

In October 1985, the company received an order to supply black plastic water tanks to East Africa. The original contact for this order had come to Kleine's via a personal friend of Joseph's, who worked for the World Health Organization. Although the initial tooling costs were high, Joseph considered the investment worthwhile, for the potential long-term benefit to the company was considerable. The water tanks would contain a supply of fresh drinking water for refugees and Joseph reflected, with some sadness, that somewhere in the world there would always be refugees, made homeless by either war or want. What Africa needed today, India might well need tomorrow.

As Joseph watched the installation of the new moulding machine which would produce the water tanks, he was struck by the irony of the situation, whereby a small company in England could be made more profitable by the destitution of East Africa. He reflected on the pictures of starving children in Ethiopia, which had appeared frequently on television. As he did so, he thought of David, his 24-year-old son. Far from starving, David was actually rather overweight.

Yet, Joseph was enormously proud of his son. Bright, but not brilliant, David Kleine had obtained a BA degree in economics from Acton Polytechnic, followed by a diploma in management studies. Although Joseph had had little formal education, he had always encouraged David to study, in the firm belief that tomorrow's managers would need a sound academic background in order to cope with the increasingly sophisticated business world. He was very impressed with David's qualifications and felt sure that he would one day take over as managing director of Kleine Plastics. In fact, David was already employed by the company and was presently working on cash-flow forecasts and patent investigation. Joseph had received good reports of David's work from the company accountant, Alan Foulkes, who considered that David had an aptitude for detailed administrative work of this nature.

Walking back to his office, Joseph decided that now was the time to take his wife on a long-promised holiday. He had always said that when he could afford to take time off from the company, he would take her on a three-month cruise to the Far East. Now the pipedream looked as though it could shortly become reality. Business was thriving. David was showing himself to be capable and responsible – would there ever be a better time to take that well-earned break? Reaching for the telephone, he booked the holiday.

Before leaving that evening he went to see Alan Foulkes. He smiled with pleasure as he told Alan that he finally booked the cruise and explained that, while he was away, he intended to put David in charge of running the company. However, while he wanted his son to gain experience, he realized that he would need help and support and therefore asked Alan to keep an eye on him and provide guidance where necessary. He then sought out all his other departmental managers, told them his plans and asked for their full cooperation and support. Finally, he spoke to David. He told him that he was pleased with his work, emphasizing his progress during the past months. Then, he told him about the forthcoming cruise and explained that he felt that David would be well able to take over the day-to-day supervision of the company in his absence, with the guidance of Alan Foulkes and the full support of the other managers.

The next morning, Joseph called all his managers to the board room. 'As you all know, I rarely call meetings,' he began. 'That's not my way of doing things. However, I feel that on this occasion, a meeting is called for. I have already seen you individually and told you about my holiday. Well, this morning, I would like to formally introduce my son to you as my deputy for the next three months. We all know that this company practically runs itself. That is because you are all so good at your jobs. In fact, I don't suppose you will notice that I have gone. However, someone has to sign the letters! That someone will now be David, and I would once again ask you all to give him the support you have always given me.' On the last Sunday in November, Joseph and his wife left for the Far East.

On Monday, 2 December, David Kleine installed himself behind his father's desk. His first action as deputy managing director was to telephone Alan Foulkes and ask him to bring in the job costing sheets for the last six months. Next, he phoned Victor Keane, the sales manager, and asked for the monthly sales records for the past 2 years, broken down by region and by product. Finally, he called Ian Breed, the production manager, for a complete summary of production schedules for the last three months and plans for the next six weeks. As the various pieces of information reached him, he worked closely on the figures, closeting himself in his office all week. Before leaving the office on Friday evening, he dictated a memo to his father's secretary, asking all department heads to meet him in the board room first thing on Monday morning. The memo did not contain any agenda for the meeting.

QUESTIONS

1 How is David likely to handle this meeting?
2 What issues are likely to be raised by David at the meeting?
3 Will the senior managers be enthusiastic/not enthusiastic about tackling these issues?

4

HERR MAYRHOFER

Philippe Poirson

THE APPRAISAL INTERVIEW CASE STUDY

The background

Bertrand is a company which was formed in 1830 by Nicolas Bertrand who built a foundry in a small town 30 kilometres north of Lyon, France. This company, which is situated in the Beaujolais wine-growing and agricultural region, became more and more specialized in the manufacture of machines aimed at the processing and refrigeration of food products. By 1960, it had become the leader in the French market for professional kitchen equipment, and in 1965, it was bought by a large French group of companies, in the electronics industry, as a part of its diversification strategy. Up until 1984, the firm experienced considerable development: the backing of a large group enabled it to invest a great deal, to build up a very considerable dense network of dealers throughout the country, as well as to develop its exports.

In 1985, the company employed 1,600 people and manufactured capital goods (refrigerated display units, mass catering kitchen units, automatic dishwashers, cold-storage units, cold rooms) which were designed for two types of customers: local communities and the food retailing industry (supermarkets, hypermarkets and traditional shops). The company's employees are distributed between three main locations: the sales management is located in the Paris area; the factories which produce the professional kitchen equipment are located in the Lyon area; the commercial refrigeration production units are to be found in the south-west of the country, just south of Bordeaux.

Because of history and geographical location, the company has always been in contact with the traditional food trades. In fact, a part of its activity consists of providing a servicing function: in particular, the installation and maintenance of refrigeration equipment. The traditional values of Bertrand & Co. and of its customers were founded on common, physical tasks, friendliness and a strong support for the service provided. The glass of wine shared after the work was done was a sign of belonging to the same world.

24

Naturally, this firm grew and grew, became structured, recruited graduates as managers, and gradually organized itself in a 'modern' manner. However, the values arising from the old culture still remained, particularly in the heart of the areas where the smallest retailer-installation specialists were to be found.

In 1987, the French group of companies on whom Bertrand depended, with a desire to reposition its activities within the 'heart of its trade', decided to sell off this firm to Wengen (a German group). The 'local communities' division recorded a turnover of 400 million francs in 1988 and the company had a low rate of profitability. It was French leader in the mass-catering kitchen sector, but the competition was very keen in this market, which was shrinking slightly, and where there was a large number of small competitors.

The construction of new facilities (schools, hospitals, etc.) had already considerably slowed down over the past few years. Now demands for replacements or for refurbishing constituted the major share of the market. Contracts for the installation of complete mass-catering kitchen units were hotly sought after by all manufacturers, thus causing profit margins to be reduced. Consequently, the sales effort needed to focus on the prospects of small-scale customers. As this market sector was less crowded with competitors, better margins could be achieved on products for which there were low, or no preliminary installation costs.

Sales management structure

A simplified organization chart is shown in Figure 4.1.
Product distribution is carried out in two ways:

1 Large nationwide customers (the army, the post office/telecoms, central purchasing offices, etc.) are looked after by six national account executives.
2 In each French department (or county), the Bertrand company has one or several exclusive dealers, who are responsible for selling, installing and repairing the equipment.

Fifteen area sales managers (most of them self taught) are responsible for motivating and backing up the dealer network. On average, each of them is in charge of a dozen or so dealers over an area of 6 to 7 countries. The latter are generally the managers of companies employing between 5 and 30 people. Many of them are former refrigeration technicians who have set up their own businesses. They attach substantial importance to the design and quality of the facilities they install, as this represents the 'noble' aspect of their profession.

Many of them have worked with the Bertrand company for twenty years or so. Beyond straightforward business relations, many of them feel an emotional attachment towards their firm, some of them are former salaried employees of Bertrand & Co. In 1956, the company decided to transform its agency network into a network of independent dealers. The sales manager is M. Cordier, a 53-year-old, self-taught, former agency employee who worked his way up through the ranks before reaching his present position. Last year, on the advice of the managing director, he took on a deputy, Herr Mayrhofer, a 30-year-old former student of a German university, in order to relieve himself of some of the workload and to ensure smooth executive succession. Herr Mayrhofer is responsible for supervising the team of area sales managers. For the coming year, he has been entrusted with the task of increasing turnover by 12 per cent (after inflation) and profit margins by an average of 2 per cent (i.e. from 25.5 per cent to 27.5 per cent). The area sales managers are paid a fixed salary. However, individual pay rises, from which they may benefit once a year, depend largely on the sales results of their geographical area. They are mainly evaluated on the changes in turnover and in profit margins.

THE PROBLEM

It is the beginning of December. A year ago, before the same period, Herr Mayrhofer arranged to meet each of the area sales managers for an annual interview. He has already seen seven of them. An appointment has been made for 3 p.m. on 12 December with Jean Bonnardel. M. Bonnardel is 28 years old, holds a post-graduate degree in marketing and has been a salesman with the firm for 5 years. He is a lively character with a brisk nature and he enjoys being out in the field. He is always ready to lend a hand and most of the dealers appreciate him. He takes great pleasure in telling people about the spectacular sales coups he has pulled off in the past. He appreciates M. Cordier's rather paternalistic style of management. Jean Bonnardel did not have an individual pay rise last year. For an area sales manager with a post-graduate degree and 5 years' experience, his current salary is about average.

Herr Mayrhofer, on the other hand, is more of a man for figures. He is well aware that, in Jean Bonnardel's sector, turnover is 2 per cent above sales forecasts (and this puts him in fifth position among the fifteen area sales managers). However, the average profit margin in this sector is nowhere near as good. And yet, during his regular meetings, which take place every two months, he continually tries to make his area sales managers sensitive to the problem of decreasing margins. By studying the figures he has at his disposal, Herr Mayrhofer noticed that Jean Bonnardel had produced two-thirds of his turnover with 5 dealers out of the 13 in the geographic area for which he is responsible. They are in fact retailers and installation specialists who are the biggest in size. He fully intends to make good use of this interview in order to better understand the working methods used by his subordinate.

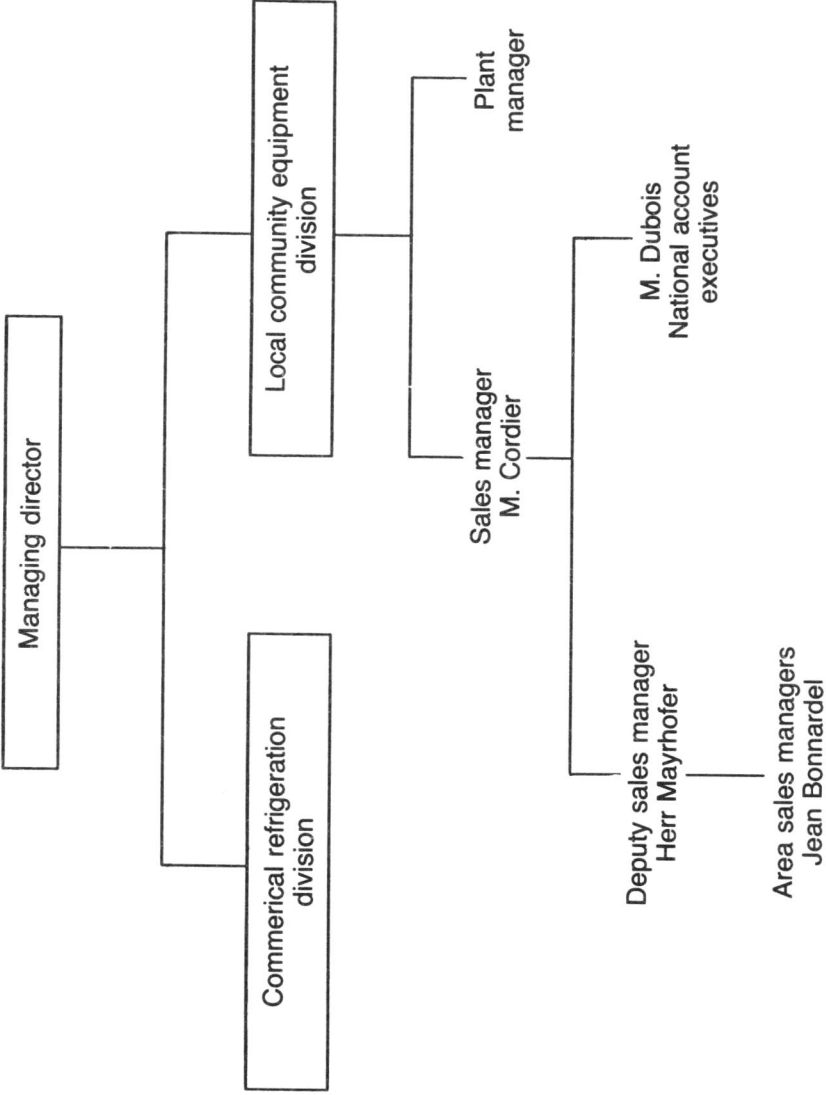

Figure 4.1 The Bertrand Company: simplified organization chart

QUESTIONS

1 In your opinion, what is at stake in this interview between Herr Mayrhofer and M. Bonnardel?
2 Draw up a detailed interview plan.
3 In your opinion, what preparations should be made before the interview?
4 How should the interview be conducted? What assistance would you expect?
5 Suppose your objective is to have M. Bonnardel modify his customer portfolio, how would you proceed during the interview?

5

THE INDUSTRIAL DEVELOPMENT AUTHORITY

Andrew Kakabadse

In the early 1960s, an Industrial Development Authority was established in order to stimulate business development in the UK. It was considered vital by the then political party in power, that industrial growth and development be conducted on a planned and organized basis. The influential politicians of all the major parties agreed that the organization should be created to promote nationally based industrial growth and thereby generate employment opportunities.

The authority identified a number of activities to pursue, ranging from technical/managerial courses to offering financial assistance and a back-up consultancy service to small businesses. Fifteen years on, politicians and influential business people generally agree that the authority has done a good job. However, needs have changed. The financial assistance and subsidy to small businesses is considered inadequate to meet present needs and the consultancy service is hardly utilized. The results of a recent survey indicate that proprietors of small companies consider the service provided as both inadequate and out of date in terms of meeting their needs.

The authority's income stems from two sources: central government and a compulsory levy imposed on all businesses. Influential members of the business community have indicated that they resent paying the levy because they could not see how they benefited from such expenditure. The minister accountable for the affairs of the Department of Industry issued an ultimatum to the Industrial Development Authority: offer a service that the business community finds valuable or else the levy will become voluntary instead of compulsory. In essence, the minister stated: change or be closed down.

The senior directors of the authority responded rapidly. Working parties and committees were established to try to identify alternative strategies and activities which the authority could pursue. As a result of these meetings it became clear that the middle management were, and had been, dissatisfied with their bosses and the total organization. Certain outspoken middle managers, in offering their views to the committees and working parties, stated that in order to get on and be promoted in the authority all that was required was to be 'political'. Competence and hard work came secondary. Further, many of the problems identified by the committees had already been recognized by the more capable middle managers. Certain managers even ventured to question how the authority could be any different in the future if the same senior managers remained in post.

It also became clear that certain departments and units in the authority had become accustomed to 'doing their own thing'. In particular, certain departmental managers had not bothered to inform their bosses of particular projects. Senior management was expected, by influential middle managers, to rubber stamp their activities. A report was submitted to Jim Carthy, the director general (DG) of the authority.

'What the hell is happening in this organization?' demanded Jim Carthy at the next directors' meeting. 'The politicians are right. This organization is riddled with splits and disagreements, people running off in all directions and nothing of value being done. The authority has become unmanageable! This all has to change!' exploded the DG.

The other functional directors shuffled uncomfortably in their seats.

INTRODUCING CHANGE

Jim Carthy recognized that something had to be done in the authority. He saw that to introduce change, it had to be achieved in a planned and organized manner to prevent the present anomalies from ever arising in the future. In an attempt to introduce change, Carthy held discussions with each of his functional directors. The one functional director most sympathetic to his boss's views was Henry Mitchell, the director of personnel. He recognized that change was necessary and argued that his department should become the agents of change. However, he and Jim Carthy realized that the personnel managers in his department were not considered particularly proactive or innovative. If the personnel department was to become the catalyst for change within the authority, then certain changes needed to be made within the personnel department. After substantial discussion, both agreed that they required an outsider to stimulate change within the personnel department. After an extensive search they identified a highly recommended consultant, Noel Green, whose specialism was the introduction and management of change.

Noel Green was told that his 'assignment' involved attempting to stimulate the managers within personnel departments to become more proactive as agents of change. Line managers in the organization needed to develop greater sensitivity and awareness of market conditions and become more assertive in their dealings with their business clients. Essentially, the consultant's task was to change the personnel managers from operating solely as administrators, to acting as internal change agents/catalysts so that they in turn could help line managers to improve their performance. In addition, Noel Green was asked to cooperate closely with Peter Davidson, the management development manager. Davidson had for some time argued that personnel should play a central role in the change and development of the authority. It was considered that Davidson would eventually assume the role of internal consultant.

Green and Davidson began their assignment by talking to a select number of managers in the personnel department about their work, ambitions and the role of the department in the future. It quickly became clear that most of this select sample wanted no change. They were content to remain as administrators. They seemed to be more concerned about their job, role, degree of authority and status differences among themselves, than about the future of the department. Green and Davidson concluded that most managers in the personnel department did not wish for change. How then to go about introducing change?

It was clear to them that before any meaningful discussion could take place as to the future role of the department, it was necessary to attempt to change these managers' attitudes. Their lethargy had to be broken! Their need to identify with the status quo had to be substituted by a wish to explore and become effective at stimulating change in other departments in the organization. In order to change attitudes however, Green and Davidson needed to identify the values, attitudes to work, thoughts, feelings and potential of each individual manager in the personnel department.

Hence their strategy was:

1 Organize a series of workshops in order to gain a perspective on how the personnel managers viewed their situation and what would be their future direction and objectives for their department;
   (a) the managers attending the workshop were asked to identify present problems and also draw up practical solutions to those problems;
   (b) the results of the workshops indicated that the lack of drive to do anything new was as much a result of both training and development of the personnel department's manager;
   (c) Green and Davidson consulted Mitchell as to their next steps. Of course, the problems in the department went far deeper than merely a lack of effective interpersonal skills. However, training needs had been identified and the training process could be used as the mechanism for helping the managers change their attitudes, ideas and skills.
2 Organize a series of three-day interpersonal skills training programmes during which managers would have to complete numerous personality tests and leadership/management style type questionnaires.
3 Green and Davidson, with Henry Mitchell's joint agreement, secretly kept a copy of all of the personality and management style test results that were administered on the programme.

4 The two consultants sketched out each individual's personality profile, managerial style, preferred approaches to work, qualifications and task skills. They drew out a comprehensive map of the personalities in the personnel department.

5 They began to match people together by personality type, work preferences and managerial style.

6 They told Henry Mitchell that the series of three-day courses were a tremendous success. The next step, in order to capitalize on such useful training, would be to initiate a number of small projects whereby people could be given the opportunity to experiment with their newly found skills. They gave him a 'hit-list' of the names and their test scores, recommending that they should be transferred out or sacked.

7 Henry Mitchell agreed, allowing the two consultants to set up a few experimental project teams. At the same time, he transferred or made redundant over 70 per cent of the people on the hit-list.

8 Having removed the most troublesome managers, Green and Davidson organized a few project teams, whose brief was to examine the problems faced by other departments in the organization, recommend solutions and if necessary help apply these solutions. Most members of the project teams had all been carefully matched together from their map of the department.

As time passed, the training programme seemed to have made quite an impact on the managers in the personnel department. Most of the project teams completed their work and as they had worked on problems faced by the authority, they displayed their value to the organization by providing practical, workable solutions to the problems they addressed. Certain of the personnel managers were subsequently asked to assist other departments in the authority in solving both short- and longer-term problems.

Peter Davidson took over from Noel Green and continued to organize workshops and training programmes to suit the needs of particular managers or groups in the authority. Davidson's brief extended beyond the personnel department. Henry Mitchell was seen by most of senior management as the man who made it all happen. In the authority's newsletter, Jim Carthy publicly congratulated Mitchell for his efforts in developing the personnel department.

Henry Mitchell learned a great deal from the intervention of Noel Green. He began to understand his own strengths and weaknesses as well as those of the managers in his department. He appreciated how necessary it was to be skilful at influencing others, especially at a time of rapid organizational change. Most of all, he learned that to be effective it is necessary to influence others without being identified as a threat. That was a valuable lesson to have learned, for the recommendations he was about to put before the director of the authority were threatening.

THE REPORT

Henry Mitchell submitted a report to Jim Carthy indicating that for the Industrial Development Authority to become anywhere near effective, redundancies were necessary. Further, the authority lacked individuals who possessed particular skills, hence, in addition to the redundancies, Henry recommended a recruitment campaign. On reading the report, Jim Carthy became anxious: 'Look Henry, I understand what you are trying to tell me and why, but for God's sake, see it from my point of view; the unions will crucify me,' exclaimed the DG of the authority. The discussion did not last much longer. Jim Carthy said he would have to shelve the proposals.

Henry Mitchell did not give up. He recognized that his boss was highly role and status conscious. Henry began to replan his influence moves concerning the reorganization of the authority. He approached Jim Carthy once more and suggested that if the above proposals were accepted, the status of the DG within the organization and amongst the nation's politicians would increase dramatically. He might even be seen as a world leader in the planning of industrial growth and development. As a secondary issue, the organization would also benefit.

After further discussions, and within the next six months, the DG of the authority accepted most of the personnel director's proposals. In particular, the proposals included selected redundancies and redeployments, the continuation of the project teams and establishment of new projects, and a major eighteen-month management training programme for most senior and middle managers. Henry Mitchell had succeeded in launching one of the largest in-organization change programmes in the UK. Mitchell realized that he could not solely rely on Peter Davidson and thereby rehired Noel Green.

THE CHANGE PROGRAMME

'The only thing I'm certain about around here is that everything is changing. I don't mind change, but when you get too much of it with little or no support, or training, or anything, I'm tired of it – I just want to stop,' stated a senior manager to the director of personnel. The two had met in the corridor on their way to lunch.

The comments worried Henry Mitchell. The senior manager was a supporter of the change programme, but his support was now waning. In fact, the personnel department had recently been heavily criticized for not providing sufficient help and support during the various phases of change and reorganization.

Henry decided to call Noel Green. 'OK, let's do that! Let's have a series of short one- to two-day training programmes for our senior and middle managers as we did for the personnel managers,' agreed Henry Mitchell on the phone. He had been talking to Noel Green over the phone for the past twenty minutes.

'I agree. Remember when we get together to plan the programmes in detail we must be very careful about whom we invite on each seminar. Getting the right people together who will talk to each other, share their problems and help each other back at work after the programme, is absolutely vital. You and I know that the informal groups are in fact a more powerful force than the formal structure in terms of getting things done or just blocking and making sure nothing gets done. Let's use the existing informal network for training,' finished Noel.

A few days after their telephone conversation, Henry and Noel met. They identified a series of two-day programmes for the senior and middle managers of the authority. At the senior manager seminars, the DG of the authority would give an hour's presentation identifying the needs for change and reorganization and then spend a further hour answering questions and responding to comments from the senior managers. The consultant would then run the programme for the remaining day and a half discussing organization strategy, organization structure and the importance of developing effective teams. The last two hours on the second day would be devoted to action planning whereby the senior managers would be split into pairs, helping each other draw up a six-month action plan each senior manager could implement on his return to work. It was hoped that by enabling senior managers to generate action plans, that would commit them to doing something positive within the organization. Further, by talking through with colleagues key issues during the process of action planning, the managers would form close relationships and hence help each other implement their action plan.

The seminars for the middle managers would concentrate more on team building, and the generation of action plans. It was considered that the middle managers would benefit more from team development and interpersonal skills training as most of their time was spent within team settings.

The senior managers considered their seminars as tremendously successful as it was widely felt that their needs were met. It was quickly established that the senior managers had little knowledge of subjects such as strategy and structure. Gaining more knowledge helped the senior managers understand how and what to improve. The participants on the programmes further considered the process of action planning to be invaluable. Most stated that they never realized that others were facing similar problems. Using each other to talk about work problems, and from there to identify solutions, helped to form positive working relationships amongst the senior managers. The director of personnel later discovered that many of the senior managers continued to meet and share problems with each other on a fairly regular basis. Six months on, one senior manager commented to the director of personnel:

'Your programme helped form one of the best "old boys clubs" I have ever experienced. You realize that the old man [Jim Carthy] won't be able to cough without asking for our permission.'

Henry Mitchell managed to force a polite smile to that last comment. 'You mean, he won't be able to cough without asking for my permission,' thought Henry.

THE EXECUTIVE MERRY-GO-ROUND

Ray Leonard, director of business development in the Industrial Development Authority recognized the growing influence and stature of the personnel department. Ray, the youngest of the five functional directors in the authority, was in charge of the most sought-after directorate – business development. Four years on the job, Ray was both feared and respected. His colleagues saw him as clear thinking, intelligent but difficult to talk to and somewhat untrustworthy. Most people considered that at the end of the day, Ray always got what he wanted.

In Ray's eyes, the balance of power within the Authority had shifted. The personnel department was now more powerful than business development. Personnel was now dictating the pace of change within the authority. Personnel was calling the shots. Ray made an appointment to see Jim Carthy.

'One thing is for sure, Ray, everyone recognizes the impact you've made on business development. Whilst you've been there, what is it, something like four and a half thousand new businesses have started with your support and help. You also introduced a consultancy service for medium-sized and large organizations, which is the most profitable part of this whole outfit, although strictly speaking we're not into profit making,' said Jim Carthy.

The two men had been talking for over one hour.

'But you think after four years, it's time for a move,' reflected the director of the authority.

'As you know, it has been practice to move our directors round every 4 or 5 years. It allows for change and vitality in the organization.'

Pause.

'You think you'd like to have a go at personnel – you'd welcome some experience of running a service function.'

Pause.

'OK! Look, Ray, leave that with me. As you know, I'll have to talk to Henry. With all these changes taking place, it may be opportune to switch our directors around as well. Thanks, Ray. Speak to you soon.'

The meeting finished. Ray left the director's office. Jim Carthy remained seated in his chair reflecting on the conversation. That morning, he had held a meeting with senior civil servants from the Department of Industry. He received a clear message from the civil servants: Henry Mitchell, the director of personnel in the Industrial Development Authority, sooner or later had to go. Apparently, Henry had made himself unpopular with some of the civil servants, especially Sir Robin Didson. When he disagreed with Sir Robin, he said so; what made it worse was that Henry was usually right. Further, Henry and Jim had been contenders for the post of DG of the Industrial Development Authority; Jim won, Henry lost. At the time, certain civil servants had been pressuring the Minister not to appoint Henry. Those same civil servants, championed by Sir Robin, were now pressuring Jim to ease Henry out of the organization.

Of all his directors, Jim Carthy respected and trusted Henry the most. Since Jim's appointment, Henry had been his loyal supporter. Moreover, he had done an excellent job as director of personnel, especially during this latest and far-reaching reorganization. Ray had also done a reasonably good job but he too had his critics, though most were inside the authority.

Jim could see no alternative, Henry had to be moved, otherwise the pressure on him from the civil servants would be too great. He decided on a straight swop between Henry and Ray. He made appointments to see Ray and Henry in that order. Ray accepted the post of director of personnel. Then, the appointment with Henry.

'Henry, as you know, it's custom for our directors to move around every four years or so. I've asked you to see me to explore whether you'd be willing to leave personnel for the time being and take on business development. There are particular problems there that need attention – attention that Ray has not been able to provide through no fault of his own,' stated Jim Carthy.

'It's flattering to be considered. Jim, but I feel there's a lot more to do in personnel, especially in seeing through this reorganization that we started,' replied Henry.

The two men continued talking. An hour and a half passed.

'Henry, my position is clear. Our training centres need sorting out. The training staff are poorly qualified, poorly motivated and incapable of meeting present-day needs. Also training centres are under the wrong directorate. You know this organization as well as I do. If I took training centres and put them under business development, all hell would break loose between Tony Rivers and Ray. Tony does not like losing, and even less to Ray. However, losing training centres to business development with you in charge is a different matter. I feel you two have always got on and could work together to improve our training centres' service,' said Jim.

'Jim, I agree with your logic. However, my problem is more personal. You know how unpopular I am with the bureaucrats in the Department of Industry. Taking on business development, especially with the increased responsibility of training centres, is high risk for me. If I am seen to perform poorly, they'll start putting pressure on you to have me out of this organization,' stated Henry.

'Henry! No more talk like this. You are one of the most valuable managers in this organization. Irrespective of what happens or what you decide, I'll always support you,' confirmed Jim Carthy.

The two men continued talking.

'OK. I'll take it on. You're right. Training centres need to be taken into business development. I'm probably acceptable to Ray and to Tony Rivers, and that'll make Ray's and my transition a smooth one. However, I'm suspicious of the Department of Industry. I suspect I'll be asking you for help before too long,' said Henry.

'Henry, let me assure you here and now that if anyone from the Department of Industry puts you under pressure, you'll have my support,' stated Jim Carthy.

The meeting finished shortly after that.

That evening Jim Carthy attended a dinner at the Department of Industry. He had been in deep conversation with a senior civil servant.

'So, it's official then,' remarked Jim, 'Sir Robin Didson will be in charge of Manpower Services. That means our training centres will be under his remit.'

'How come you know so much about his appointment then?' enquired the civil servant.

'Oh, I was one of the people consulted on who should be in charge of Manpower Services. I, like so many others, recommended Sir Robin,' stated Jim.

'Then you've known for some time?'

Jim Carthy nodded.

TIME I DID SOMETHING ABOUT MY SITUATION

'He knew. Yes, of course he knew!' remarked Henry Mitchell.

It was 11.00 p.m. and Henry was at home, seated in an easy chair in the lounge, talking to his wife. Henry had spent a particularly harassing day at a meeting with Sir Robin Didson in the chair, a group of civil servants and Jim Carthy. At the meeting, whatever suggestion Henry Mitchell offered was criticized and finally rejected. Further, Mitchell was heavily criticized for not 'sorting out' the training centres. Mitchell knew that improvements concerning the training centres would take 3 years. He was only four months in post.

'Jim did at times, try to support me today, but he was just too quiet,' reflected Mitchell. 'Yes, he must have known about Didson's appointment when I was offered the business development job,' he continued.

'That does not sound like Jim Carthy. I always thought he was a straightforward sort of man. I also thought you two got on so well,' said Evelyn Mitchell.

Pause.

'Just shows you how wrong anyone can be. What a situation. Jim Carthy working against one of his own top directors,' continued Evelyn Mitchell.

'I'm not sure that Jim Carthy is that political. I think he's just stuck. At the time, Didson was the best. Carthy had to recommend him for the job. The relationship between Ray Leonard and Tony Rivers is worse than ever, but the training centres needed reorganization. I was the most likely candidate. Perhaps at the time, Jim Carthy thought he could handle all the pressures and now finds he can't.'

Pause.

'I just don't think Jim Carthy is that political,' finished Henry Mitchell.

Silence.

'Forget Jim Carthy. What about you? What are you going to do?' enquired Evelyn.

'You remember my telling you that I met someone from rail transport at a lunch about two weeks ago. Well, he kept telling me that a senior position was about to become vacant, but he did not say what. I wonder if that was a hint,' said Henry.

'Well that would be the ultimate! You going back to manage the railways after what, 20 years?' laughed his wife.

'Yes, I left the railways to help form the authority,' said Henry Mitchell.

'Give him a ring. Invite that chap to lunch or dinner here at home. You certainly have nothing to lose,' stated Evelyn.

'Quite right! Time I did something about my situation.'

TASK

Split into your study group and discuss the following questions. Please use a flip chart or black/white board to note the key points of your conversation for discussion in the plenary.

1 If you were Henry Mitchell what would you do next?
2 How effective do you consider Jim Carthy to be as director of the Industrial Development Authority?
3 Identify criteria that you would consider suitable for assessing the performance of a senior manager in any organization. To what extent do your criteria seem to be applied in the Industrial Development Authority?
4 From your experience, how important, desired and necessary, is an awareness of the politics played in any organization? Give reasons as to why!

6

D'ARCY AND KEY

Andrew Kakabadse

PART I

'So, it's agreed.'

'Yes', responded Peter Thorn, Chairman of D'Arcy and Key, the subsidiary investment bank of Global, known as the clearing bank with ambition.

Crosbie stared at his drink as the two men sat together in one of the many cellar pubs frequented by the businessmen of the City. Crosbie de Veaux, managing director of D'Arcy and Key, was a young, aggressive merchant banker whose meteoric rise had been more than noticed by the City pundits. He came from a wealthy family who could trace their connections to the French nobility as far back as the Battle of Agincourt. Although Crosbie made little of his family's background and wealth, he projected a somewhat arrogant and self-assured image, which those less confident found irritating. He was very different to Peter Thorn who, as a considerably older man and the son of a railway inspector from Tyneside, had an undramatic but steady rise as a clearing banker, having only ever worked for Global. He had switched to investment banking ten years previously, and in his safe but sure way, recently secured the position of chairman of D'Arcy and Key.

'You know how many people we are going to have to hire?' asked Crosbie.

'We will have to grow at least three times our current size of seven to eight hundred people,' responded Peter.

'Yes, that feels about right,' whispered Crosbie. 'It is going to be a hell-of-a-job for us, even though our partnership has produced the results in the past,' continued Crosbie.

Pause.

'Together with the parent, we have to grow into becoming a major world player. The name "Global" actually means something to them, and from now on, even more to us. You know it's not going to be easy.'

Peter Thorn nodded.

The two men continued their discussion, mixing business with social chit-chat until well into the evening.

THE 'OPS' MEETING

One of the many complaints in D'Arcy's was about meetings. Meetings to discuss current clients' contracts, meetings on new products or ventures, coordination meetings, premises meetings; for those involved, the list seemed endless. However, there were two meetings that were absolutely sacrosanct – the chairman's meeting and the 'Ops' meeting. Peter Thorn chaired the chairman's meeting every Monday morning on behalf of the management committee, to review events over the past week and to discuss developments over the following week. The Ops meeting was chaired by Crosbie, again on behalf of the management committee, to address current concerns, whether of an operational or strategic nature.

The key members of the management committee included:

Peter Thorne	Chairman, D'Arcy & Key
Crosbie de Veaux	Managing director
Neil Price	Deputy managing director
Jeremy Mortimer	Director, investments management
Caroline Hayle	Director, information technology
Lionel Kane	Director, capital markets
Penny Latimer	Director, development capital
Michael Stone	Director, corporate finance
Isra Boone	Director, treasury
Geoffrey Fields	Director, fund management
Rupert Sayer	Central administration
Jack Flint	Director, equity securities

Additional members of the committee existed, but their involvement fluctuated according to whether Crosbie invited them or whether the other members of the committee considered it appropriate to instigate changes of membership. The membership fluctuated between the basic 12 and a total of 21 people according to the numerous reorganizations instigated by either the chairman or managing director.

'Despite the number of items on the agenda, three must be fully discussed: the integration of our proposed acquisitions of Hoggett Barr and Myddleton & Co., our plans to acquire Securities and Investments and Finance Royal, and of course, the new technology issue,' said Crosbie.

The four pending and proposed acquisitions were brokers/jobbers, designed to strengthen the sales/marketing of the securities part of the business.

'I think we're making the right decision to undertake small to medium-sized acquisitions, as integrating them into our culture is not going to be easy. Anything large would make it impossible,' commented Jack Flint, the dour Welshman director of the function.

'That's all very well,' responded Penny Latimer, 'thinking small because you want a comfortable life, Jack. The point is, we want a presence in the equities markets, just like we have to make an impact in the debt [capital] market arena. You cannot get away from it, buying and selling shares, and similarly with government debt and currencies, both are no small-time or amateur operations. We are competing with the Americans and Japanese and they are organized because their markets deregulated some time ago!'

'I know, Penny. I know!' exclaimed an exasperated Flint. 'You and I go round this topic time and again. I know we have to have a major presence in the equities and capital markets, but you must also invest to build up slowly. There is absolutely no point in buying big to find that the fish you have just caught nibbles and swallows you, as opposed to the other way round,' stated Flint.

Other members of the committee offered their views and suggestions, the comments varying between making a major acquisition in order to command a presence in the securities markets, and buying small in order to progressively capture market share. By the look on Crosbie's face, what other people called discussion, to him must have seemed like squabbling. It was Michael Stone who broke the deadlock.

'Yes, we need a presence in equities and what the shit whether we buy small or large – we've got the skills to make it there. It is capital markets that are going to drag us down. It has been said in private so often – shift the bastards and treasury to the parent.' Stone was known for not being the most tactful of the group.

The embarrassed silence was broken by Crosbie. 'There's no point in denying it, we are divided on the issue. The reality is that we are buying two and then two more. Jack, I would wish you to update management committee periodically over the next nine months on how integration is developing', said Crosbie.

Flint nodded. Crosbie indicated he was moving on to the next item on technology. 'We need to give Caroline far more support than she is getting in the process of new technology introduction', said Crosbie.

Silence.

'Look, just like everything else, we seem to hold polarized views on this. We are not just a merchant bank introducing some more sophisticated, computerized credit-control procedures, we are going to become a major world-player investment bank that needs an effective control function from new technology as well as a sophisticated communication network,' explained Crosbie.

'Our businesses are very different. Mine is as different from Michael Stone's as it is from Penny's. We need technology to suit our businesses; not to satisfy central control,' said Jeremy Mortimer.

'Jeremy, you, Michael Stone and I have talked about this before. When the functions spend money on technology, we inevitably lose more money,

41

as the functions do not have the skills to understand, let alone develop, the technology. Such piecemeal activities are expensive, as they inevitably are one-offs, which makes integrating the various technologies among the functions a costly nightmare. Centralizing technology means getting an overall view, not controlling what the functions are or should be doing.'

'I am here to make money for the bank and my function does that,' said Stone, staring first at Caroline and then at Lionel Kane. 'Why the hell should I be paying for passengers who cannot pay their way?'

Crosbie allowed the discussion to continue. Eventually, he somewhat abruptly indicated that he was satisfied from what he had heard of the discussion that no changes in the strategy for new technology should be introduced. He continued with the other agenda items.

'F . . . ing meetings', muttered Stone to Isra Boone, as the two walked down the corridor at the end of the Ops meeting. 'How the hell can you get on with real work, if all you do is attend f . . . ing meetings with that lot!'

THE BANKERS AND THE BROKERS

'I agree, Jack. Personnel should be involved in bringing together the brokers and bankers,' said Dick White, personnel manager.

The two continued to discuss a plan of action as to how the new and proposed acquisitions could readily be integrated, especially with the securities function which was most likely to be affected.

'Val Ginns, our training officer, and I will interview the various personnel, try to understand their problems, and with you, draft organization charts. You see, the reason I want Val involved is that she can look after any training requirements. From what I am hearing already, there is likely to be a need for workshops or seminars even just to inform our new colleagues about D'Arcy's.'

Flint nodded in agreement.

Valerie had just completed her fifteenth interview at Hoggett's. 'You really feel there is no future for you in D'Arcy's?' she reflected.

'Well, I can't see it,' commented the young broker team leader. He continued, 'I'm looking after this section which overlaps considerably with the work of two sections in D'Arcy's. I can tell you who is going to be worse off – me and my people. All this business about integrating, and seminars, and getting to know each other and, of course, personal statements from good old Crosbie saying we're all in it together – it's bull! We're going to get the chop. Well, I'm not hanging around for that. I'm leaving, and advising my people to do the same.'

'I see.'

Pause.

'Well, thank you for the interview,' smiled Val, somewhat weakly. Val had completed six interviews that day. She felt tired and her mood was low. On her return to her office, she detoured to see Dick White in order to swap notes. Dick was still at his desk.

'Well, how did the interviews go today?' he enquired.

'It's much the same. Despondency and gloom. Always wanted to be separate little brokers and jobbers. No one wanted to be part of D'Arcy's. Many feel they are going to get the sack, and some are ready to resign,' she finished.

'I've just finished drawing up the organizational plans for Jack Flint. Far fewer are going to depart than was first expected, but the demotivation is considerable. I am expecting far more resignations than sackings. You know, generally the whole of the investment bank is demotivated. Staff turnover is increasing, and the statements recently made by Crosbie as to the sort of people the bank wants are simply making things worse!' said Dick.

'Oh you mean this business about we want entrepreneurs and they have to be Aggressive For the Business In Going About Their Business?' she asked.

'That's right. All that's happening, as far as I can see, is that we are hiring the really aggressive types who bargain hard for their package and bonuses; who see only what *they* want, not what's best for the bank; who are building Chinese walls between the departments; and who, when they've got what they want, leave to take up even bigger and better-paid jobs here and in the States. I know we are ambitious and we want to grow, and are growing, fast, but Crosbie, I think, is making a mistake in management style.'

'I suppose for our little brokers, things are not made any better by the way Godfrey Pullen is being treated,' commented Val. Dick nodded in agreement.

Godfrey Pullen was the young and flamboyant chief executive of Hoggett Barr. Unlike his counterpart at Myddleton – who was offered a high salary with bonuses, a status title, but in reality a position in the bank of little consequence – Pullen was offered considerably greater remuneration and a seat on management committee.

However, for Pullen, market flair, making money and being outspoken were natural bed partners. Not only Crosbie, but Thorn and a number of others on management committee were on the receiving end of Pullen's tongue. Significantly, Pullen had not attended the last two committee meetings, and there was rumour of his imminent departure.

'I don't know what Crosbie is really playing at – you can grow quickly, but that does not mean you can sustain it over time,' reflected Dick.

THE DEALERS AND THE SELLERS

The more serious and thoughtful financial journals had begun the year with favourable comments and articles concerning Crosbie, Peter Thorn, and the ambitious growth plans of Global, within which D'Arcy played a significant part. Even up to three months ago, a feature on Reeve Ballard, the group chief executive of Global Bank, highlighted his brilliance as a businessman and his sensitivities in selecting people, especially the talented pair of de Veaux and Thorn. However, the mood of the press was changing. Hirings at very high rates – one headline ran, 'Only 22 and Only £200,000; Poor Little Rich Boy' – sackings, and a number of minor scandals concerning client accounts not being properly controlled, had now become headline news, and of course Crosbie was to blame. The message basically was: 'here was a young upstart who thought he could turn the whole financial world over with rapid growth and just buying in people!' Certainly, the next story to hit the headlines tarnished further de Veaux's public image. The headline ran: 'The Bank with No Loyalty'. The story was concerned with how the head of the dealing room and his team walked out, giving vent to their feelings of how capital markets were mismanaged in the bank.

The origin of the problems in the dealing room stemmed back to the appointment of Joel Mant, an American headhunted from the formidable American finance house, 2nd Wisconsin. Joel got most of what he wanted, and on that basis accepted an offer of appointment from D'Arcy's. Joel was made head of dealing in capital markets, brought over many of his own people from 2nd W, and in the dealing room, and with his seat on management committee, attempted to stimulate the environment which would establish a formidable dealing operation. Mant, however, was out-spoken and took a strong line on most issues, in his eyes, to support the bond and currency dealers. As far as others were concerned, Mant was narrow minded and took only a selfish perspective on virtually everything. In fact, the dislike for Mant was and had been growing considerably. Mant was equally responsive in his irritation with others, especially when he lost his seat on management committee in one of Crosbie's reorganizations. All that Crosbie said was, 'Joel, you are more than ably represented by Lionel Kane as your head of capital markets, and anyway, the committee is too large and I have to reduce the numbers!'

Mant was no committee man and so felt no personal slight at his loss of status. It was the fact that he lost a position of power where he could truly represent the issues that faced his bond and currency dealers – especially one issue in particular – the fact that he was not head of the dealing room. The dealers sat at one end of a large rectangular room and the sales/distribution force at the other. Mant's people purchased the products in the debt securities market as well as undertaking certain currency transactions. The other side, ideally, was there to sell and distribute the products and currencies purchased. The relationship between the dealers and sales, however, was so poor that in Mant's eyes, his people also had to sell without having the benefit of a distribution network within which to dispose of products. Within such a competitive market and on tight margins, naturally the dealers were losing money. Mant felt he could never get on with Tony Peale, head of sales.

Mant's natural impatience took over, and late one afternoon, he stormed into Kane's office, cataloguing his complaints about Peale and sales. Quite by chance, Peale happened to be away on a business trip, to be faced on his return the following afternoon with an irate Mant and irritated Kane. As happens in so many successful finance houses, Peale was as highly-strung and quick-tempered as the two confronting him. He launched into a fierce attack on Mant, accusing him of being product-driven and certainly not client-centred, of buying up any old bonds, of playing the Futures Markets, and dumping on to the Sales force such junk that any distribution network would have difficulty off-loading. Worse still, Peale's operation was as fledgling as Mant's and at the time when the sales operation should be given quality products in order to attract and build up the necessary client base, he was given, as he put it, 'Shit.' 'What's real funny is that the Yank buys shit which nobody wants, and so does his own sales – badly. I can't get the products I want, so I do my own purchasing, which means I do not have the contacts, so I do not get enough quality products to go round, so I disappoint my clients and they piss off to someone else, all because of you two bastards!' he shouted at Mant and Kane.

With that, Peale laid into Kane, accusing him of being a hopeless manager with a totally inappropriate style, of not understanding capital markets, because if he did, Mant would not have been appointed and apart from everything else, Kane was just thick. Even Mant looked embarrassed at Peale's choice of language. Little was achieved at that meeting other than an agreement to cool off and meet the next day. Little was achieved at that meeting or subsequent ones and within the month, Mant had resigned and on the day of his resignation went straight to the press. Within the next three months, Peale resigned, and he too gave a version to the press.

Now, not only the financial press but also the more serious dailies were giving D'Arcy's considerable attention, and especially Crosbie.

THE MANAGEMENT CONFERENCE

Crosbie's position was becoming ever-more difficult. The four acquisitions had not been as successful as he had hoped, as many of the staff he had wanted to keep, left, and those not required were made redundant. The demoralizing effect of considerable numbers of people leaving made a significant but unfortunate impact on the rest of the bank. There was no doubt about it, staff turnover was on the increase.

Certainly, Crosbie's recent pronouncements on what it takes to make the bank successful were generally considered not to have helped matters. Crosbie was identified as championing a more aggressive management style which was intended to attract single-minded entrepreneurs who would make money for the bank. Those who left, described the bank as a cold, ruthless place to work, where teamwork and basic good manners no longer existed. Such sentiments, coupled with rapid growth and large numbers of people entering and exiting, left even the most loyal oldtimers dissatisfied.

'We used to know people in the old D'Arcy's, so that we could naturally do business across boundaries. Now you just don't know people any more, and with everyone trying to make a quick profit to get their bonuses, its Chinese walls that really run the place', were the comments of one well-established D'Arcy merchant banker on his retirement.

The press were certainly giving D'Arcy's ever-more attention, much to the discomfort of Crosbie. The overall theme was the poor management of the bank, internal dissatisfaction, and weak controls which had lead to a number of scandals. Accounts had been allowed, more through inadequate supervision, to be overrun, losing in relative terms insignificant sums of money, but as a result, gaining considerable adverse publicity. Three separate incidents of accusations of insider dealing added fuel to the growing speculation of total mismanagement and anarchy. The fact that in all three cases no evidence of insider dealing could be established was not even being given a mention.

Rumours, staff turnover, adverse publicity and constant bickering on the management committee pushed Crosbie to a confrontation with his management committee.

'The publicity the bank and I are receiving is abysmal, which most unfortunately bears no relation to the fact that we are well capitalized and investing in our growth and success. The fact that we are not showing a profit is neither here nor there; it is exactly as expected in our growth plans. What is of concern to me is that we as a team are not of similar mind – we really have to sit down and thrash this one out,' stated Crosbie at the end of one of the weekly 'Ops' meetings.

Sullen silence. 'There is no point in saying nothing. We all know how divided we are,' continued Crosbie.

The ensuing silence was finally broken by Stone. 'Yes, you're right, the differences are great. What the hell sort of bank we are; how we should do things and how we should operate are major issues which, as you know, remain unresolved.'

Pause.

'Even over you. A number have wondered whether you should stay. You were probably the best "getter of deals" of all of us, but as MD I'm not sure you're that great,' finished Stone. Stone always ended up speaking his mind, and despite the uncomfortable silence experienced by all, Crosbie knew Stone was speaking the truth.

Yes, I do like doing deals, and I'm fed up with all this hassle. Nobody appreciates what I've done. I wonder who the hell could have done better, under these particular circumstances, thought Crosbie to himself, whilst maintaining a poker face to his colleagues.

'Although what you say is uncomfortable, you're probably right about the bank's problems and me,' reflected Crosbie.

Silence. 'You know, we probably need a management conference,' continued Crosbie. 'Staff turnover is high and morale low. Why not have all E [executive] grades 7 and upwards attend a two-day management conference whereby we can present a united way forward, listen to and thrash out the problems the E7s and above face, and hence improve morale. The mood here in the City is going to spread to the overseas offices and we just cannot afford that at this point in time.'

The following discussion indicated approval of the idea.

'Alright, here's what we do. A group of five of us not only plan the conference, but think through any organizational and policy changes that may need to be made prior to the conference, present them to this committee for approval, and announce them prior to or at the conference. Peter, Neil, Lionel, Michael and I should form the planning group.'

The group met on three separate occasions. The issue of Capital Markets was not addressed, as much due to Crosbie's ability of manoeuvre. However, the group decided on the following.

1 The reporting relationships concerning the overseas offices should clearly be stated once and for all. At the outset, the New York dealers reported to Kane; the head of the Australian operation, to Neil Price; with a number of dotted-line relationships existing to the various UK functional heads for each of the different Australian functions; the head of Singapore to Price; and Hong Kong to Kane, as the largest function was debt securities for Asia Pacific. However, the overseas general managers felt their issues to be inadequately represented and so insisted on reporting to Crosbie, which they did. The planning group decided to revert to the original reporting relationships and announce that at the conference.

2 Management training for E3 (supervisory) grades and above would be introduced throughout D'Arcy's. The group concluded that many of the people and organizational problems were as much due to poor management as arising from rapid growth.

3 A new committee and organizational structure was to be announced which involved minor changes, in that certain senior managers (not directors) from development capital, corporate finance and treasury were to lose their seats on the committee, which in turn would be taken by the four overseas general managers. The intention was to appease overseas management for no longer reporting to Crosbie.

4 The directors and their deputies of each of the major functions would make a presentation on the plans, objectives and expected performance of their function in keeping with D'Arcy's corporate policy.

5 The management conference date was set for the November, which

left four months for the management committee to ensure that their presentations were in keeping with the overall corporate view. A date was set in early October for a dry run for each of the presentations.

Management committee accepted each of the recommendations.

In total, 107 managers from the UK and overseas attended the conference. The morning of the first day dragged on, whilst each of the directors systematically went through their presentations.

A buzz of excitement went round the conference room when Crosbie stood to speak. He spoke of the ambitions of the bank, of the recent acquisitions and their integration, of the unity of the directorate, of the need for management training, of the need to maintain quality staff, and generally of the need to adopt a far more professional managerial attitude and approach, as with growth and success arises a strong need for competent management, and finally Crosbie announced the organizational changes. Peter Thorn finally presented a strategic view of the bank's future and reiterated the need to account for and respect the organizational, managerial and human resources issues and values highlighted by Crosbie. The managers were then split into working groups to discuss the issues outlined in the morning, and to identify and present these and other issues relevant to them. The afternoon, and the rest of the next day were set aside for small-group discussion and plenary presentation.

The first group to present late in the afternoon were the overseas managers, and they outlined their deep resentment towards the organizational changes. From their point of view, their issues never had been adequately represented until they began to report to Crosbie, and their request was to scrap the new organizational changes and to continue their present direct reporting relationship to Crosbie.

'But that means I will have about twenty-five direct reports,' responded Crosbie.

The spokesperson for the overseas managers shrugged his shoulders. The overseas managers' presentation and ensuing discussion continued for longer than expected and, hence, it was decided to address the issues of the other groups the next day and devote the evening to the conference dinner and socializing. The dinner went well, but as the evening wore on and ever-increasing amounts of alcohol were consumed, certain of the underlying tensions began to emerge. Crosbie walked into a private row between Stone, Kane and Boone.

'You're telling me that you could not take capital markets and treasury into the parent and run them as part of a traditional clearing bank operation?' enquired an exasperated Stone.

'Of course you could, but it takes time to incorporate our function with the other overlapping functions in the bank; time to build up a dealership and sales network, which is best left to us to handle rather than having the hand of a large traditional bank trying to manage what are esssentially strong-willed and quick-tempered entrepreneurs, and we just have to make it work because that is how we've declared ourselves to the market, and at the moment our image needs boosting and stability, not more change,' responded Isra Boone.

'You and your f . . . ing stability and your f . . . ing staid image make me want to throw up, Isra. The problems is that you two bastards are nothing more than product-driven salesmen – somebody points you in one direction and says "sell" and you just do it. You've got to have brains to think and be concerned about what your client needs. You two know only too well that any of my clients who wish to enter into the capital markets area, I don't expose them to you. I just leave the issue with them, unaddressed, and why? – I don't trust that either of you is any good, and why? – I make profits for the bank and you tell me you need time to invest to grow, and all I see is money going down the drain and an unwelcome change from the merchant bank I used to know.'

Lionel was about to let fly at Stone when Stone said, 'Ah, the boss – hello, boss, this is your happy family!' Stone laughed for some time. Crosbie looked at his three colleagues, said nothing, sat down and poured himself a drink.

Early the next morning, Crosbie was wakened by a phone call from Neil Price. 'Crosbie, you'd better see this in the financial section of one of today's dailies.'

Crosbie put on his dressing gown and went to Neil's room and read the headline: 'REVOLT IN D'ARCY'S – de Veaux cannot manage the satellites'. The story outlined how the organizational changes concerning the overseas offices had been rejected and that Crosbie was outmanoeuvred, outnumbered and isolated. The story continued by recollecting the ails and scandals of D'Arcy's and how Crosbie's aggressive style and lack of managerial skills and sensitivities were largely responsible for the current ills.

Crosbie stared at the article. 'Neil, would you ring Peter, Michael and Lionel, asking them to meet me in half an hour in our executive conference room. I should be grateful if you would be there as well.' Neil Prince nodded in agreement.

The five sat in the conference room. 'Judging by today's paper, I seem to have lost all credibility outside. Would you say it's the same for me inside?' enquired Crosbie.

Peter Thorn shuffled most uncomfortably, but it was Michael Stone who spoke. 'I know you and I have had our differences, but at least I have always spoken the truth and, outside the bank, supported you absolutely, so I shall be honest. I think you have lost all credibility. I think you have no option but to resign.'

'I feel awful saying this, but I think we have reached that position,' muttered Peter Thorn.

Lionel Kane nodded.

Only Neil Prince held a different view. 'I think you've done a lot for D'Arcy's. You promoted the growth plans and gave the bank a vision. You were heavily involved in negotiating and holding together the overseas offices and most of all, holding together the management committee and hence the bank, when everyone resented that. I feel we should stand behind you now.'

Crosbie smiled at the last comments. 'Thank you, but I think Michael is right. I think my credibility in the market is damaged and, internally, is gone. It would be destructive for me and for the bank to continue our relationship. Peter and I should see Reeve Ballard before I formally resign. We've got to continue with the conference, so we will arrange to see Reeve this evening.'

The other four nodded in agreement.

The conference delegates must have read the article, for the day was muted. No real controversial items emerged, and discussion focused on matters of operations and detail. Crosbie commented little. That evening, Crosbie and Peter Thorn met with Reeve Ballard, and within the hour, Crosbie had resigned, removed all his belongings and moved out. Crosbie's resignation was announced the next day.

QUESTIONS

1 Identify the business and organizational concerns that need to be addressed if D'Arcy's are to be successful as a bank. Please identify what you mean by 'success'.

2 Imagine yourself in Crosbie de Veaux's position as MD of D'Arcy's. Would you have resigned? If so, why? If not, why not?

3 What impact, if any, is Crosbie's resignation going to have on the bank and on the management committee? Please be quite specific in your response.

4 Assume you have just been appointed as the new MD of D'Arcy's. You have *no* track record of banking, but have had considerable success in retail:

   (a) identify the questions you need to ask in order to find out what you really need to do as MD;

   (b) indicate how you are going to go about finding out what is really happening in the bank, and how long this process of discovery is likely to take;

   (c) armed with this information, what are you going to do as the new MD?

Read the case ($\frac{1}{2}$ hour) so that you are fully familiar with the issues, events and concerns of D'Arcy and Key. Spend approximately:

1 $1\frac{1}{2}$ hours on discussion within your study group.
2 15–20 minutes preparing a presentation which will be made by a member of your study group.

7

GRAYLE ENGINEERING

Ron Ludlow

Grayle Engineering was established in 1936, and was now a public limited company, in which the Grayle family owned the controlling share interest. Throughout its existence, it had relied solely on Ministry of Defence (MoD) contracts for its source of income. Until 1980, these contracts had been placed on a 'cost plus' basis, but with the Conservative government's policy of reducing public expenditure, the method of placing contracts had been changed to 'fixed price'. Simultaneously, the size of the contracts had been reduced. Instead of the large contract, involving over a hundred employees or more for up to 5 years, the company was now being asked to handle contracts which frequently involved less than 15 employees for a duration of under 2 years. Between 1974 and 1985, personnel levels had fallen from 1,500 to 900. Staffing levels in the electrical engineering department had fallen from 45 to 26 over the same period. Between 1981 and 1984, redundancy announcements had resulted in the loss of over 300 employees.

Norman Graham, project manager in electrical engineering, had joined the company in 1977, as a senior electrical engineer, and for the first 5 years of his employment had worked on one large project. He had not enjoyed this long-term project commitment, and in 1982 had been relieved to find himself transferred to smaller projects. After working on 12 such projects, he was promoted to the position of small projects manager in January, 1985.

During his 8 years of employment at Grayle Engineering, he had frequently requested management training, but had only succeeded in getting on to two management courses, one held externally and one in-house, each lasting for one week. Prior to joining Grayle, his industrial experience, extending over 20 years, had started with an engineering apprenticeship, followed by 6 years with a large computer company and 9 years with the Science Research Council. He was professionally qualified with an ONC mechanical (endorsed by the Institute of Production Engineers) and an HNC in electronics.

GOING COMMERCIAL

Climbing the stairs to his office, one Wednesday morning in January 1986, his thoughts went back to the day he had been appointed small projects manager. He had then put forward his ideas to expand the electrical department by 'going commercial', and tendering for contracts outside the MoD, something Grayle had never done before. While this had received the agreement of his head of department, Norman was well aware of the problems facing the introduction of small commercial projects, in a company such as Grayle where operations were, and had always been, defined by MoD procedures.

The company had high fixed overheads, exemplified by the quality assurance (QA) system, mandatory for MoD work. The MoD required that all components should be traceable by their batch number, even back to the source of the raw material. Every deviation from the issued drawing had to be recorded and 'concessed' by the head of design. Scope for 'judgement' was not permitted by the inspectors – it was either correct to drawing or not correct. Norman realized that one of his first problems was to introduce some scope for 'judgement' if small commercial projects were to be viable.

Grayle had no experience in tendering for commercial projects. MoD contracts required approval documentation with contributions from many department (systems analysis, stress, reliability). A commercial project did not. It would therefore require considerable effort on Norman's part to prevent these departments 'jumping on the bandwagon', particularly as new work was scarce for all departments, in the current economic situation.

Norman was also concerned about staffing levels. The Electrical Engineering Department's involvement in minor projects could be anything from 3 months to 2 years in duration. Yet extra staff could only be recruited if it could be shown that there would still be a shortage in 12 months' time. Despite 4 years of monitoring the situation, the electrical engineering department was always 25 per cent understaffed at any one time because of the difficulties involved in the forward planning of the work load. The recruitment policy remained unchanged. Norman estimated a need for six more engineers. Staff morale was falling. New graduates joined and required training. The 'over-forties' in the department trained the new graduates.

However, there was a dearth of experienced engineers in the 25 to 40 age group, as a dramatic shortage of engineers generally made it possible for them to exploit good salary enhancements outside Grayle. New graduates saw a 20-year age gap between themselves and their seniors and felt that promotion was impossible. They left at the earliest possible moment.

The sales operation was also a cause of serious concern for Norman Graham. It was staffed by ex-service officers, who responded to general staff requirements issued by the MoD. They sold only that which the company had already produced and had had approved by the MoD. They did not explore the market, in order to assess its future needs and initiate internal research and development (R&D). The new business committee only responded to invitations to tender; such invitations were then passed to the marketing department, for assessment. The marketing department received information from the company's agents in foreign countries, who fed back 'needs' to Grayle.

A further problem arose in the manufacturing department. The continuity of large projects meant that the staff employed at the end of one fiscal year would be employed at the start of the next. The finance department therefore had become accustomed to delaying the issue of works order numbers by up to six weeks into the new fiscal year. Minor commercial projects had to be sanctioned anew after the start of the new fiscal year, and this took several weeks after presentation to the new business committee. The manufacturing could not proceed without a valid works order number.

The drawing office was required to produce drawings to the strict requirements of Defence Standards. Indeed, it was regularly audited to ensure that it did so. The wider tolerances and the suitable alternative components, permissible in commercial work, produced a laborious drawing burden. The chief draughtsman insisted that draughtsmen worked to the written instructions of the engineer. It was his belief that draughtsmen had no reason to visit the workshops during manufacture. Norman realized that it would be a major task to break down the custom of 'isolationism.'

The personnel department moved slowly. Several weeks could elapse between an interview and the issue of an offer of employment. They seemed to be unaware that experienced engineers were at a premium, and that new graduates steadily left after 2 years, thus exacerbating the age gap. Despite the 'seller's market', salaries of electrical engineers were pegged to other disciplines to avoid 'creating a precedent'. Norman's present staff on small commercial projects numbered four; three were new graduates and one was an engineer with 5 years' experience.

As Norman reached his office door, he ruefully reflected that so far out of the seven tenders for new small projects, submitted since he became project manager, no contracts had yet been placed. Five of these had been for fixed price MoD contracts and had become 'deferred decisions', a policy decision of the Ministry, but of the two purely 'commercial' tenders, one had gone to a company in Germany (a job for South America) and the other (a job for the Middle East) was still in abeyance. The current commercial work in progress consisted of a contract for Africa.

Norman was determined to get more work into the department and to increase staff levels in order to handle it. He was determined that he would initiate action today in order to achieve this. His first priority was to write a proposal to senior management, via his head of department, to increase his authority as project manager on minor projects, so that other divisions would be accountable to him for their performance. He wanted to change the project management structure so that small commercial projects would no longer be organized, as seen in Figure 7.1, where the small projects manager could only get input from the various disciplines by making a request upwards via his head of department, and once such input had been sanctioned, he had no direct control over it on a 'daily basis'. Instead, he wanted to adopt the management structure which already existed for large projects, as seen in Figure 7.2, where the projects manager had staff from various disciplines seconded to his project, and had full control over their input, on a daily basis, for the duration of the project. This would specifically give him more control over finance and marketing operations.

He also wanted to stress the need for additional staff, and estimated that his immediate need, regarding commercial projects, was a minimum of two experienced main-grade engineers. However, his head of department was well known within the company as a man who always put off until tomorrow a decision he should have taken today – his 'in tray' was referred to as the Bermuda Triangle. Therefore, Norman decided to side-step normal company procedures, and to send a copy of his proposal to the chief engineer.

THE DAY BEGINS

The telephone rang. The progress department informed him that the paint, required for the transit cases on a current MoD project, was two weeks out of shelf life. As a result, quality assurance had impounded it into the stores to prevent its disposal. Would he please write a memo, accepting it. The alternative would be one month's delivery for a new batch, and a £100 minimum order charge. He had to decide quickly what should be done, and advised them to use the out-of-date paint.

A knock on his office door heralded the arrival of the safety officer. He explained that he could not sign an operational procedure for some test equipment on an existing project, because it did not contain the 'standard paragraph' on the Health and Safety at Work Act. He asked Norman to arrange for its inclusion, or to confirm that there was a disclaimer in operation. Norman promised to check and advise him further that afternoon. He wondered whether or not to delegate this job to one of his new graduates but, after consideration, decided to do it himself, for speed.

The telephone rang again. Purchasing department advised him that a subcontractor had suffered fire damage, which would delay their delivery of some parts for an MoD small project by twelve weeks. Was this acceptable, or should they go to another firm, which was not MoD approved but could deliver in six weeks, but with a cost penalty. Norman advised them that he would prefer the earliest delivery, but that he would have to see quality assurance for a concession. He promised to call purchasing back in the afternoon with an answer. Glancing out through his office window, he noticed that his staff seemed to be engrossed in their work. 'Oh well,' he thought, 'better not disturb them.' Rising from his chair, he made his way to quality assurance.

It was almost 10.30 a.m. He got up to get a cup of coffee, but as he reached the door, the telephone rang again. This time, it was finance department, querying the booking of personnel from marketing department on works order numbers issued to Norman Graham. He informed them that, in the case in question it was quite in order, and hastily replaced the phone to get his coffee.

As he returned from the coffee machine, he heard the phone ringing once more. This time it was publications, advising him that the presentation material for the sales 'push' would have been ready if the slide copier had not broken down. They asked if he could use an overhead instead of a slide projector. The material was all ready, and they wanted to know who would pick it up. He said that he would come over and pick it up straight away.

At publications, he joined in a discussion of their technical difficulties, and received their profuse apologies for their failure to supply him with the material, in the form he requested. He had always enjoyed good relations with them, and consequently allowed them to take up more of his time than he could really spare, given that his morning had been one of constant interruptions.

Arriving back in his office, he dumped the presentation material on the table and noticed that a drawing had been put on his desk, with a memo, requesting him to check it through for errors. Having found one small dimensional error, he reached for his pen and corrected it. He then walked to the drawing office and returned it to the chief draughtsman, informing him of his action, and thinking how much time his modification would save. It took at least a week to get modifications done in the drawing office.

Returning to his office, he looked at his 'in tray'. He noticed a letter from a subcontractor which required his urgent attention. He groaned inwardly, remembering that letters always took at least two days to be processed through the typing pool. Reaching for some headed paper, he wrote the letter himself.

It was now almost 11.30 a.m , and he had not yet chased up the mechanical engineers working on the current commercial project. He knew they were having problems, as one of his subordinate electrical engineers had relayed the information last night. 'Better check it out now,' he muttered, and left immediately for the mechanical section, situated in an office block some 400 yards from his own. 'This is where I could do with more experienced subordinate staff,' he thought, 'but then, would I really want to delegate this sort of thing? A good manager should always keep his finger on the pulse, and there is no better way of doing it than by being seen to be doing it. Besides, I enjoy the contact with other disciplines, it makes for good interpersonal relations.'

On his way back to his office, he was stopped by one of his young subordinate engineers, who told him that he had just become a father for the first time. He congratulated him warmly, and spent a few minutes discussing the joys and burdens of fatherhood. When he finally reached his desk, he dug out the local telephone directory from the pile on his filing cabinet and telephoned Interflora, asking them to send the happy mother a bouquet. He was always interested in the lives of his young subordinates, and believed that a manager should show such concern. Besides it made them feel important, and he hoped it would help promote company loyalty and stem Grayle's staff 'leakage'.

No sooner had he put the phone down than it rang again. This time it was main-gate security, informing him that Mr Coleman from CAB Ltd had called. He apologized for not making an appointment, but he had located a supplier of some material which he knew, from his previous meeting with Norman, was being sought. Norman said he would meet him in the foyer. As he descended the two flights of stairs to the foyer, his feelings were ambiguous. He was annoyed at this further interruption but, at the same, time, he was very grateful to Coleman for his help. Having taken note of the details supplied by Coleman, Norman glanced at the foyer clock. It was 12 o'clock. 'Well, that's the morning gone,' he thought to himself, and inviting Coleman to join him, he made his way to the visitors' dining room for lunch. Lunch there always took longer, because of the waitress service, but then Coleman had been extremely helpful and he could hardly say goodbye to him at that point in time, without seeming very ungracious.

AFTER LUNCH

It was just after 1.30 p.m. when Norman returned to his office. He immediately returned to the task of working through his 'in tray'. He had just completed reading the first page of a specification document when the telephone rang. It was the secretary of the new business committee, informing him that Wednesday's meeting had been brought forward to Monday because the managing director would be away on Wednesday. He confirmed that he could attend on Monday but that he had not yet received reports from either the planning, progress or finance departments, and he needed to collate this information before attending the meeting. He telephoned each department, asking if they had their reports ready for him. Planning and progress departments confirmed that theirs were ready, but finance department informed him that theirs would not be available until Tuesday. He felt a mounting sense of frustration, as he realized that the collation of these reports had been a job he planned to do on Monday, ready for the Wednesday meeting. Now he would have to collect the two reports that were ready, and begin work on them this afternoon, if he was to be ready for the Monday meeting. Moreover, he would have to go to the meeting without the report from the finance department. His collated material would be incomplete, and his input into the meeting unavoidably curtailed. He quietly cursed the managing director for bringing this situation about.

Putting the specification to one side, he rose to visit the planning department. As he reached the door, the telephone rang once more. It was one of his four subordinate engineers, phoning from the inspection area. The assembly of an electronic unit had been undertaken to use available components, but had not been completed because some were long lead items and were still awaited. Unfortunately, the order of assembly did not comply with the planning sheets, even though both the workshop and inspection agreed that it was sensible in the circumstances. Norman's subordinate engineer felt 'out of his depth', with the chief inspector, the workshop foreman and the planner, all arguing. He therefore asked Norman to come quickly, as the situation needed sorting out!

On his way back from the inspection area he called into the planning department and then climbed the stairs to the progress department to collect their reports. While in the progress department, he stopped and discussed two other jobs with them. He regarded good relationships with the progress department as an important part of getting things done. He decided to call in on finance, to see if there was any chance of speeding things up but only secured a half-hearted promise that they would try to have it ready by Friday night. 'Oh well,' he thought 'I could read it over the weekend, instead of the Sunday papers!'

Returning to his office he managed to finish reading the specification and made some notes, which he would have to flesh out in the morning. Glancing at the clock, he realized he had not rung back the safety officer. He rang the safety officer to tell him that a disclaimer was in operation. On being told that he had only just caught him, Norman glanced at the clock. It was 5.30 p.m.

AT THE END OF THE DAY

Norman locked his filing cabinet, grabbed his coat and opened his briefcase, to put the remaining paperwork from his in-tray into it, to read later that night. As he did so, he spotted that his briefcase still contained two documents that he had read the previous night. He switched the new for the old, silently promising himself that he would clear all his paperwork in the morning.

At 5.36 p.m. Norman Graham left his office, anxious not to be late home. It was his twenty-fifth wedding anniversary and he had planned a surprise dinner for his wife and family of three at a local restaurant. He got into the car for the drive home, only too aware of his failure to complete that which he had set out to do that morning.

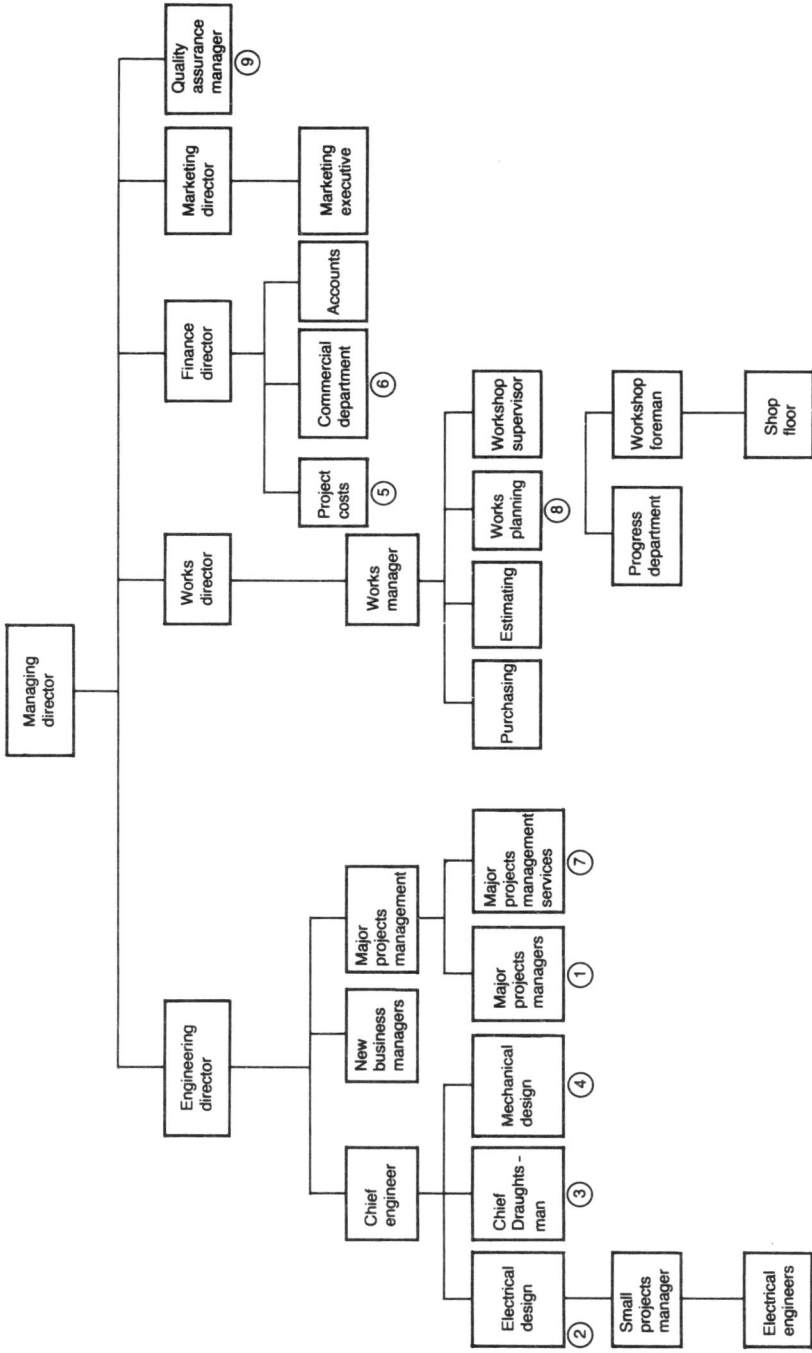

Figure 7.1 Minor project management

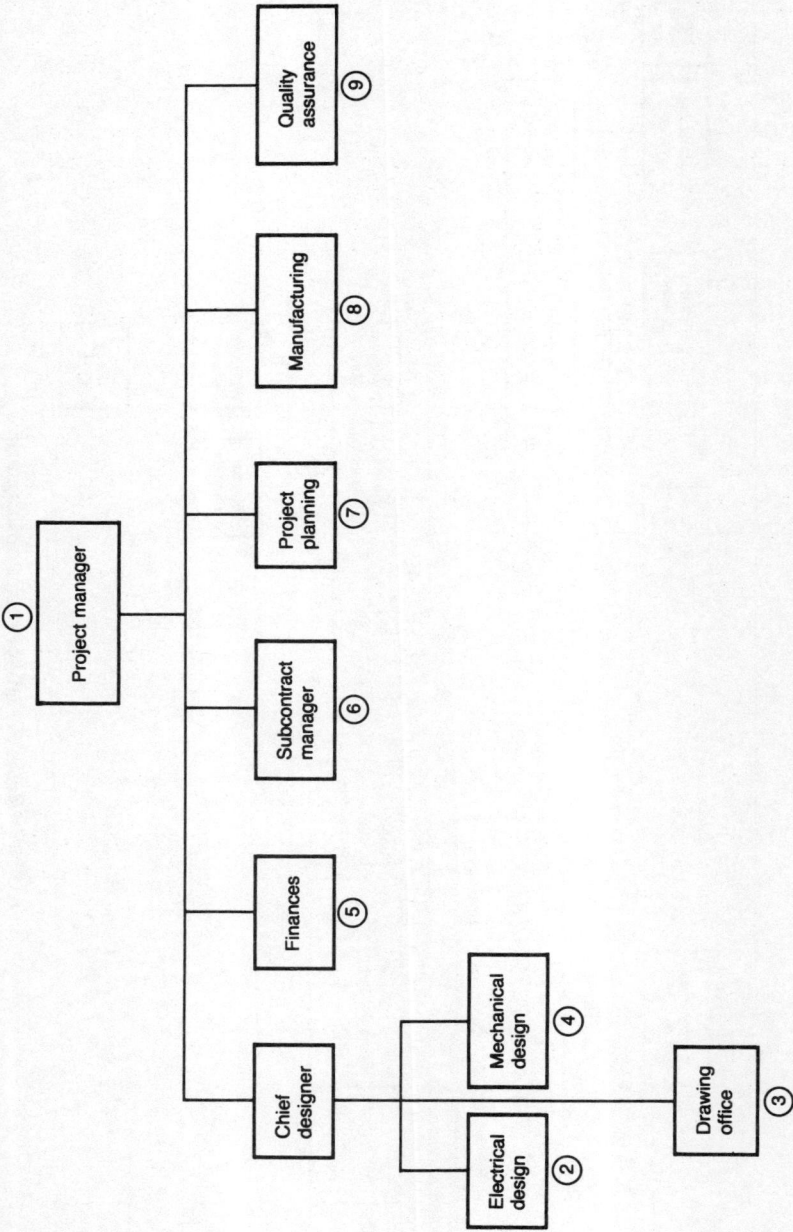

Figure 7.2 Major project management

As he drove home through the pouring rain, he had time to review his situation, and question his own competence. 'Am I an effective manager?' he asked himself, aloud. He reflected that he had been instrumental in creating the prototype wiring shop, as an offshoot from the formal shop. He had also introduced the 'roving inspector' and 'process inspection' when end-of-product inspection was inadequate. Had he not also supported the case for radical changes in the electrical 'goods inwards' inspection? Had he not also introduced the 'running errata sheet' for a complete assembly, to overcome the 'one deviation – one concession form' syndrome, which was the custom in inspection? Had he not forced through the drawing office a drawing system which saved 30 per cent of draughting time on printed circuit boards?

With his knowledge of the existing system, and a fair record of sacrificing 'sacred cows', the management considered him the most likely man to succeed in creating a new internal procedure to facilitate commercial projects. Yet, at the same time, he was well aware of senior management's criticism of his methods of dealing with his subordinates. He was thought to be too friendly; senior management believed that managers should adopt a more remote style of management. Norman disagreed; his style had always got things done. His friendliness made people more willing to 'do him a favour', even when this went against company procedures.

That night, returning home with his family from the restaurant, he reflected on his long and happy marriage. However, he was also reminded of the fact that he was now 50 years old. Switching on the 10 o'clock news, he sat back to catch up with what was happening in the outside world. He heard, without undue surprise, the announcement that Michael Heseltine had resigned. As he rose to switch off the TV, he smiled wryly, thinking that whoever became the new Minister of Defence would make little difference to his own situation at Grayle. Things would not change as far as MoD contracts were concerned. The amount of work might vary, but the system would remain the same. Pouring himself a double whisky, he reached for his briefcase.

QUESTIONS

1 Evaluate Norman Graham's effectiveness as a manager.
2 Describe his style of behaviour and analyse the reasons for it.
3 What can be done, if anything, to improve Norman's effectiveness? Explain why.

PART II

STRATEGIC
MANAGEMENT

The term strategy has been used in a multiplicity of ways in the management and organization literature. Strategy has been applied at the individual level to indicate the approach(es) a person adopts in order to address particular problems and issues. From an organizational perspective, strategy has been identified with those interests and actions which help achieve the mission and objectives pursued by the organization in its market place. Equally, the term has been utilized to both describe and epitomize the tensions and pressures at the interface between the organization and its external environment, especially during periods of change.

Even taken from an organizational perspective, strategy has been interpreted in two distinct ways. Under the normative school, all-embracing models are formed in order to explain the making and effective application of strategic decisions. The emphasis is on a scientific approach to contingency forecasting, in order to draft plans, designs and generate strategies that fit with predetermined criteria. In contrast, the incrementalist philosophy projects an intermittent, loosely linked pattern to strategy formulation and implementation, as much influenced by those executives involved in the strategy formulation process, as by organizational, market or external environmental forces. The cases offered in this section address both philosophies, covering the more haphazard, subjective processes of the incrementalists and the planned, rigorous, objective stance of the normative school.

The case of *The Syntax Corporation (Part 1)* examines the interpersonal processes involved in the development of a newly formed group of senior executives as they progress into becoming a more effective and mature management team. The importance of the behaviour of the team members and other senior executives (non-team members) in the organization, on the organization and its business, emphasizes the importance of understanding what constitutes effective performance at senior organizational levels. The case is sequential and hence parts 2, 3, 4 and 5 can be found in the teaching manual.

The role of the consultant in the process of strategy formation, especially when key executives hold different perspectives concerning the future of the business, provides the theme for the case of *The Celtic Woollen Company*. In situations where tensions need to be overcome in order to form business strategies with which senior management can identify, the issue of ethical/unethical behaviour arises, which provides an additional interesting aspect of the case.

The processes of strategy generation, implementation and the contribution that can be made by a consultant is continued, but from the particular perspective of data feedback, in the case of *The Public Welfare Agency*. The steps to gathering relevant data and its feedback to managers in the organization in order to assist strategic decision making, are crucial learning points in this case.

Continuing with the theme of strategy formulation and implementation, the case of *Kabi Pharmacia* concentrates on strategy implementation with particular focus on downsizing. In addition, where the company should be located and how to cope with redundancies when no redundancy policy exists in the organization, are interesting learning points.

The themes of strategy formulation and implementation are continued in *The Bank of Ireland* case. From an organization that was losing 1 per cent market share annually to now being a significant financial player in the world banking scheme, a broad range of issues are highlighted in the changes experienced by the organization. A particular point of interest is that the chief executive officer is highlighted as a key change agent. The Bank of Ireland case provides for a comprehensive overview of the change process. The case is sequential. Parts 2 and 3 are to be found in the teaching guide manual.

The individual as the key driver of change is a concept that is contained in the *Vinny Wallace* case. The case explores the role of general manager, specifically from the role holder's point of view. The perceptions of the role holder as to the key issues to address and how to address them are fundamental to understanding the case. In roles where considerable discretion exists concerning what to do and how to do it, perception is a vital determinant of decision making and decision implementation. The case is sequential. Parts 2, 3 and 4 are to be found in the teaching guide manual.

Effectively addressing and managing the processes of strategy generation, decision making and implementation is in part influenced by the management development exposure individuals experience. The case of *Eurodollar* examines management development strategy addressing both senior and middle management concerns.

Having explored the processes of strategy formation/implementation and thereby discussed the range of criteria for assessing executive performance, the case of *Fosbar Electronics* examines the management development requirements of senior management. Particular management development solutions are requested as part of the case study tasks.

Vanguard provides an overview of strategic processes by examining a broad range of communication related issues. Within the analysis, the role of human resource departments within the processes of communication is explored.

Similarly, *The Epicurus Leisure Group* case requires that a broader industry perspective be adopted before examining in detail the situation in the company. Having identified the desired strategies for the future, it is important that a human resources strategy be identified and developed which can adequately support the newly shaped corporate plan.

8

THE SYNTAX CORPORATION

Andrew Kakabadse

PART 1

Syntax is a multinational, advanced computer technology corporation offering a wide range of hardware and software computer products, such as the new micro VDUs on the hardware side and up-to-date packaged management training programmes on the software side. In addition, the corporation has diversified into other areas such as the production of high-quality aircraft instruments and vehicle instrumentation and medical and laboratory equipment. Currently, the corporation is split into four divisions, with its head office in Culver City, California.

Medical and laboratory division (MLD)

Our attention is focused on the activities of MLD; specifically that part of the division known as 'Rest of the World'. The general manager responsible for MLD split the division into two – the USA and Rest of the World. The president for rest of the world is an American, Jeremy Bryant, based in London, but servicing the UK and Eire, Europe (including the eastern bloc), the Gulf states, Africa and the Asian bloc, including mainland China and Japan.

In his current job, Bryant has an impressive track record. He regularly returns a healthy profit. In addition, he holds a reputation in the corporation for picking the right man for the job. His two latest successes are former Lancashire textile worker, Peter Ashcroft, whose selling skills have made him a legend in the corporation, and David Hall, generally recognized as intellectually highly talented. Ashcroft holds the position of sales vice president (Rest of the World) and seems to be achieving the impossible – selling advanced medical and laboratory equipment to the Japanese in ever-increasing quantities. Hall has a Ph.D. in physics, a former young university professor, but with an eye for business and product development. Of the two, it is considered by the other influential managers, that Hall will be the one who will take whatever 'big jobs' become available in the USA.

Hall's responsibilities are two-fold:

1 To participate as a full member on the product strategy team (PST) which meets periodically in Culver City to decide on the product portfolio of the division. Amongst others, such as the President, MLD/USA (Bryant's counterpart), Bryant himself and representatives from Japan, Europe and other factory sites in the USA, sits Corgill, the General Manager responsible for MLD. On this committee, Hall's task is to represent the British contribution in terms of product design and development, manufacture and the worldwide marketing of all MLD products.

2 To promote product design, development and manufacture of British goods at three sites in south-west England, Taunton, Yeovil and Marlborough, and a further site in Carlisle. Hall's position is that of UK production vice president.

At present, Hall is the sole UK representative on the prestigious PST.

Both Hall and Ashcroft report directly to Bryant. A third member provides the full complement to Bryant's entourage, Eammon O'Sullivan, the Dublin born, finance and administration vice president for Rest of the World (see Figure 8.1). Unlike the commonly accepted stereotype of an Irishman, O'Sullivan is dour, quiet, a non-drinker and efficient. He meets deadlines.

MLD, to an outsider, could be seen to operate a somewhat unclear management structure. For the employees, lack of clarity is in reality, confusion, at times leading to disillusionment. The problem is that two structures operate simultaneously, a traditional hierarchical structure and a team structure.

On the hierarchical structure side, appraisals are conducted by the line managers; promotions and pay increases are determined by established procedures and guidelines. Most work, however, is conducted by teams. Teams exist for virtually every contingency – long-term strategy teams, medium-term resource allocation teams, segment teams that examine the needs of particular segments of the market, task/production teams that manufacture particular products and leader teams that attempt to identify new markets and their potential. In fact, MLD operates an intricate matrix structure that looks more like a spider's web than the more traditional two-dimensional, functional/mission based matrix structure.

Any individual could hold membership to two or more teams whose interests may not be well aligned and yet be supervised by a line manager with whom they may spend less than 15 per cent of their time. Line managers, naturally, turn to team leaders for performance appraisal information in order to accurately assess their subordinates. Such a practice has caused problems, for on numerous occasions, team leaders have provided negative appraisal reports to line managers, which the individual felt was unjustified. The issue is that individuals could hold membership to two or more teams whose interests may conflict. The poor appraisal reports often concern the individual's inability to fit as a team member. From the individual's point of view, the problem is one of a conflict of role expectations.

Although particular problems exist such as, a conflict of interests, poor appraisal performance data, switching team membership, being taken off one project on to another before project completion, the morale and motivation among employees (both operatives and management) is high. Starting early, working late, not claiming for extra remuneration and a general preparedness to be responsive to change, has become a norm in MLD.

The birth of a management team

Murray McConnell, Personnel Director, Syntax UK (a subsidiary within MLD) had noticed that a number of coordination and communication problems existed in Syntax UK. A few important issues that affected the performance of a number of teams were not being addressed. This was not so much due to negligence, but rather because no one person or team had been briefed to handle these problems. One reason for this, was the now traditional lack of communication and rivalry that existed between the Yeovil and Taunton sites. Yeovil was the bigger of the two as it had the largest production facility of the UK sites, and housed Hall and his team. Taunton, although smaller as a site, housed the marketing, sales and accounts group. Further, for McConnell, Bryant's style of management did not help the situation. Bryant, quite deliberately, had developed an almost perfect delegative style – to the unsophisticated, he sat back and let things happen. McConnell knew that Bryant was aware of the coordination and communication problems but had done little to improve matters. Why should he, he was president for Rest of the World; the fact he was based in London did not mean he had to attend to all of Syntax UK's problems. On that basis, McConnell approached Bryant, indicating that something should be done about the coordination and communication problems in the company.

'Murray, I hear what you're saying. Why not pick a team to handle these problems. I won't interfere. Teams get things done – you know that!' stated Bryant.

McConnell did just that and invited six influential managers (Tony Capella – manufacturing; Robert McSweeney – product development; Jerry Jones – sales; Andy Taylor – accounts; Damien Carter – marketing; Russell Peters – sales) to sit with him on a newly formed team. All but McConnell reported to Ashcroft, Hall or O'Sullivan. McConnell invited these managers for four reasons: they were well known, influential and respected in Syntax; they represented each of the major functions; also they were well known to each other and shared McConnell's concern for the problems facing the organization.

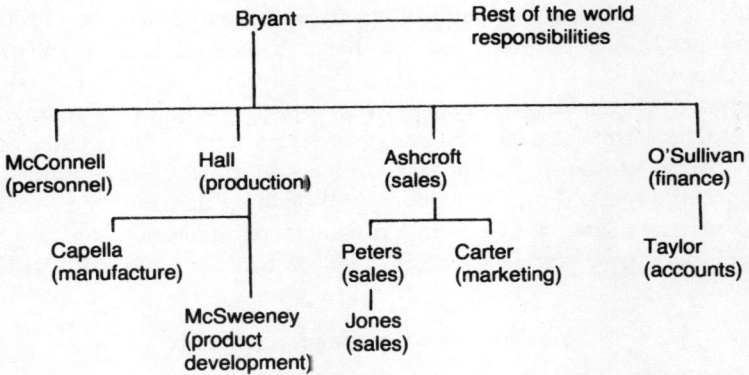

Figure 8.1 Syntax (UK) organization structure

'Hell, we are not just an operational group, we are a management board,' thought McConnell.

So was formed Syntax (UK) management board, on which neither Bryant, Ashcroft, Hall nor O'Sullivan sat.

QUESTIONS

1 What would you consider the nature of some of the co-ordination and communication problems mentioned?
2 What particular problems and issues are McConnell's team likely to face?
3 What criteria would you consider appropriate for assessing effective team performance?

9

CELTIC WOOLLEN COMPANY[1]

Andrew Kakabadse

'As you can see, we were a very traditional company with still some changes to come,' finished Jim Peters, personnel director of the Celtic Woollen Co. Jim sat back in his comfortable black leather chair, awaiting a response.

Jim had been talking to Neville Sims, a senior consultant of Management Associates, a large consulting firm offering a number of different services ranging from marketing surveys, feasibility studies, organization design and structure, personnel consultancy, recruitment and selection to management training. Neville Sims specialized in organization structure and design, the management of change in organizations and management training. The Celtic Woollen Co. had frequently used the services of Management Associates for marketing surveys, feasibility studies and recruitment and selection. This was the first time Neville Sims had been approached by the company.

Sims reflected on Jim Peter's account of developments in the Celtic Woollen Co. He examined the organization chart of the board of the company that Peters had drawn for him. The Celtic Woollen Co. had been transformed from a small family business based in Dumfries to an organization of considerable size and repute by Hamish McArdle, grandfather of Rory McArdle. The McArdles had been wool manufacturers for five generations but serviced only local needs. Despite the 1930s recession, Hamish recognized the potential of the American market and negotiated short-term contracts with the more reputable Chicago and New York department stores. The American retailers considered the products of the company to be of high quality, manufactured at the right price, but in short supply. More through the persuasive powers of the American retailer, than Hamish's desire for considerable expansion, did the company take a calculated risk and purchase two further factories in Inverness and Motherwell. In fact, the risk was small. The American retailers recognized the market potential of traditional manufactured woollen clothing goods imported from regions such as Eire or Scotland. The 'Made in Scotland' label was suitably large and placed on each item of clothing.

Hamish's second son, Robert, showed the flair, capacity and potential to take over the company. In 1950, he was duly elected MD of the Celtic Woollen Co. in succession to Hamish. Robert considered the company's dependence on only certain American retailers to be a risky policy. For a start, Hamish's counterparts in the USA had either retired or died. Robert had neither the time nor inclination to negotiate the same trusting, informal relationships with the new generation of professional manager retailers as Hamish had done with the owners or family representatives of the American retail outlets.

Further, Robert had questioned why just the American market? What about the English or even European markets? The House of Fraser, a well established Scottish family business, had purchased a considerable number of retail outlets in England, the most notable being Harrods.

During the 1950s and 1960s, Robert negotiated numerous long-term contracts with several retail outlets in England, notably the House of Fraser, the Burton group and the Austin Reed chain of men's retailers. In order to service this increased demand, Robert opened a fourth factory in Glasgow. In addition, he invested considerably in modernizing the other three factories. Unfortunately, Robert had to retire prematurely due to a heart condition and his eldest son, Rory, was elected MD in 1974.

Rory McArdle and his father had, to say the least, a somewhat strained relationship. At the age of 36, portraying the image of the young, energetic, competitive, 'about to change everything' executive, Rory took over the company with the expressed intention of introducing changes to the company's product portfolio. Although over two generations the company had grown, increased its manufacturing capacity and negotiated lucrative retail outlets, the product range had hardly altered. The company manufactured chunky woollen knit sweaters, scarves, woollen hats and pure wool kilts. Apart from minor design changes or changes of colour pattern, the product line remained the same. It was Rory's intention to introduce new designs, and to enter the upmarket cashmere sweaters, cardigans, scarves and coats, and women's fashion market. Further, Rory considered the current manufacturing technology to be outdated, labour too expensive and the management too traditional and set in its ways to introduce the drastic changes he desired.

From 1974 to 1981, Rory worked on two fronts:

1 Introducing new and updated manufacturing technology and information systems.
2 The opening of two new plants in Nicosia, Cyprus, and in Galway, Eire, manufacturing cashmere sweaters and scarves.

The traditional clothing making skills, the abundance of cheaper female labour and the attractive subsidies offered by the home governments had made Eire and Cyprus two particularly favourable areas for the location of additional manufacturing plants. The cashmere product ranges were selling well in upmarket stores such as Harrods and Debenhams in London, top stores in Brussels and the Marshal Fields group of stores in Chicago and New York. Rory considered the manufacture of cashmere coats to be the next addition to the cashmere product range, to be manufactured in Nicosia and Galway.

Although he introduced substantial changes to the production side of the business, Rory made little impact on the management structure of the company. He had met with considerable opposition from his own board to the Galway and Nicosia projects. Unable to act without the support of his board, Rory made considerable concessions to the three long-standing directors in the organization.

David Price	Production director
Alex Campbell	Marketing director
Alistair McIntyre	Sales director

All three were in their late fifties or early sixties, had started as apprentices in the company and were the appointments of Hamish or Robert McArdle. The only changes Rory had introduced onto the board were the appointment of Jim Peters as personnel director, ex personnel manager from Phillips, the rapid promotion of Jonathan McArdle (Rory's cousin) to finance director and the introduction of an entirely new functional directorate – product design, under the directorship of Aelish Patterson, another of Rory's cousins, previously married to an American, now divorced. Aelish's skills and experience were particularly relevant as she had been product designer with one of the more experienced American fashion houses but returned to Scotland shortly after her divorce.

It was common knowledge in the organization that on most issues Rory would face most opposition from the production, marketing and sales groups.

'You say Rory wants his managers to be more capable of managing change. Also your managers have not really undergone any form of management training and you would at least like to consider what sort of training would be useful and how much it would cost, reflected Sims.

'Don't forget, Rory would like to look at the needs of the production and sales department first and then marketing and finance. The personnel department has been charged with masterminding the whole programme, but where do we start?' enquired Jim Peters.

'Look, I can't see the point of training your managers to appreciate all the various aspects of business. Why not train them to handle what you, I and they consider to be the problem issues? Why not hold a series of workshops with say, six to eight managers at each workshop for them to identify their needs? We can then create whatever programmes are necessary from the ideas and issues these guys generate,' said Neville Sims.

'Sounds a good idea. Look, why not come to Dumfries and meet Rory and any other members of the board that may be there,' responded Jim Peters.

'Good! Why don't I give you a few dates and then you can see which of them is most suitable to the others in Scotland. Finding dates is such a problem. Well here's mine. I'm free on . . .'

'Mr Sims. Do come in. Nice to meet you. I hope you had a pleasant flight from London. Yes, do sit down.'

Pause.

'I've arranged for a number of my colleagues to meet you at lunch. Any further discussions that are necessary, perhaps you could conduct on a more individual basis after lunch,' said Rory McArdle.

Rory then re-told Neville Sims the history of the Celtic Woollen Co., its current state of affairs and its need for change.

The luncheon meeting was a lively, friendly and informative affair for Neville Sims, attended by David Price, Alex Campbell, Rory and Jonathan McArdle and Jim Peters. The group discussed the company's present state of affairs, its need for change and the need for improved managerial skills in the organization. Jonathan McArdle indicated that the company had not explored different market sectors sufficiently. Whatever developments had taken place, the company was still in the high-quality woollen knit garments business. Alternative markets that should and had not been considered, were men's wear (e.g., jackets, trousers and suits) and the more giddy world of women's fashion such as dresses, blouses, skirts, tops, etc. Rory stated that the company was not ready for such expansion. During the conversation, Jim Peters spoke quietly to Sims stating that a meeting between David Price, Alex Campbell, Peters and Sims had been arranged for after lunch. Sims thanked Peters for organizing the meetings as David Price had hardly contributed to the luncheon conversation but most of the initial workshop activity would involve a substantial number of managers from production. The lunch meeting finished with Rory pledging his support for the workshops and any ensuing activities.

Neville Sims and Jim Peters made their way to David Price's office.

'Gentlemen, enter,' said Price. 'Perhaps if I can outline the purpose of the meeting. Well, what I want is to know what you intend to do in line with Rory's statement on making our managers more sensitive and capable of managing change.'

'I think it's important that before anything is done, you, the directors, know what we are trying to do. Towards this end, it's crucial that the problems, constraints and opportunities faced by the various levels of management are identified and understood. Although Jim and I have not specifically mentioned this, we would have thought the top managers of the organization should be included in this initial process of investigation,' said Neville Sims, turning to Jim Peters.

'Yes, I see. Uhmm ... to what extent have you been briefed on the developments in this company?' asked Price.

'I'd say fairly fully with no punches pulled,' responded Sims.

'So you appreciate some of the basic issues facing this company, and especially this board!'

'Yes, I have been told what's happening,' stated Sims.

'Then why start mainly in production and partly in marketing departments?' asked Price.

'I can answer that,' responded Jim Peters. 'You see, the parts of the organization that are likely to be affected most crucially by change are principally production and to a certain extent marketing and sales. I think whatever we as a board decide, the greatest impact will be on your people.'

'Yes, that I appreciate. How do you intend to proceed, Mr Sims?' questioned Price.

'Initially, to identify key and infuential managers in production and marketing who would be sympathetic and interested in talking about and identifying present and future problems. Then invite them in small groups of two or three, to one-and-a-half-day workshops. The findings of these workshops would be presented to you and other interested directors. From there on, the directors can debate what should be done,' finished Sims.

'That's interesting: get the managers to identify their own problems and their own solutions, by the sound of it. Mmmm. OK. What do you need from Alex Campbell and myself?' asked Price.

Campbell had not commented throughout the meeting.

'What we need are the names of people whom you would consider suitable for the workshops. For instance, they could be people who are sympathetic to change, those opposed to change, those who are influential in the organization; you know, a complete cross-section.'

Pause.

'Thinking about it, we would also need a few representatives from sales, finance and personnel. In that way we will have a complete cross-section,' commented Sims.

'That's fine by me,' said David Price.

'You may find Alistair objecting to some of his sales boys taking part. As for the idea itself, that's OK with me,' stated Alex Campbell.

'I'll speak to Alistair and Jonathan,' interjected Jim Peters. 'Although I can't promise anything. As far as my people are concerned, I think it's a good idea that some should attend the workshops.'

Four 1½-day workshops were organized and held at monthly intervals. The venue was a comfortable hotel in the Highlands of Scotland equipped with full conference facilities. Neville Sims, as workshop leader, stated the objectives of the workshops and then split the plenary into a number of subgroups.

Each group was asked to identify the problems facing the company. From these findings each group was then given the specific responsibility of identifying particular courses of action which the company could adopt.

The workshop participants used flip charts to make their presentations. At the end of each workshop, Sims collected all the flip charts and wrote a short report, concentrating on the key issues/problems identified and the proposed courses of action to overcome those problems. Each workshop participant received a copy of the report, as did the members of the main board.

After the fourth workshop, Sims drafted a summary paper for the members of the main board. The paper contained the following comments.

KEY ISSUES FACING THE CELTIC WOOLLEN CO.

1 *Relations between management and staff*
   (a) Industrial relations between management and labour force are poor.
   (b) Managers consider that the trade unions have weak full-time officials who lack control over shop-floor workers.
   (c) Managers feel that the workforce is at times better informed than management.
   (d) There exists a general indifference to authority on the shop floor.
   (e) It is considered that there is a reluctance on the part of the trade unions to identify with the management of the organization.
   (f) The company is seen as very much concerned with the development of its managers.

2 *Diversification and new developments*
   (a) The company has experienced a number of changes over the past few years which have caused anxiety amongst its employees.
   (b) Further change, in terms of utilization of new technology, is likely.
   (c) Demand for certain of the company's products is likely to stabilize or decrease. In particular, the chunky knit products are likely to decrease and cashmeres are likely to increase.
   (d) There is a need to explore new market areas, such as fashionable male/female clothing, but using other fabrics – silks, linen, rayon, etc.
   (e) An expected increased variety of goods means an increased workload for management and work force, thereby creating remuneration problems.
   (f) Costs of machinery, raw materials and products are likely to increase.

3 *Work opportunities and career development*
   (a) There is no master plan for career development within the organization.
   (b) Managers tend to be moved to different jobs with little initial training in their new post.
   (c) Currently, the lack of formal career development is not viewed as

problematic. It is considered that the better managers occupy the more responsible jobs.

(d) The company is still of a size that the better managers are personally known to various members of the board.

(e) If the organization plans to grow further, career development is a key issue which requires immediate attention as current practice will be unsatisfactory.

(f) There is a need to recruit further personnel into the organization due to the potentially ageing work force.

(g) Succession planning needs to be considered as an issue in career development.

4 *Relations between departments and production units*

(a) Communication problems are identified between departments and production units leading to lack of cooperation and antagonism between important sections of the organization.

(b) The main board is identified as being divided and split on certain key issues. If the main board members are unable to cooperate why should others?

One point in particular concerned Sims, namely the lack of impact on the organization by the personnel department. True, the company faced a number of strategic problems which needed confrontation and some training and development work was needed with the main board. However, the workshops highlighted a number of key human-resource issues that should have, in Sims's opinion, been addressed some time back. Sims wondered whether he should highlight the lack of penetration by the personnel department into the organization. Up to now, Jim Peters had been Sims's client. Sims recognized that the relationship between the two would be severely shaken if the personnel department was seen to be criticized by the consultant they hired in the first place.

Sims delayed submitting the report to give himself time to consider how to report the personnel department's involvement in the organization. He had, for some time, been dissatisfied with Jim Peters. In fact, most of the criticism levelled against the personnel department was criticism of Jim Peters. Peters seemed unable to grasp quickly the key issues in a problem and certainly did not present himself well at the workshops. On the other hand, he had recognized the problems faced by the organization and forcefully argued for and supported Sims's intervention. In this split, diversive and somewhat bitchy organization, Jim Peters had taken a considerable risk in inviting Sims.

Sims decided to have an informal talk with Rory and not to emphasize Personnel's deficiencies. Sims submitted the report to Jim Peters to circulate to the other board members. The main board meeting to discuss the report was set.

'Having now talked it through, the issues facing us are not just what business areas do we or don't we enter, but also what sort of managers, their skills level, and I suppose what sort of organization we want,' commented Rory. The main board meeting discussing the Sims report had now entered its second hour.

'I think the issues are more linked than that. For example, the sort of business you want to be will dictate what sort of managers you require. Let's face it, you are a functionally structured organization that really is fairly centralized in terms of decision making. You talk about profit centres and giving greater responsibility down the line. That's not just a training problem. You may wish to restructure your organization. In reality, you as a main board, may not wish to become that decentralized,' responded Neville Sims.

'I think what's interesting with this report and our discussion is that a number of problems have been highlighted. Our image as a board is not that great. Our managers have spotted our internal squabbles all too readily. Production in itself is not seen as a particular problem but new technology and new areas of business could severely influence the way the whole of production is managed. What's more, personnel have not come out as the shining heroes. I've been saying this for years, and yet production has been blamed for most of the problems in the organization,' snapped David Price.

The heated debate continued. Throughout the discussion, Sims noticed the tension between Rory and Jonathan McArdle. Rory seemed to be stressing staying with the present product lines and increasing the marketing activity in those areas. Jonathan was arguing strongly in favour of entering new market sectors, especially the world of women's fashion, ranging from formal to casual and even trendy sports attire for women. Throughout, Jim Peters was being criticized for his lack of planning and development of managers and the labour force in the organization. Two hours later, the meeting finished. The board members decided that the following two action points should be pursued:

1 Jim Peters, together with Neville Sims, would work out a manpower plan for the organization with particular emphasis on training and career development.
2 Jonathan McArdle, together with Aelish Patterson, were asked to explore new market sectors. Jonathan indicated he would commission particular consultants to conduct feasibility studies in particular markets.

Rory asked for a short meeting with Neville Sims after the meeting. 'Neville, be honest. You heard what was said at the meeting. What's your opinion of Jim Peters: You've worked with him,' said Rory.

'Probably most of what was said of the personnel department, and Jim in particular, is true and accurate,' replied Neville.

'I was afraid you'd say that. Jim's been with this company a long time.

He's loyal and always supported me. However, I'm not too sure he really appreciates what his job is all about.'

Pause.

'It'll probably come as no surprise to you that I've been thinking of moving Jim out of that job. Problem is, to move him into anything else would be to downgrade him. I reckon it has to be early retirement. I know you've worked closely with Jim and I would like you to continue doing so on this management development blueprint thing. However, I also need a new personnel director. Would you be willing to start, informally and very confidentially, a search process for the right man?' asked Rory.

'Yes. Yes I would. I'm not sure you have any other choice,' replied Neville Sims.

'You don't need to say anything to Jim; I'll talk to him. OK?'

'Fine,' responded Neville Sims.

Jim Peters and Neville Sims embarked on the project of drafting a management development blueprint. Each job in the organization was analysed in terms of task content, objectives to be achieved, skills required and the training needs of the incumbents. Numerous meetings and discussions were held with the managers of various departments and units.

One day Jim Peters commented to Neville Sims: 'I had a meeting with Rory yesterday evening. We talked about the changes required for the future and why we need a younger management, especially on the board. He suggested I might consider early retirement after I finish this project and another one he's got in mind for me.

'I see,' came the reply.

'I must tell you, I'm not too happy with the situation. Financially, no problem. This company is still old fashioned enough to look after its employees, even when it sacks them. What aggrieves me is that it would have been impossible to do anything substantial until now. Can you imagine David Price allowing personnel to take a look at his part of the organization? Who would have bothered turning up to workshops? Who was capable of running workshops? It took all my time to get Rory's support for you to come into the organization,' said Jim.

'Mmmm. Yes, I can see that,' mumbled Neville.

'I also understand from Rory that he's asked you to search for my replacement.'

'Yes, that's true.'

'Are you doing this because you agree with him?' asked Jim.

'Yes. I'm afraid that's true. I do agree with him on this issue,' responded Neville.

'I see,' said Jim quietly.

Jim Peters turned away and left the room.

The management development blueprint was completed and the report presented before the board. The board accepted the key recommendations of the report. Shortly after, Jim Peters was appointed project director to manage the start-up of a new factory in Portugal which was to manufacture cashmere sweaters. This project, championed by Rory, had been commissioned and agreed before Neville Sims had been approached by the company. Within a year, Jim Peters was retired. Tony Waters, the training manager, was placed temporarily in charge of the personnel department. Within two months, the new personnel director was in post.

Neville Sims was commissioned to implement certain of the proposals accepted in the management development blueprint. Sims initiated an assessment centre available for all levels of management, training programmes for managers and shop-floor supervisors and completely reorganized the entire performance-appraisal documentation and instituted appraisal training in an effort to ensure more effective appraisals were conducted down the line.

During this period, Jonathan McArdle submitted his fashion-wear feasibility study, which was strongly supported by Aelish Patterson, David Price and Alex Campbell. Jonathan highlighted three particular issues:

1 Fashionable sports and leisure wear.
2 Fashionable clothes for the executive woman.
3 Evening wear for men and women.

Rory, together with Alistair McIntyre and the new Personnel Director, refuted certain of the recommendations made by Jonathan. After substantial debate and two extraordinary board meetings, it was agreed by majority vote that the company should enter the markets of sports and leisure wear, and fashionable clothes for the working woman. By now, the majority of the cashmere products were being manufactured in Portugal.

The Galway plant was being run down. The bulk of the sports-wear items were sited for manufacture at the Galway plant. The fashionable female executives' clothes were to be manufactured at a new factory to be opened in Connemara in Eire. State financial support in Eire for new business was generous. The Celtic Woollen Co. made use of all the facilities offered in the Republic.

After the start-up of the Connemara plant, Rory called in Neville Sims and indicated that David Price would be taking early retirement. Neville was commissioned to search for his replacement. At the next board meeting, Jonathan McArdle questioned why David Price was opting for early retirement and why Neville Sims, in particular, had been asked to find his replacement. Jonathan was heard to have muttered that there were better hatchet men around.

Within six months, David Price's replacement was identified, appointed and in post. Neville Sims is substantially involved with the Celtic Woollen

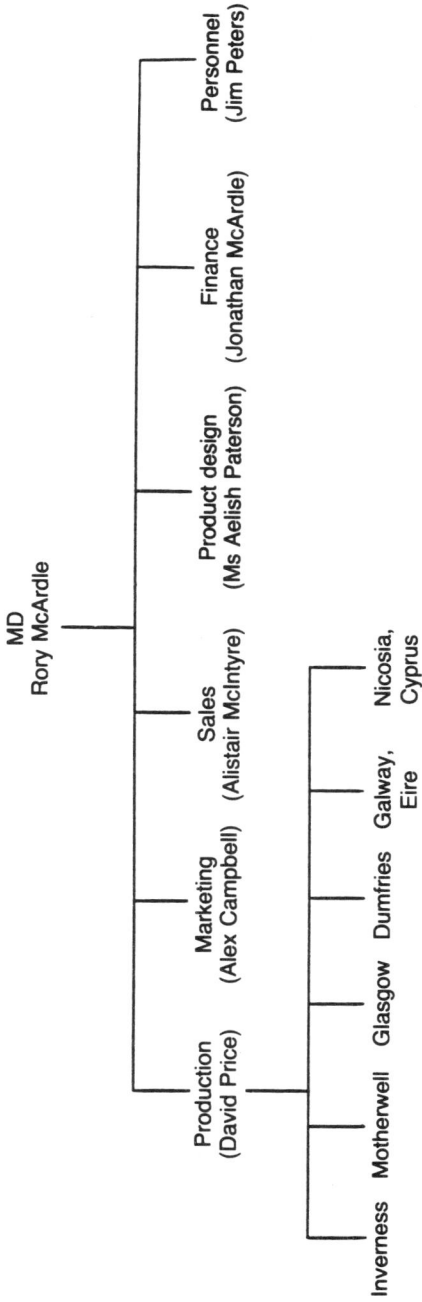

Figure 9.1 Celtic Woollen Co.

Notes: Total number of employees, 2,280; turnover £102m; profit £9m.

Co. as he regularly runs training programmes for them and is the only person qualified to administer the psychological tests used in the assessment centre. Jonathan McArdle has submited another paper to the board, arguing that the company should enter the fashionable evening wear market. So far, only Aelish Patterson has publicly supported the proposal.

QUESTIONS

1 If you were the consultant, how would you have handled the situation?
2 How would you define 'ethics' in business?
3 How important do you consider the ethics of consultancy practice?

NOTE

1 This is a true case, but not based on the woollen industry. Hence the name, Celtic Woollen Co. is fictitious and thereby no commercial relationship exists between the Celtic Woollen Co. and any other organization mentioned in this case.

10

THE PUBLIC WELFARE AGENCY

Jacqueline Drake and Andrew Kakabadse

PART 1

The director of social services of the Public Welfare Agency had been worried for some time. She had tried to talk about her concerns with her colleagues but they had shown little interest. It was the director's view that social services was becoming inefficient and ineffective. One Thursday, at a meeting with her directors, she voiced her complaints again.

'Our social workers have been known to go directly against what we stipulate and, at times, this has been with the support of their supervisors. The field staff in general don't seem to fill in the necessary forms so we do not have accurate or up-to-date information on what we are doing with clients, with children in care, or with old people in residential accommodation. Equally important, we do not know how much money we are committed to spending. We have to become more efficient but that's a minor problem in comparison with the fact that our staff do not seem to respect us. We are simply losing control of this organization!'

'Come on Joan, things aren't that bad. It's never been an easy job and with the recession it's got even tougher. Our people are doing their best,' soothed George Allen, assistant director, administration and accounting.

'Trinworth has been particularly badly hit, what with the closure of Bailey Components and the Stenley Works not taking on any more apprentices . . . they used to take a lot of young lads between them – got nothing now,' Trevor Keating, area director for Trinworth explained.

'Don't talk to me about youth employment, idle little tykes! Don't want to work, more like it,' burst in Chris Brown, red in the face. 'Prefer their mothers to go out and work all the hours God sends while they get up to all kinds of monkey tricks. Our paper work will never be up-to-date with the likes of them. If anyone needs discipline, it's them – not us. We've been taking too soft a line for a long time. I've said it before, I'll say it again, some proper authority, like we used to have, that's what we need out there . . . and in here,' he added, half under his breath.

Despite being made area director for Ipstone, Chris Brown had never fully accepted the reorganization Joan had pushed through shortly after her appointment.

'Let's not all get exicited now,' came back George Allen 'there probably is room for improvement, so why don't we all look into our own departments and see what we can do?'

There was general agreement and a sense of relief that someone had provided an escape route from what seemed to be something of an hysterical outburst by the director. 'Typical of a bloody woman,' thought more than one of the managers around the table.

Joan felt thwarted. She knew they were brushing their problems under the carpet. They wouldn't do anything even though performance was not what it should be. A problem existed, she was convinced of that. An irritating sound brought her back to the meeting. It was Lionel Edgely, clearing his throat.

'While I am perfectly prepared to look into efficiencies in my department, I should like to make it quite clear that as assistant director for residential services, I know (1) what is going on in my area; and (2) what financial commitments we have made. I would be disturbed to think it might be otherwise.'

Two weeks later the Simpson case broke. Fourteen-month-old Jennifer Simpson was beaten to death by her father. The social services had long been involved with the Simpson family. The social worker and his supervisor had made an error of judgement in releasing the child from care to her parents. The director of the social services department showed just how angry she could become at the next management team meeting.

'Everyone here knows that the Simpson case need never have happened' ... Pause ... 'And why did it? Because the field staff are a law unto themselves. I've been stating that fact for too long. Up to now you've persuaded me otherwise. Well, I tell you, I've made up my mind what I am going to do. First, I've asked Harry Francis to take responsibility for a special project on problem families. He will have a roving brief and report directly to *me*; and, second, I'm going to call somebody in to look at our organization, just to tell us where the problems lie!'

The others looked at her. The assistant director, residential services, spoke first.

'I don't like people poking their nose into our affairs. The press have just done that; one more snooper will destroy all our good work. Anyhow, who are you calling in, someone from Whitehall or is it some slick management consultant?'

'Neither, it's a university researcher whose specialism is public welfare administration,' she responded.

Shortly after the meeting finished, Lionel Edgely turned to one of the other assistant directors in the corridor and stated.

'Just how is that stupid woman going to solve any problems by bringing in some know-it-all academic? Apart from which, I just don't trust her.'

Everyone heard his comments but no one responded. The assistant director, residental services, was even more unpopular than the director of social services.

Joan Armstrong prowled around her office feeling that she had a problem. She considered that most of her assistant directors (members of the top management team) and area directors (the middle management) neither liked nor trusted her. Not that she really blamed them. On being appointed director, she had introduced some dramatic changes. She removed two levels of advisory management, reducing what was, in effect, a seven-level organization to a five-level organization. She also introduced a policy of decentralization, creating six geographical 'areas' from what had previously been five. The combined effect of these two major changes was planned to increase the number of people working in the field. It also dismantled what Joan considered to be a 'bureaucratic nightmare of an organization' so that it could better fulfil its primary mission, that of providing a helping service to members of the community. Nobody lost their jobs in the reorganization but Joan Armstrong felt the resentment. People saw themselves as demoted. Many felt they had lost their status. Others did not wish to go back to fieldwork activities; they were quite content to administer the system.

What made matters worse was that she, at an earlier stage of her career, had been employed as a social worker in that very same social services department. Some of the managers in the organization remembered her as a rebel, a person who complained that the bureaucracy in the organization was 'getting in the way' of good social work. Joan then left and practised social work in the USA for a number of years. On her return to England, she was appointed director of the same department. Certain managers found it difficult to accept such a role reversal with her. Two area directors in particular found it difficult to accept that a woman, who had been their subordinate, was now their boss.

Joan bore her colleagues no resentment; in fact, she quite liked them. She wanted her policy of decentralization to work and also for personal relationships to improve. Two of her supporters had urged her to fire at least two of her opponents. Joan flatly refused to follow such a line. She saw her colleagues as basically honest and sincere people who had not yet 'seen the light'. However, opposition to Joan was increasing and her policy of decentralization was not being implemented to her satisfaction. What should she do?

In order to maintain her policy of introducing major change while sticking with her existing group of managers, Joan recognized that she lacked information as to what was going on in the organization.

'What do people feel about me, my managerial style and how committed are they to the reorganization?'

She decided to call in Saul Becker, a bright young professor from Cornell University (USA) on sabbatical at Oxford University. Joan first met Saul when she had been working in the USA.

'Saul's the only one I know who would know how to handle these guys and get them to answer these questions,' thought Joan.

'Hello Saul, nice to see you again', said Joan, shaking hands with Saul Becker as he was ushered into her office by her secretary.

'Something very English, would you like some tea?' asked Joan.

The two of them talked about old times.

'Y'know Joan, the issue is not just getting some relevant information together, its deciding from whom to get it. I could be more of a hindrance than help asking them to complete questionnaires. People will become more suspicious than they already appear to be, according to the way you have described the situation. We need to discuss who you think I should interview and why, and how I should approach them.'

By now the conversation had become serious. Joan asked her secretary for a copy of the organization chart (Figures 10.1 and 10.2). She explained to Saul why she reorganized, the logic behind the new role structure and her opinion as to the strengths and weaknesses of key people in the structure.

'As far as I can see, Joan, there seem to be three groups that we must get on our side: the assistant directors, the area directors and the supervisors. The assistant directors are vital because if any one of those people does not agree to let me into his department, the project is virtually dead,' stated Saul.

The two continued to talk about each of the personalities in turn.

'Look Joan, I know you want to get this thing going, but I urge you just to be a little cautious. Try this out for size. You organize a buffet lunch for the assistant directors so that they can meet me under fairly informal surroundings. With a bit of luck, I will be able to arrange to see each one in his office some time after the lunch. I don't think we need to be that sensitive to the Area Directors and supervisors. Why don't you identify those Area Directors and supervisors that are forceful characters, those that are likely to support the project and those that may be a bit 'anti'. We can then organize a couple of one-day workshops and invite a handpicked number of area directors and supervisors to attend. We can get these people to talk about the problems they see in the organization and their jobs, introduce the project to them and even get them to think about how to carry it out,' said Saul.

'Good thinking! That's probably the way to do it,' responded Joan.

The lunch and workshop seminars were organized. All went well. Saul, however, faced problems with both the assistant directors and the area directors.

First, and as expected, Lionel Edgely raised his objections at the lunch.

'This isn't New York, Mr Becker. Far from it. I don't know how you think you can tell us what to do. Your knowledge may be all very well over there but things are very different in this country.'

'Sir, I recognize things are very different over here. I have no intentions of "telling you how to do your job", nor is that what I was brought in for. My technical expertise helps me to understand what's happening and what alternatives may be open and I will share these with you as and when appropriate, but my *primary* role here is to help you to identify and work through your own problems. Now, to do that we need to work together and I look forward to that.'

The idea of a survey was mooted by Saul who soon had the support of most of the assistant directors. However, he did not have everything his own way. Edgely persisted in his objections to the extent that Saul suggested that a steering committee be formed to review the results of the survey and indicate what further steps, if any, should be taken. Lionel Edgely was invited to act as chairperson to the steering committee. Saul made it clear that each individual's responses would be kept confidential. Only Saul would have access to each person's data. The committee's responsibility would be to help interpret the overall data in terms of trends, provide administrative and other assistance, if and when required, and generally to explore the implications of the findings in terms of the structure and management of the social services organization.

Second, the area directors proved to be more difficult than Saul or Joan anticipated. Their problems emerged at the workshop. They suffered a lack of role clarity and role identity. Since the reorganizations, the area directors did not understand what was expected of them and what, in essence, decentralization meant to them. They also suspected Saul's presence in the organization and the workshops as a manipulative attempt by Joan to introduce further change. Saul concentrated on helping the area directors identify the supports, constraints and key activities in their roles. By the end of the workshop, the area directors seemed comfortable with the process.

'Saul, I think this is a valuable exercise. I will arrange for you to see all my supervisors and social workers,' enthused Chris Brown.

'Will you be putting them through a workshop, or seeing them one-to-one, or what?' enquired Trevor Keating.

'Oh. It will be one-to-one. I need to gather the data fairly quickly now,' responded Saul.

'I suppose it will be much the same as we have had; questions on people's work, their working relationships, job satisfaction, their views of the team and of the organization in general. Is that right?' asked Brian Eversley, area director for Brympton, the smart part of town.

'Yes, very similar indeed,' replied Saul.

'Then I'm in favour. I think we should all give Saul Becker every possible assistance,' chimed in Trevor Keating.

Director of
social services

(Joan Armstrong)

Assistant directors

Administration and
accounting

(George Allen)

Field
services

(Philip Watson)

Residential
services

(Lionel Edgely)

Chief development officers

Geriatric, handicapped
remand, homeless

Community
development
officersª

(Harry Francis)
(Mary Hollins)

Administration
staff

Accouting
staff

Children's homes

(Frank Clark)

Area directorsᶜ

Trinworth

(Trevor
Keating)

Handbury

(Peter
Mead)

Brympton

(Brian
Eversley)

Woodlake

(Alan
Peters)

Hollybush House

Head

Deputy

Section heads

Principal officersᵇ

(Helen Ashton)
(Tom Bishop)
(Chris Carey)
(Bill Denton)
(Judy Elsmore)

Supervisors

Fordham

Stone

Brown Corbett Wilson

Social workers

Popham   Mills   Weller   Scott   Humphries

Resident
social
worker

Cook Housekeeper

Kitchen
staff

Cleaners
Handyman
Gardener

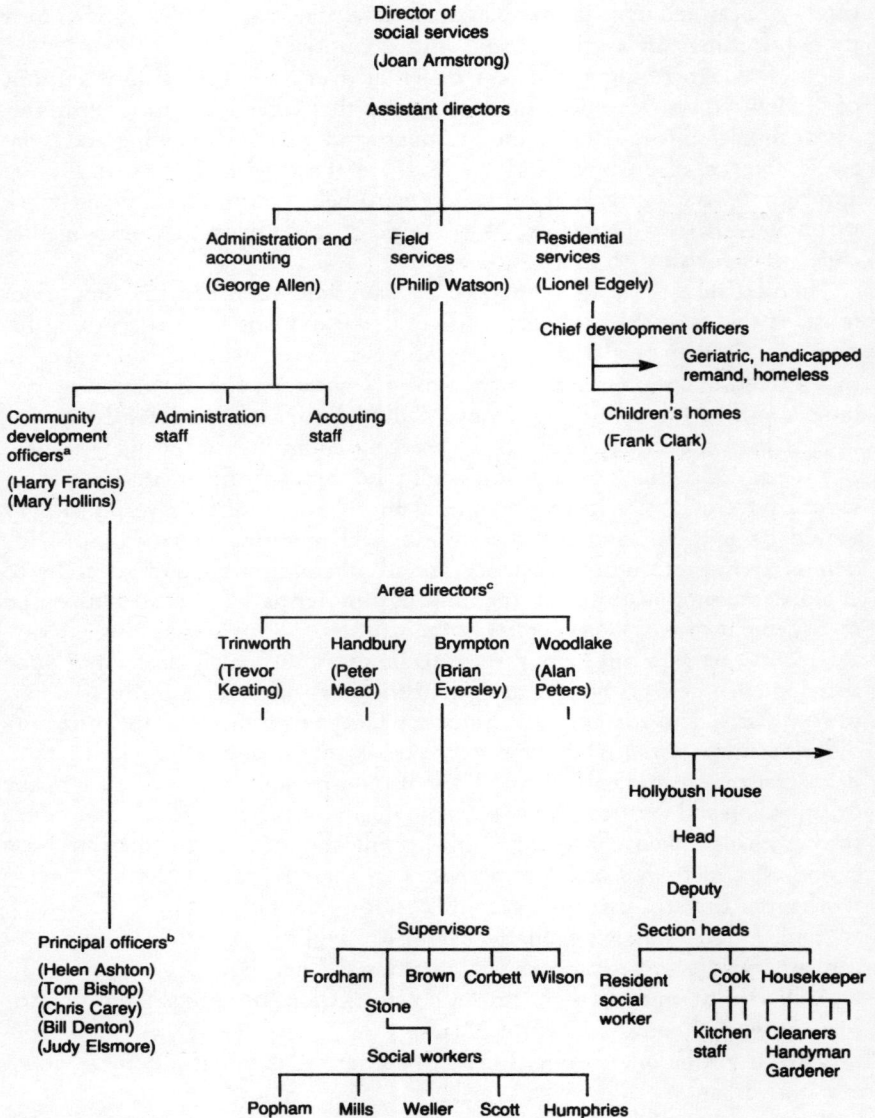

Figure 10.1 The Public Welfare Agency organizational structure: pre-Armstrong
reorganization

Notes: ª Professional specialists; advisors to assistant directors;
ᵇ Specialists in drug abuse/alcoholism, child welfare, marriage guidance, psychiatry,
home teaching for the blind. Advisors to area directors, supervisors and social workers.
ᶜ Each controls a sector of town, being line manager to five supervisors. Each supervisor
is line manager to five social workers.

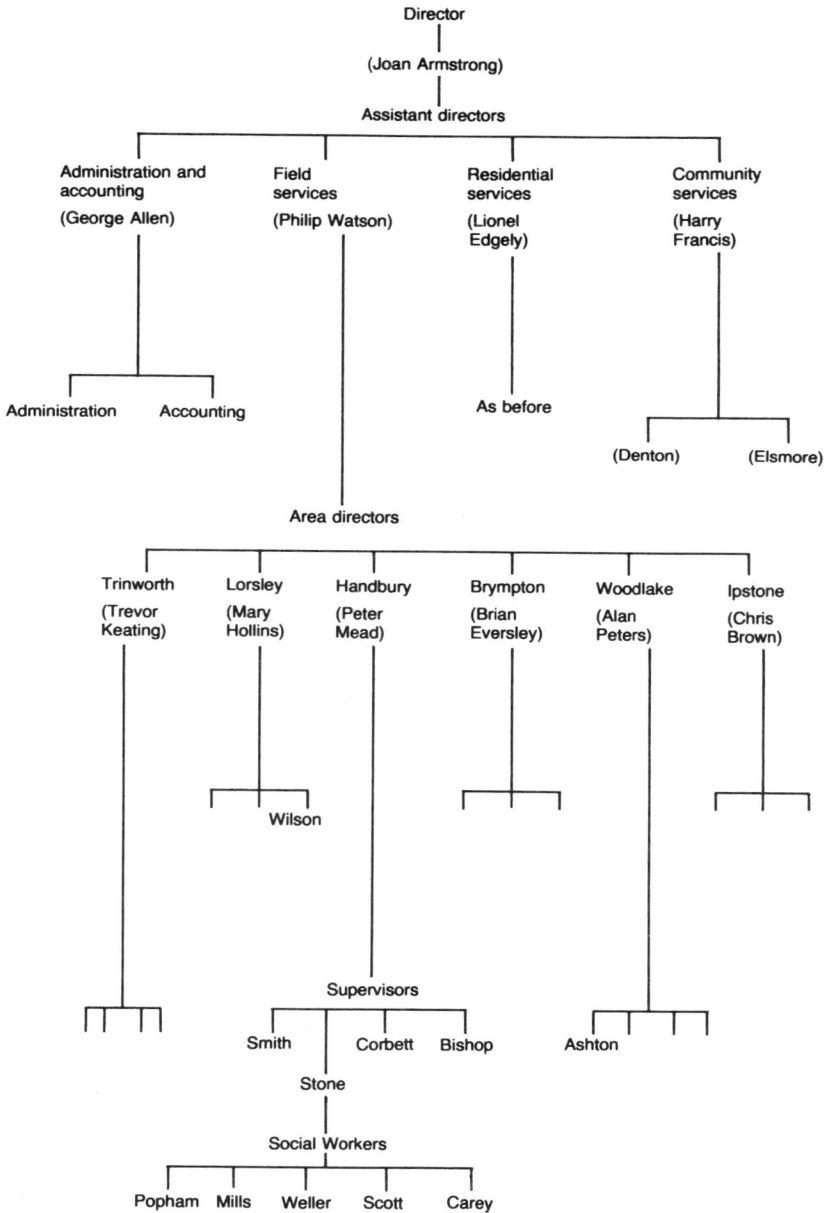

Figure 10.2 The Public Welfare Agency organizational structure: post-Armstrong reorganization

QUESTIONS

1 What has happened so far:
   (a) Is there a problem?
   (b) Is it important?
   (c) Whose problem is it?
2 How effective do you consider Joan Armstrong to be as the director of the Public Welfare Agency?
3 What strategy should Saul adopt in order to address the problems facing the Public Welfare Agency? In your answer identify the factors Saul should be taking into account.

11

KABI PHARMACIA

Solveg Bruce-Stupples

KABI PHARMACIA: BACKGROUND

This case is set in 1990. It focuses on the problems that arise when there is a need for restructuring and downsizing due to a merger. The merger occurred between Kabi owned by Procordia, and Pharmacia with Volvo as its main shareholder – both Swedish companies. This was the largest corporate deal in Swedish financial history.

The key to the deal was Provendor, which was owned by Volvo, but which deflected the management effort and resources from its mainstream activities. This was an ideal target for Procordia to expand its consumer-product business. Volvo also had a partial stake in Pharmacia. It could be anticipated that Pharmacia's pharmaceutical business might be appropriate for an arranged marriage with the Kabi company already in the Procordia group. Pharmacia therefore was used as a make-weight to sweeten the Volvo–Procordia deal.

The merger between Kabi and Pharmacia was significant for the people in Kabi and Pharmacia and was seen as an imposed change. The merger occurred in May 1990. The result was to create not a bigger Kabi Pharmacia but two new companies: Kabi Pharmacia responsible for the pharmaceutical business and Pharmacia Biosystem which mainly concentrates on the biotechnology market and diagnostics products for hospital laboratories. This case will focus on the merger in the UK between Kabi and Pharmacia's pharmaceutical business and the central resources: finance, EDP, warehouse and business services.

LOCATIONS AND ORGANIZATION

Kabi had just moved into new premises in Bourne End, Buckinghamshire. The organization chart which follows (see Figures 11.1(a) and 11.1(b)) shows the structure. They distributed the products directly to the hospitals and pharmacies. There were 75 field based staff and 75 office based staff, out of which there were 25 managers. The organization was divided into three

91

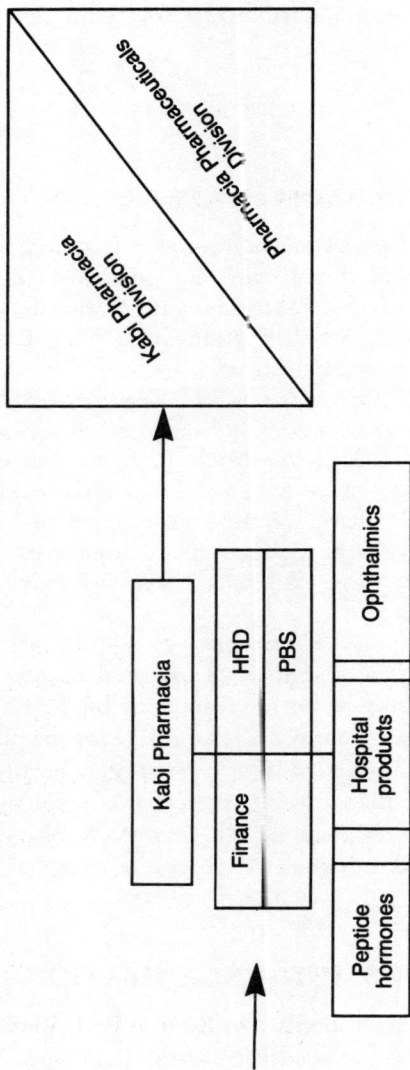

Figure 11.1(a) Organization chart: Kabi

Kabi
Number of employees 150

Managing director

Administration

Human
resource development

Finance

Peptide
hormones

Pharmaceutical

Hospital
products

Turnover of £30 million

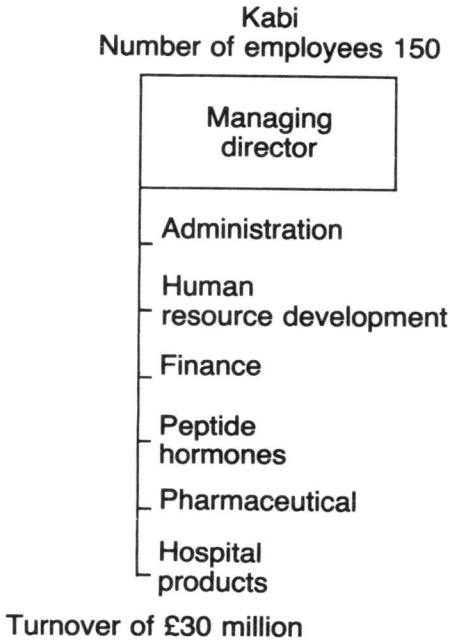

Figure 11.1(b) Organization chart: Kabi

divisions; the Peptide Hormone divison, the Hospital Product division and the Pharmaceutical division.

Pharmacia employed 250 people before the merger out of which 120 were in Biotechnology and Diagnostics divisions, 70 in Pharmaceutical division and 60 in finance, EDP and personnel and business services; around a 100 people were field based. Pharmacia's premises were located in Milton Keynes and they were also in the process of constructing a new building, an investment of £10 million (Figure 11.2).

There were two managing directors and two management teams. There were too many field staff, both managers and sales people. There were two administration organizations and two human resource managers. Kabi had grown during the last three years and was very profitable mainly due to the introduction of new products. Pharmacia's profitability was declining due to a changing market place but also because of recent acquisitions. There were no unions involved.

The brief to the managing directors from the Swedish headquarters was

Pharmacia
Number of employees 250

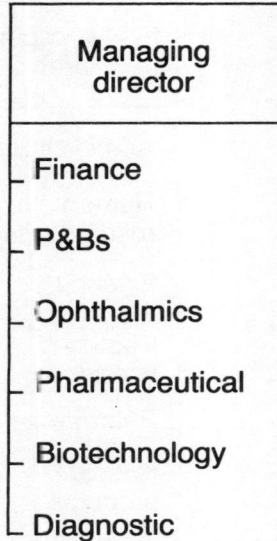

```
┌─────────────────────┐
│     Managing        │
│     director        │
└─────────────────────┘
  ├─ Finance

  ├─ P&Bs

  ├─ Ophthalmics

  ├─ Pharmaceutical

  ├─ Biotechnology

  └─ Diagnostic
```

Turnover £30 million

Figure 11.2 Organization chart: Pharmacia

to establish two companies in the UK according to the new Swedish structure; Kabi Pharmacia and Pharmacia Biosystem, and to create the most effective organization for the UK pharmaceutical market (Figure 11.3).

HUMAN RESOURCE DEPARTMENT

In Kabi a human resource manager was appointed in 1989 for the newly established position. Traditionally, all personnel matters were handled by the finance director. The new HR manager had grown up in the company and had previously a position as marketing manager. The business had a personnel development manager which was the equivalent to HR manager in Pharmacia who was on job rotation from Sweden on a three-year contract that was due to expire in January 1991. Her responsibility was to establish an HR department and to head up the personnel and business service, this being general administration. Her background was in international marketing,

94

Kabi

- Administration
- Finance
- Human resource development
- Hospital products
- Peptide hormones
- Pharmaceuticals

Pharmacia

- Finance
- P&Bs
- Ophthalmics
- Pharmaceuticals
- Biotechnology
- Diagnostics

Kabi Pharmacia

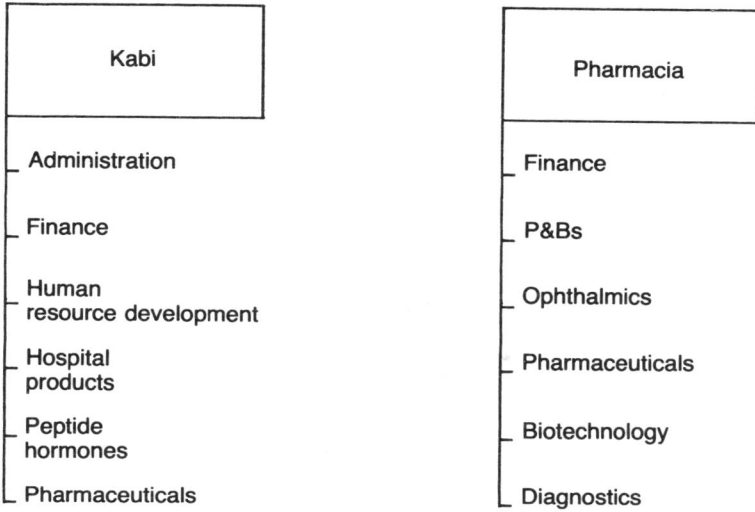

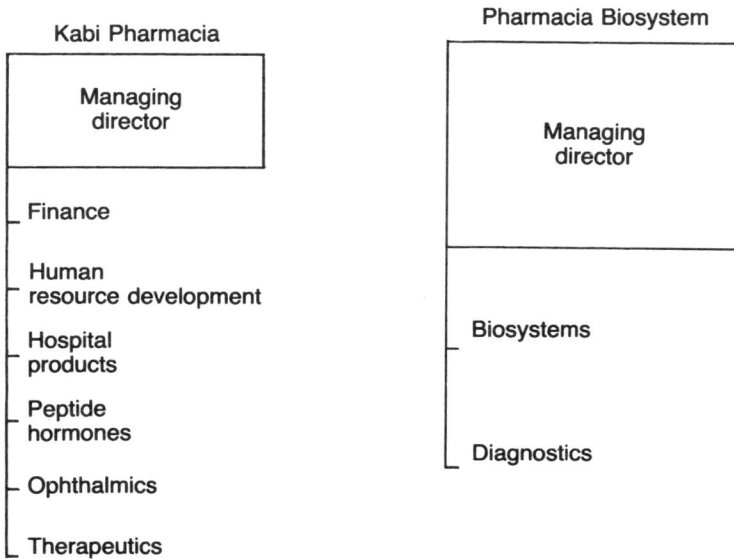

Managing director

- Finance
- Human resource development
- Hospital products
- Peptide hormones
- Ophthalmics
- Therapeutics

Pharmacia Biosystem

Managing director

- Biosystems
- Diagnostics

Figure 11.3 New structure of Kabi and Pharmacia

with a previous position as a division manager, but with an interest in human resource matters. She had been with Pharmacia for thirteen years.

PROBLEM AREAS

A merger is a major event in a company and the two organizations and its management were facing change of which they had little experience. Sweden decided on the main structure (see Figure 11.3) and appointed the managing director who was previously the MD of Kabi. Kabi Pharmacia was to sell services to Pharmacia Biosystem and share managing directors.

1 *Location*. Both organizations wanted to stay where they were. This was a very unsettling time for the staff. There were three alternatives: Kabi Pharmacia could stay located in Bourne End, Pharmacia Biosystem could stay in the old Pharmacia building, or all could move into the new building. The cheapest alternative was for both organizations to move into the new building in Milton Keynes. If a company has to relocate, this raises the question of redundancy.

2 *Organization*. The structure of the organization was relatively straight-forward and based on customer groups. Three divisions were staying the same. There was a need for a financial department including EDP (data processing) and warehouse, human resource department and general administration.

3 *Appointments of managers, field force and office staff*. There was a general concern amongst staff concerning who would obtain the jobs. Both management teams were concerned regarding not only the legal aspects but also the handling of the process as far as the feelings of the employees were concerned.

4 *Communication (internally and externally)*. There were rumours and misunderstanding causing demotivation and depression. People were looking for alternative jobs outside the companies.

5 *Harmonization*. The harmonization of terms and conditions of employment was an urgent matter.

ACTIONS REQUIRED

The HR manager, who was ex Pharmacia, was made responsible for the process of downsizing the organization. The other HR manager was also involved in the process. The brief was to have the organization in place and all the appointments/redundancies made by 6 July 1990 starting on 21 May. The managing director (ex Kabi) wanted the problems solved quickly so that no sales or momentum were lost. He also pointed out that it should be done 'with a cool head and warm heart'. Good compensation was available for the people who were going to be made redundant.

QUESTION

What actions should the HR manager take and what should she recommend to the MD and the UK board?

12

THE BANK OF IRELAND

Andrew Kakabadse
Siobhan Alderson
Mairi Bryce
Vincent Dooley

PART 1

'That's interesting and most helpful. But would you please tell me who is responsible for implementing all that's been discussed and analysed.'

No one spoke. Mark Hely Hutchinson, chief executive, Guinness Ireland, and non-executive director of the Bank of Ireland, who had made the comment, looked around the room awaiting a response. The strained silence was broken by the chairman of the meeting indicating that Mark's comments had been most helpful and would provide food for thought for future meetings.

The topic of discussion in 1983 had been an analysis of the internal organizational and external market problems of the Bank of Ireland.

The Bank of Ireland is one of the two main commercial banks in the Republic of Ireland. Formed as a result of a merger of three banks in the 1960s – the Hibernian, the National and the Bank of Ireland – the bank experienced a period of economic growth, but since then had progressively been facing ever-increasing difficulties through the 1970s and into the early 1980s.

From the late 1960s to the middle to late 1970s, the Irish economy experienced something of a boom, with an attendant rise in borrowing and a period of growth and expansion. At the beginning of the 1980s these trends were quite rapidly reversed against the background of a world oil crisis and further increased national borrowing. During this period, the Bank of Ireland in common with other banks experienced a massive increase in bad debts, and a slump in the lending market. These problems had not been previously encountered to such a degree. Recession continued right through until the late 1980s, when a slow economic improvement began, and is continuing, although the national debt is still high. Further, Irish membership of the European Community, and the European Monetary System, means that all Irish financial institutions face the same challenge of European legislation on financial institutions, and their rights of entry into, and competition in, international markets.

In the mid-1970s foreign banks began to arrive into the Irish market, and their number has steadily increased. These banks have not captured a significant segment of domestic banking business, but they did begin to make an impact on the corporate banking sector. There has also been an increase in the number of new Irish financial institutions, including building societies and savings-based insurance institutions.

Political events in Ireland, changes of government in particular, have not had major economic impacts, since the ideological difference between the two major parties, or coalitions formed between them, is not great. While the continuing conflict in Northern Ireland does not have a direct significant effect on the southern Irish economy, there is some evidence of an impact on investment attractiveness in the Republic.

Socially, the evolution of the Bank of Ireland coincided with the growth of the television medium in Ireland. Advertising has become a growth industry among all Irish financial institutions, and has been a major factor of influence on the Irish bank customer, who is now regarded as having an enviable choice of institutions with which to do business. There is a general view that the Irish education system is good, both at second and third level, and that the young people coming from Irish schools, colleges and universities have increasingly higher expectations of their employers. Along with these expectations and quality of education, however, is a downside of high unemployment and a high rate of emigration among young people.

In its early years, the Bank of Ireland was generally regarded as solid, reliable and perhaps a little 'stuffy' in its attitude to customers and staff. The working atmosphere of the bank in the early years was very procedures oriented, with business and internal relations always being conducted by the book.

The impact of the union

In 1966 there was a strike in all the major banks in Ireland, including the Bank of Ireland. The union, the Irish Bank Officials Association (IBOA), demanded a large pay increase and this was awarded by management. In 1970, there was another bank strike as a result of large pay demands from the union not being met. Although this strike was settled in the same way as the first, by concession on the part of the management, the competitive situation had begun to change and there was some loss of business during and after the strike. In the aftermath of each of these strikes, staff were allowed to undertake overtime work, paid at overtime rates, in order to catch up on the large backlog of work. A further, longer dispute took place in 1976. This, however, resulted in a lower pay settlement than that demanded by the IBOA. Additionally, staff were not able to compensate for the effects of the strike through overtime working. The 1976 strike did, however, still result in a major pay concession from management to the IBOA.

The UK operation dispute, (1984)

In the aftermath of the 1982 agreement on technology and change which conceded increases of 23 per cent to the union, a new industrial-relations team was formed. They saw the excessive increases gained by the union as crippling the business. They were determined to ensure the support of the executive when dealing with the union. This support was forthcoming, as the executive saw the clear need. Up to this point, the IR people involved were conscious that they had a reputation for talking about and knowing what to do but never having the support to do it. The IBOA made demands in the face of this and IR thus seemed to exist merely to serve the union's purpose. This situation caused confusion and ambiguity and made the role of the mangement's chief negotiator difficult.

The first industrial dispute situation in which the new IR team became involved concerned the UK operation of the bank. At that time, the cost of living in the UK was high, and this gave rise to a pay increase demand among workers in the UK operation. Pay rounds were forced by the threat of strike action. It was recognized that pay demands of the magnitude in question would not be feasible, and would quite probably lead to the closure of the UK operation. The IR team, and bank management were prepared to close down the UK operation, in order not to concede to the union. Management made a point of talking to all staff in the UK operation, informing them of the impossibility of meeting the costs of the pay demand.

The support for management was surprising. The stike did go ahead, but the UK operation was maintained, despite intimidation from the union. The dispute was resolved without concession in two weeks, but it was widely acknowledged that the union did not appreciate the significance of the change in attitude of the management. The union leadership and committed membership believed that the situation would be different in an Irish-based dispute.

Business development

Up to the 1970s, the commercial banks were dominant in the savings market. However, the situation slowly changed, for although the overall savings/deposits market had grown, the commercial bank's share of new savings had fallen, in both percentage and actual terms. Between 1972 and 1987, the share of the market, as held by the Bank of Ireland branch banking, fell from 23.1 per cent to 18.8 per cent. Over the same period, the building societies' share of the market increased from 9.9 per cent to 19.7 per cent. While Bank of Ireland subsidiaries improved their market share during this period, the overall Bank of Ireland group share of the market fell from 26.2 per cent to 24.2 per cent.

In 1975, banks and assurance companies captured 47.8 per cent of the personal-sector new savings total of £601 million for that year. As far as the commercial banks were concerned, this resulted in their sharing £282 million, of which the Bank of Ireland's share was approximately £106 million. By 1985, when the personal-sector new savings for that year amounted to £1920 million, the banks' share had fallen to 11.4 per cent or £219 million, of which the Bank of Ireland's share was approximately £66 million. As far as lending is concerned, during the period between 1972 and 1987, the commercial banks' share of lending fell from 51.5 per cent to 40 per cent. The Bank of Ireland group's share fell from 28.1 per cent to 24.4 per cent. Further, the bank itself suffered a fall in market share from 24.4 per cent to 17.6 per cent despite an increase in its share of the home loan market.

Surveys conducted throughout this period gave insights into why these trends occurred. Basically, the bank had not been competitive in rates. Further, traditional loyalties were breaking down. With customers becoming more aware, they were actually seeking better rates for their money.

One survey indicated that:

1 Fifty-three per cent of account holders are dissatisfied with bank interest rates.
2 Men tend to be more uneasy about bank interest rates (56 per cent) than women (50 per cent), and dissatisfaction levels peak amongst those in the 35–49 age group – namely those with the highest levels of financial commitment.
3 Middle-class income earners also tend to be more critical of bank interest rates (58 per cent) than skilled working-class people (47 per cent) or those from unskilled working backgrounds (43 per cent).
4 Dissatisfaction with interest rates tends to be almost as high amongst the farming community as it is amongst middle-class people generally.

However, the bank had shown some success. The bank did experience reasonable growth in its deposits taken. Much of the growth was in the large (> £100K) more expensive deposits, with the major element being paid above standard rates. Growth in the smaller deposits (< £100K) was achieved only by selectively paying rates significantly above standard. In fact, deposits in this category fell sharply.

In a memo, one executive wrote:

'In the competitive environment in which we operate, growth in our deposits can be achieved only by offering rates to depositors which are significantly better than our current standard rates. We have done this, on a selective basis, over the past year at a considerable cost to our profit margin. We cannot possibly afford to continue on this basis. To be in a position to offer competitive deposit rates into the future, we must secure a significant reduction in our operating costs. The impact on the bank of a continuation of the market share trend outlined earlier would be traumatic. The consequentially serious impact on the size of our network is obvious. These trends will not change of their own accord – they must be made to change. So long as we continue to be uncompetitive to the extent we are at present, we cannot realistically expect to reverse these trends.

'The essential problem which the bank faces is that its cost structure is such that it requires an unsustainable margin between the cost of its funds and what it earns on these funds if it is to cover its operating costs and generate a profit. But market forces will not permit us to maintain such a margin other than at the price of an accelerating reduction in our market share and our business base. At present we need a margin of approximately 7 per cent to survive. Building societies typically operate on a margin of around 2 per cent. It might, of course, be argued that we can maintain margins through charging more for lending, while increasing rates for depositors. We have already shown that our share of the lending market has shrunk because of competition. We are experiencing continuing pressure on lending margins (at both wholesale and retail levels) which makes the maintenance of present lending margins quite problematic. The key to survival is therefore a sustained reduction in operating costs so that we are equipped to compete and survive in the emerging environment.'

Traditionally, the Bank of Ireland's competitors were the other commercial banks. Over the 1970s and into the early 1980s, the situation changed. The main competition was, and is, organizations as much outside as within the traditional banking system.

Building societies, that had extensive branch and agency networks with lower costs bases, became major competitors. Building societies had become active in the deposits markets. As the 1980s continued, the building societies expanded their activities to include unsecured personal lending, business and agricultural lending, credit cards, money transmission, and foreign exchange. These activities were further expanded to include the provision of foreign currency facilities, and personal and commercial lending. Overall, the commercial rates of the building societies were 1 per cent below the bank's rate, a significant amount, given the price and cash-flow sensitivities of the private sector. Certain branches of the Bank of Ireland reported that the Irish Permanent Building Society offered Bank of Ireland customers personal loans at rates as low as 8.25 per cent and the

Educational Building Society offered car loans at 11.25 per cent. For such loans, the bank's minimum rate was 13.5 per cent.

1 An Post (the Post Office) became more aggressive and more successful in the deposits markets. They not only enjoyed favourable tax discrimination for some of their products, but their cost base was lower than the Bank of Ireland's, and their network significantly larger.
2 Insurance companies, with their facility to market tax-effective deposit instruments, made major inroads into the deposit markets. They targeted large depositors within the Bank of Ireland network, and made full use of their extensive and relatively inexpensive network of branches, agencies and representatives.
3 Intermediaries such as financial consultants, agents, solicitors and stock brokers equally targeted valuable segments of the commercial bank's markets with specific financial packages, resulting in a further erosion of deposits.

As indicated, union activity was pronounced. The IBOA had managed to secure close to 100 per cent membership within the Bank of Ireland. In fact, at one point all but the top twenty bank executives were members of the union.

As a result, there has been a history of low levels of cooperation between management and the union. All union negotiations were carried out on an industry basis and the successful record of strikes seemed to give the union confidence that they would lose little or nothing by taking industrial action, or from banning specific activities or changes.

As a result, the bank became *change resistant*, as the union had successfully negotiated pay increases or bonus payments for its members on the introduction of virtually any change. Fundamentally, change became too expensive and too much of a strain to seriously contemplate unless that change was deemed absolutely necessary. It did seem as if the union believed that the increasing presence of non-traditional competitors in the banking market would not damage the oligopoly between the principal commercial banks. The situation became so tense that the union objected (at times successfully) to management even discussing change with staff. The union claimed that they were the sole communication channel with staff.

One senior executive in an interview remembered that in 1978, 60 per cent of his time was being spent on industrial-relations issues. In fact, on the information technology and computer software front, lists of software packages were submitted to the unions for them to agree as to what could and could not be purchased. One discernible trend to have emerged in this culture was the meaning behind the term, 'to manage'. To manage became synonymous with banking – the provision of professional services to the lay and financial community. People issues, industrial-relations issues and personal services issues became the remit of the personnel department, a centralized function which had become the key agent in dealings with the union.

'That's interesting and most helpful. But would you please tell me who is responsible for implementing all that's been discussed and analysed?'

All eyes turned towards Mark Hely Hutchinson, the recently appointed (1983) chief executive of the Bank of Ireland, chairing a meeting of the board. Mark had been listening to a presentation in 1983 outlining the bank's problems and possible ways forward. Mark looked at his colleagues, awaiting a response.

QUESTIONS

Split into your study groups in order to address the following issues.

You have been appointed as internal consultants by the new CE, Mark Hely Hutchinson. Your remit is broad: to assist the processes of the introduction and management of change. Discuss as a group:

1 What areas of the bank require attention?
2 What strategies do you consider appropriate to implement in order to facilitate change within the bank, and why?
3 How would you go about implementing such strategies. In your presentation, identify what obstacles you would expect to overcome and how you would overcome them?
4 How long is it likely to take to introduce meaningful change into this organization?
5 What role would you expect the personnel function to play in the change process and what skills would you expect the personnel manager to display?

Make your answers as detailed as possible. Draw upon each other's experiences, in the preparation of your responses. Prepare a formal presentation using flip charts, outlining the nature of the strategies for change that you propose and their manner of implementation.

13

VINNY WALLACE

Andrew Kakabadse

PART 1

'Congratulations, Vincent. I think we really do have the right man for the job,' smiled Mark Walters, group president of IEC (International Electronics Corporation).

IEC is a communications, data systems and office equipment company, primarily serving the North American market. Essentially, IEC concentrated on the telephone switching business, but was also making a considerable impact on the market in the areas of cellular mobile telephone systems as well as the more recent office equipment products. The principal areas of business happened to be in public switching, business communications (office systems), defence systems, network engineering and customer engineering supported by an R&D organization.

Vinny Wallace, a Louisiana-born telecommunications engineer, who also qualified as an accountant, joined IEC on leaving college and worked his way up the managerial hierarchy. Vinny had experience of manufacturing, customer support, and was latterly appointed vice president, strategy, IEC Research. However, his latest appointment pleased him. He was made president, IECE (IEC Europe), headquartered in the new city of Milton Keynes, north Buckinghamshire, England. His task, so aptly phrased by Mark Walters was, 'Go to it, boy and do in Europe as IEC has done to North America'.

IECE had started as a small group of sales and support engineers located in Milton Keynes. Originally run by a general manager (sales), reporting to a vice president in North America, the group had grown considerably to now encompass an R&D group in Bracknell, England (in reality, more D than R), and manufacturing plants in Scotland and France. European headquarters still remained in Milton Keynes but in reality, the bulk of the European business came from the UK.

In an attempt to make himself known to his team, Vinny made three 'fact-finding' trips to the UK and France prior to taking up his appointment, spending approximately two hours with each of his managers, trying to appreciate the issues facing each of them in their job. Once into the job, a mountain of paperwork faced Vinny on his first day. Orders that needed

105

his signature, customer complaints, requests to meet with key potential customers. Vinny's new secretary, Prunella (Pru) Seale, already looked harassed when Vinny walked into the office.

'Mr Wallace, a number of people have been trying to see you. I have made no commitments as I thought you may wish to keep your first day or so free in order to go through some of the paperwork and letters that I have for you.'

'Thank you, Pru. That's just fine . . . Oh, by the way, please call me Vinny'.

'Yes, Mr Wallace,' replied Prunella.

Vinny smiled. Vinny spent most of the day in his office, but did go round shaking a few hands and introducing himself in the staff canteen at lunchtime. All employees used the same canteen. Prior to being located in Milton Keynes, Vinny had explicitly prevented senior IECE management from having their own dining facilities.

Vinny had already arranged for an informal buffet and drinks party for middle and senior management and their spouses from all of the UK locations.

'Hello, Patrice,' said Vinny smiling. 'I'm so pleased you made it from Bracknell. Hello, Mdme Poirson'.

Patrice Poirson, vice president (VP) manufacturing, engaged Vinny for a few minutes in polite conversation. 'Well, what do you think?' asked Patrice. 'Can we get more orders in for manufacturing? As you know, the plant is under capacity and sales aren't getting the orders in.'

Cliff Winskowski, the American ex-pat, VP Sales, was well within hearing distance and turned round when he heard the comment.

Vinny noticed Winskowski's response. He wondered whether Poirson had been aware of Winskowski's presence.

QUESTIONS

1 As Vinny Wallace, what course(s) of action would you consider appropriate in trying to make a success of your job?
2 More specifically, what are you going to try to do in your first six months of appointment?

14

EURODOLLAR

Peter Norris

The chairman of 'Classic Products' plc, James Leeds, put his head
down and walked into the strong north wind as he set out from the
company's new administration block in which its head office, marketing and
merchandising functions were housed. It was an icy blast and it helped to
increase some of his feelings of disquiet. He quickly scanned the greenfield
site to which the company had moved its manufacturing operations two
years earlier and to which the head office functions had moved six months
ago.

He reflected with pride on the growth of the company but he felt some
tensions when he considered the rapidity of the changes that were taking
place in the light of what – with uncharacteristic panache – he liked to call
'Operation Eurodollar'. Were they really ready for the developments that
were taking place? Had they tried to move too fast? He knew in his heart
that to have stood still would have meant takeover or decline. He realized
his thoughts kept coming back to the management staff of the company. He
had taken a leading part over the years in their selection but were they the
right people to succeed? They mostly seemed to take too much on the nod,
not enough questioning even of his ideas. Overall, they seemed to lack some
spirit. Was this something he had failed to consider when they were chosen?
Take this quality assurance meeting he was going to now. Most of the
managers and supervisors present would be looking to him and the
manufacturing director for a lead and approval. He would be surprised if
any of them rocked any boats.

He thought of the company. As English as roast beef and Yorkshire
pudding! Now having about nine hundred employees, it had grown steadily
from the time it was established at the turn of the century. He thought of
its long family history. His grandfather Josiah, had established the company
and kept a very tight control on it until he retired in 1933. His father had
been brought into the company at the age of 16 and had learned its
operations from the shop floor up. James reflected on his own relatively
privileged entry to the firm – good school followed by a university degree
in economics. He also reflected that a lot of his father's and grandfather's

feeling for business had rubbed of on him since he still knew as much about any of the company's retail outlets as anyone.

He ran over in his mind the recent changes that had taken place. Until two years ago it was a private, family-owned company. It then became a public limited company. For some time prior to this it had been obvious that a vigorous growth programme was also necessary. Acquisitions of three companies in France and Holland were started to give the company increased manufacturing capacity but, more importantly, to have a much wider distribution and retail network. Also – not to be minimized – four new shops had been opened in south eastern England with expansion of two of the existing outlets in the north.

Despite the company's recent flotation as a plc he liked to think that it had retained the family feel and hoped that it always would. A nagging worry for James was that he might lose control to the City. The company had started out by being essentially a retail organization, with prime-position high-street shops, and Josiah had recognized from the outset that its own manufacturing capability was required since complete control over the quality of its products was vital.

Until the move to the new site, it had been based in old premises in an English Midlands town. The move to the new site had left a small, less glamourous part of the manufacturing at the old site. By most measures the company was successful. For the current year turnover is projected as £62 million with pre-tax profit of £8.9 million. The previous year's results were turnover of £57.25 million with pre-tax profits of £7.8 million which represented a 13.5 per cent improvement on the previous year. Investment in the new site during this period has been in the order of £2.85 million. James thought about this growth and whether he had steered things as he should have done. Three years ago its operations were restructured into two divisions (retail and manufacturing) and a head office function, which included the finance directorate, computer operations and the personnel directorate.

Key people in his plans for the company were the two operational directors. Philip Willis, the retail director, had been with the company for a long time and now was ill. His frequent and protracted absences had left a void and a new retail director was due to start at the beginning of the next month with Philip taking up a new assignment. The company should be 'retail led' – that's where it had always been strong. Arthur Cook, the manufacturing director, had assumed quite a high profile and had taken strong advantage of the absence of Philip Willis. James considered Arthur as aggressively competitive – he had sought and obtained own-brand orders for well-known chain stores even though marketing was part of the retail operation. While he recognized that this was good for cash flow in the shorter term, he was uncertain about whether this was right for the company in the longer run.

By now James had reached the main manufacturing building. As he stepped inside out of the cruel wind, his thoughts switched to the more immediate problems of the quality assurance team meeting. While James Leeds had been making his own mental appraisal, Clive Bowen took his first cup of coffee for the morning as a stimulus to think about his role in the company's development. He had been appointed as personnel manager for the company 10 years earlier, and had been promoted to the board as personnel director a few weeks ago. He thought that now he ought to have more direct influence upon the real personnel concerns rather than being restricted chiefly to administration and functional matters. His main present concern was what he should do about the development of managers. He had no doubt that some management training was required, but he himself was not a training specialist – most of his own experience had been in salary administration, wage negotiating, conditions of service and the administration of recruitment.

A training and development consultant he had invited to come to talk with him informally had just left after an hour's conversation. This had been both stimulating and worrying. Clive thought over what had been discussed. This centred on the following issues:

1 The tradition of long service, particularly in its manufacturing operatives, had been a mixed blessing. On the one hand there was a stability and loyalty within the work force, but on the other there was a complacency and a reluctance to confront inadequate performance. Much of the promotion, particularly in manufacturing, had been from the shop floor.
2 He recognized that no coordinated management training had taken place over the years, and this was something that now had to change. Occasionally people had gone on short courses and a few had been on three-week general management programmes at a business school as a result of particular needs being recognized. Four years ago he had introduced the use of personality testing for management entrants. This was carried out by an independent consultant. Although this was now well accepted in the company there were some strong overall resistance to management training since people seemed genuinely to have little time for this.

His analysis of the state of management in the company for the consultant was:

1 *The directors.* The chairman found it difficult to keep his hands off the detail, but not much would change him! After all, it was the family's company even though it had now floated as a plc. 'Mr James', as everyone still referred to him, gave the impression of being a little distant, but he was as sharp as a razor. He did not like long executive board meetings. His style was to listen to what the directors had to say, giving very little

response at the time. He would then adjourn and pick up the issues with individuals, sometimes days later. Unfortunately, mused Clive, he didn't always pick them up with the right people. Arthur Cook: brilliant, political, insensitive and ambitious. Few of the managers reporting to him really seemed to enjoy the relationship. True he was well regarded in the industry, perhaps better regarded outside than within the company. To those who did not know him well, he gave the impression of being hail-fellow-well-met. He was quick to make a judgement about his – and others' – staff and equally quick to change it. It was Clive's opinion that he did not always think in enough depth about issues before he brought them to the board; certainly he did not always consider the implications for the whole company. A new retail director was to join on the first of next month. Philip Willis was currently moving sideways to develop the European acquisitions. They had talked briefly of the new director – he comes from a large, well organized company where there has been considerable management development and training – and wondered how he would fit into the company's culture. Brian Thompson, the finance director, had been around for eight years and had a good pipeline to Mr James. Much of Mr James's focus was on the financial results of the business and he leaned heavily on Brian. Outside financial matters, Brian contributed little to the board discussions.

Clive Bowen had talked briefly and ruefully about the weekend course run by a business school especially for the board some three years earlier. Most of the nine people present had found it rather threatening, and the chairman had particularly found the information coming from personality questionnaires deflating and even now made passing comment about this.

2 *The 'Executive'*. Eighteen months ago the chairman decided they should have a level of executive between the board and the next level of functional management. Ten people were designated as 'executives'. These included:

(a) from manufacturing: the personnel manager, the finance manager, the planning manager, the engineering manager;
(b) from retail: the personnel manager, the finance manager, the northern regional manager, the southern regional manager, the manager responsible for planning, the manager responsible for franchise operations.

Both the personnel managers and both the finance managers were relatively new to the company, in their early thirties, and new posts had been created for which they had been recruited. The remainder of the executive had been with the company a minimum of 11 years, with the longest serving having joined twenty-four years ago. But did they really function as an executive – considering cross boundary issues and contributing to the broader management of the company? He could not recall them ever having met as a body. They all seemed to carry on in the same way – concentrating on their own functional or specialist areas.

3 *Middle management*. These were a mixed bag. Several were of the 'old and bold' having been promoted from the shop floor and in many ways still retaining the shop-floor attitudes. Some had been recruited lately to meet specialized needs. These included computer specialists and retail area managers. The supervision all came from the 'shop floor', and this included the management of the retail outlets where the range of numbers of staff employed was 12 in the largest shops to 4 in the smaller.

Clive had described the performance appraisal scheme he had introduced two years ago. He thought of this as being 'state of the art' in its principles, being 'objectives based'. He was inwardly quite pleased with it, but the consultant had looked at random samples of the forms completed for various members of staff at the last appraisal and had identified that objectives were poorly defined and that any development needs had been expressed in the broadest terms and it was impossible to do anything specific with this information. Clive felt quite hurt that its weakness, which he had not recognized, had been so easily identified.

Payment systems for managers consisted of awards being made on an individual basis by the directors. There was no objective system for relating these awards to assessment of performance. He was still uncertain about the real value of performance related pay for managers. The principle was logical enough and sounded all right, but the modest research he had carried out with other companies who used performance-related pay tended to show that there was no improvement in company performance. He really didn't think he knew enough about this and it was a very big step to introduce such an approach unless there was real certainty of it being successful.

YOUR TASK

Clive Bowen is expecting the training and development consultant to make some broad recommendations for a management development initiative. In reading this case initially try to get a feeling for the nature of the key management development issues in the company. It will help you to do this if you do not try to think ahead at this stage to detailed courses of management training action to be taken.

You are asked to put yourself in the position of the consultant. First identify the issues that must be taken into account in preparing a management development strategy for 'Classic Products' plc; then prepare a broad brief for Clive Bowen giving recommendations about this strategy for management development most appropriate for the company. This brief might also include observations about further information you would require which is not in the case study.

The syndicate work sheet is provided as a guideline for analysis (Appendix 14.1).

APPENDIX 14.1

'Classic Products' plc: syndicate worksheet

1 *Strategy*: What are the implications for management development of the directions the company is taking? How much of this direction is overt and how much is implied and needs reading between the lines?

2 *Style*: Can an ambient management style be identified and if so, what are the implications of this for management development in 'Classic Products' plc?

3 *Shared values*: Are you able to identify – or speculate constructively about – the values which predominate in this company? What are the implications for management development?

4 *Structures*: Some of the structures – such as divisionalization – are apparent. Are there any other issues of structure including the use of teams? What is the implication of structures for management development within 'Classic Products' plc?

5 *Staffing*: Describe the staffing of the company as far as you can from the information given. What more information would you need to have about staff to contribute to the plan for a management development strategy?

6 *Skills*: Consider the managerial competencies that will be required in 'Classic Products' plc to meet the requirements of the strategy. What do you think will be required at each of the levels of: (a) director; (b) executive; (c) manager.

7 *Systems*: What are your observations about the systems in the company and their possible impact upon management development?

15

FOSBAR ELECTRONICS

Ron Ludlow

Fosbar Electronics was formed in 1979, as a wholly owned subsidiary of Fosbar Engineering Limited. Initially, their work had been in fairly fundamental communication and data transmission systems. However, it had recently recognized that there was a demand for an accurate vehicle position location and reporting system (PLRS) by companies engaged in the transportation of bullion and other high value cargoes. Fosbar Electronics realized that this was an area of the market which could prove very lucrative, and it was determined to be at the forefront of its development.

However, this work involved a massive injection of capital to provide a research and development budget, computers, analysers and radio equipment. It also meant recruiting specialists who were essential to such a high-technology project. The company undertook feasibility studies, using both standard models and their own developed models. They established a reputation for technical knowledge of considerable breadth and depth, but as yet the market had not really opened up. When it did, they fully intended to be viable contenders.

ORGANIZATION STRUCTURE

Fosbar Electronics was an engineering company organized along functional lines. Its departments were staffed by engineers, technicians, scientists and mathematicians, with each technical discipline located in its own department.

All engineering aspects were headed by the engineering director, Ralph Doe, to whom the department heads reported. The line management continued to group leader, section leader, and then to the main grade engineers and technicians.

The lines of communications were clear and formal. The family tree of the department was pinned to the wall in the office of the department head's secretary, and could be seen easily through the glass panels facing the main office area.

All group leaders, but few section leaders, had side offices. However, their status was recognized by eating in a separate canteen from the rest of the factory, including the main grade professional engineers.

In 1985, Fosbar Electronics set out to bid for a contract which represented a major part of the vehicle location and reporting market. Without doubt, this was the biggest opportunity which had come to the company. A long-term project, it would restore a healthy cash flow and give financial stability for several years.

The electronics content was the largest the company had ever had to face and the department head, Reg Fryer, was instructed to fill the position of project leader with an engineer of high calibre. The position was offered to Jack Savage, who saw the opportunity as his big break. Assuming that the company's bid was successful, he believed that as the market grew so too would the electronics section. At this point, the matrix system was incorporated with all participants of the new project being located in one building and reporting on a daily basis to a project manager. Jack had previously handled all the estimating and feasibility studies in his group (group C). There were two other groups in the department, but they did not interact with C group.

Jack Savage's departure from the group left a vacancy for a group leader, which had to be filled. The new project would last at least another five years (even the proposal stage would last eighteen months). Before Jack Savage left, he was asked whom he considered the best candidate to fill the vacancy. He declined to answer, pointing out that the department head would need to work with, or delegate to, his new group leader. In the circumstances, therefore, Jack felt that the department head should choose.

The choice was between two men only. The group was run as three sections. Len Bartholomew headed the data-handling section, which covered a variety of small projects, including in-house test gear and training equipment, and was the section which had been most involved with the workshops and marketing division.

The second section was headed by Gareth Stevens and handled the software requirements of the group, electromagnetic compatibility (EMC) studies, and the effects of radio frequency radiation on electrical and electronics systems. The third was undermanned, having no designated section leader, but handled the detailed analogue design work.

The problem was that the background and characters of the two section leaders were totally different. Gareth Stevens was 42 years old with a BSc in electronics, and had been at the company for 10 years, 6 of which had been in the electronics department. The first few years had been spent in a theoretical studies group, before a lateral transfer. He had a thorough knowledge of the effects of high frequency radiation microwave theory and he was a sound mathematician and theoretician. His software knowledge was broad, but not deep, and he thoroughly enjoyed 'putting it on the computer', which was always done with careful analysis but lacked clarity of presentation. He had a background of analysis in the aerospace industry and experience in formal reporting of experimental data. One of his shortcomings, however, was that he was almost totally humourless and, to some, too dogmatic on every issue.

Len Bartholomew was totally different. At 48, he had 12 years' experience with the company behind him, all in the electronics section. Academically, he had obtained three O-levels at school and had proceeded to the Civil Service, followed by national service (a period in history unknown to everyone else in his department except the department head). At night school, he had acquired an HNC in electronics and an ONC in production engineering, while 'rising through the ranks' from workshops to design office, via the drawing office and experimental laboratory of a small electrical company on the south coast. His background was in hardware, with a flair for ergonomics. It was varied, but not specialized, and he could see the broad picture. Yet, he was not good at detailed work, much of which he dismissed as 'nit picking' and 'exercises for word-smiths'.

Unfortunately, he had not done any computer programming; indeed his software knowledge was virtually zero. Despite a notoriety for 'not suffering fools gladly', he also had a reputation for possessing negotiation skills and patience. He was often described as being able to 'think on his feet and talk his way out'. During a period of rapid staff turnover, he had become the section leader and unofficial training officer for the new graduates (a position which Gareth had steadfastly refused) but his irreverent sense of humour perturbed Reg Fryer. Yet, at the same time, he admitted that Len always had his feet on the ground.

Reg Fryer went to Ralph Doe who accepted his choice of Gareth. Ralph had some unspoken doubts, but conceded that it was Reg who would normally deal with Gareth. He also acknowledged that Gareth did have the more formal education behind him.

The following day, a new issue of the family tree appeared on Reg's secretary's wall. Len's attention was brought to it by one of the technicians in the laboratory. Len was not happy and objected to being 'leap-frogged'. He pointed out that in the previous year, when there had been staff turnover turmoil, he had carried the group. Gareth had refused to have even the software people reporting to him, until he was virtually ordered to. Len's annual report recorded how he had responded to the situation. Reg accepted that Len had a wider variety of skills, but he wanted more depth in his department. He accepted that the group needed 'a Len Bartholomew', but not as their leader. Gareth had, after all, taken on the work involved in applications for capital equipment, which Reg felt was very important. His decision stood. He expected Len to report to Gareth in the same way that he had done to Jack Savage.

Len continued to work, reporting to Gareth as he had done to Jack which was, 'I'll shout when I need help.' This had always suited Jack, who trusted

Len not to get out of his depth but also not to 'get in his hair'. He wanted Len only to shout when he really meant it, and he, in turn, would provide help. Len's progress reports were short and succinct. Gareth, however, wished to know the details of the task, which Len regarded as intrusive and insulting. Gareth regarded this response as uncooperative.

To combat his lack of computer experience, Len proposed to Reg that he should have a budget to convert his estimating system and format for proposals into a departmental standard. This would put his methods clearly on paper for others to follow, as well as giving Len some hands-on experience of minicomputers. Reg was sympathetic and enthusiastic, but the new project was currently soaking up all the available funds. He did have some money, but the requirement did not fall into the correct category.

Len then asked if the categories included another of his pet ideas – to produce a set of modules for use on data-transmission systems. the need for these had appeared in four spin-off proposals the previous year, and the design and development costs could not be written off over the four proposals. They had to be carried by one, and the development costs were making the estimates too high. This too was refused on the grounds that the R & D budget did not include it. Len interpreted these refusals as deliberate blocks: first, in an area where it was acknowledged that he was not proficient and second, in an area where he was considered to be constructive. He attacked his department head for being obstructive and negative.

Four months later, the annual review of staff took place. The form had a space for 'work undertaken in the previous twelve months' which the individual concerned filled in. Beneath this was the assessment format. The centre column was marked 'normal for the grade and position', and had two squares above and two squares below it. These were normally filled in by the immediate supervisor; in Len's case, Gareth.

Len proposed that he should fill in his own assessment, as a self-appraisal. That would only have left the difference between the appraisal by Gareth and the self-appraisal, to be discussed at the annual review with Reg. Gareth agreed.

On the form, there was one slot for 'other abilities'. Len inserted, 'presentation skills' and assessed himself 'above average'. Five years of night school lecturing, plus active parts in the local drama group had, he believed, given him the ability to present information. Reg regarded such claims as 'unnecessary and extravagant'. Len claimed that engineers 'talking into their shirt buttons' created a bad impression. His remarks regarding the company's lack of training for presenters led to more heated words on general lack of training and retraining available from the company, and the annual review ended less than amicably.

In the ensuing months, Len found the development work on which he was being engaged being curtailed in favour of the large project. Works

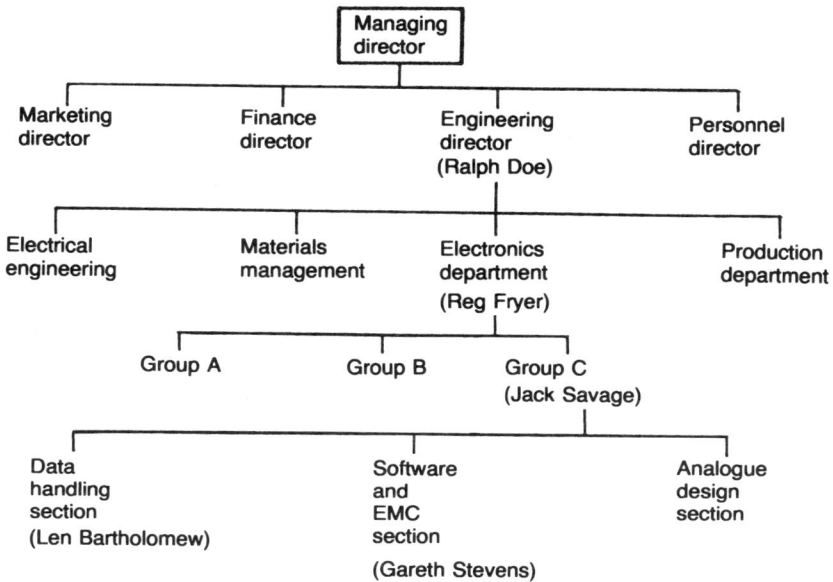

Figure 15.1 Fosbar Electronics organization chart

order numbers became scarce. Demands for a 'waiting time' number rose. Accounting for 36.5 hours per week became embarrassing.

Len required hardware to pass through the department in order to exercise his skills, but there was no hardware. This was regularly pointed out to Reg and Gareth, but the development of the total system was still incomplete. Without hardware, there would be no expansion and no promotion. Len considered his position. He was 48 yeras old; there was no hardware design planned for the immediately foreseeable future. Did he have a future at Fosbar Electronics? Reg considered the position. 'There is only one Len Bartholomew in the department,' he told Len. 'There is no one else who can do what you do; but I don't need two!'

Reg pondered. Financial strictures had prevented Len from training himself in the areas he knew to be a personal weakness, and the current climate had hidden Gareth's weakness. He could not promote Len to an equal position with Gareth, without expansion in the department; but if Len was not returned to the position in which the younger staff had regarded him, he would lose face and the new members would lose faith. If he didn't do something, he felt that Len's departure would be imminent.

Meanwhile, Len flicked through a borrowed book, *The Psychology of Management*. The book fell open at Chapter 13, 'The male menopause: a crisis of confidence'.

QUESTIONS

1 What are the implications for management development at Fosbar Electronics?
2 What steps would you take to improve the situation for:
   (a) Fosbar Electronics?
   (b) Gareth Stevens?
   (c) Len Batholomew?

16

COMMUNICATIONS AT VANGUARD

Noeleen Doherty

BACKGROUND

The Vanguard Group is a multinational organization with interests in the textile, manufacturing, process and retailing industries. Vanguard products carry world-famous names in textiles and world fashion and the group is one of the UK's principal suppliers of textile goods to chain stores and supermarket groups for sale under their own brand labels.

The group was formed in the mid-1980s as a result of the merger of three separate firms. It is now decentralized into business units, with self-contained management. The businesses are grouped into divisions that relate to major product areas. Within each division, local management boards assume responsibility and authority for the achievement of financial and other key targets. The group has an annual sales turnover of approximately £2 billion. In the UK, Vanguard is now organized operationally into 11 Divisions, employing a work force of over 40,000 people at over 100 sites within 65 profit centres. Sites are spread geographically throughout England, Scotland, Wales and Ireland (an organization chart is provided in Figure 16.1).

COMMUNICATIONS BACKGROUND

In the UK, the amalgamation of the three firms involved the combining of distinct backgrounds, cultures and communication styles – in many companies there has been a traditionally pervasive paternalistic management culture while in other companies there has been a more open management style. The group now has a centralized employee relations policy which embodies, as a key principle, the use of effective communication for encouraging employee participation and commitment.

Some formal methods of communication have been instituted within the group including the distribution of a group newsletter. Other formal methods in operation within some companies, include team briefing sessions. However, in general, there still appears to be a heavy reliance on traditional non-participative, one-way communication systems, for example, notice boards and a heavy dependence on the grapevine for information, in the absence of formal channels. This has been exacerbated in many cases by the formal communication policy at an individual site level and poor communication skills in line management.

THE MD'S OFFICE

Keith Clarke sat in his office and wondered at the events of the past few weeks. Keith had, just two months ago, assumed the position of MD of Knitwear International, a small wool manufacturing company in the Knitwear division of Vanguard. There are two sister companies in the division, one geographically close, which compete for a similar market share within the group. With increasing pressure from the board, Keith knew that he would have his work cut out trying to pull the company out of a recent slump. The knitwear industry had fallen on hard times and Knitwear International recently had the worst performance of the three companies, despite past successes relative to the others.

Keith had anticipated an element of low morale due to the present climate, but the company was small and he had hoped that the family-like business would blossom under his open-participative style of management. There was a large proportion of long-serving employees at Knitwear International who knew the knitting industry and who had shown immense loyalty and commitment to the company. These people were the backbone of the company and had served it well over the years. His plans, in due course, included a review of all functions, but he felt that one of the first key steps to increasing morale was to review communications in the company. In particular he wanted to formally introduce team briefing sessions to try to encourage more open communications and promote team building. This seemed to be well in line with the Vanguard group's employee relations policy, which the group personnel director had given him during his induction into the group. How did it read?

> The board of directors of Vanguard Group are committed to ensuring that their employees, through the provision of effective systems of communication, fully understand the performance and progress of their particular company and the group.

Having such committed backing at board level he felt that his initial task of pulling the company together would be made somewhat easier. However, he was to find that his ideas on team briefing were not greeted with enthusiasm. He knew that briefing sessions had been used in the past on an ad hoc basis but he wanted to institute them as regular forums for discussion in the company. In his first attempts to test the water, Keith had decided to arrange individual meetings with a selection of his managerial and line staff.

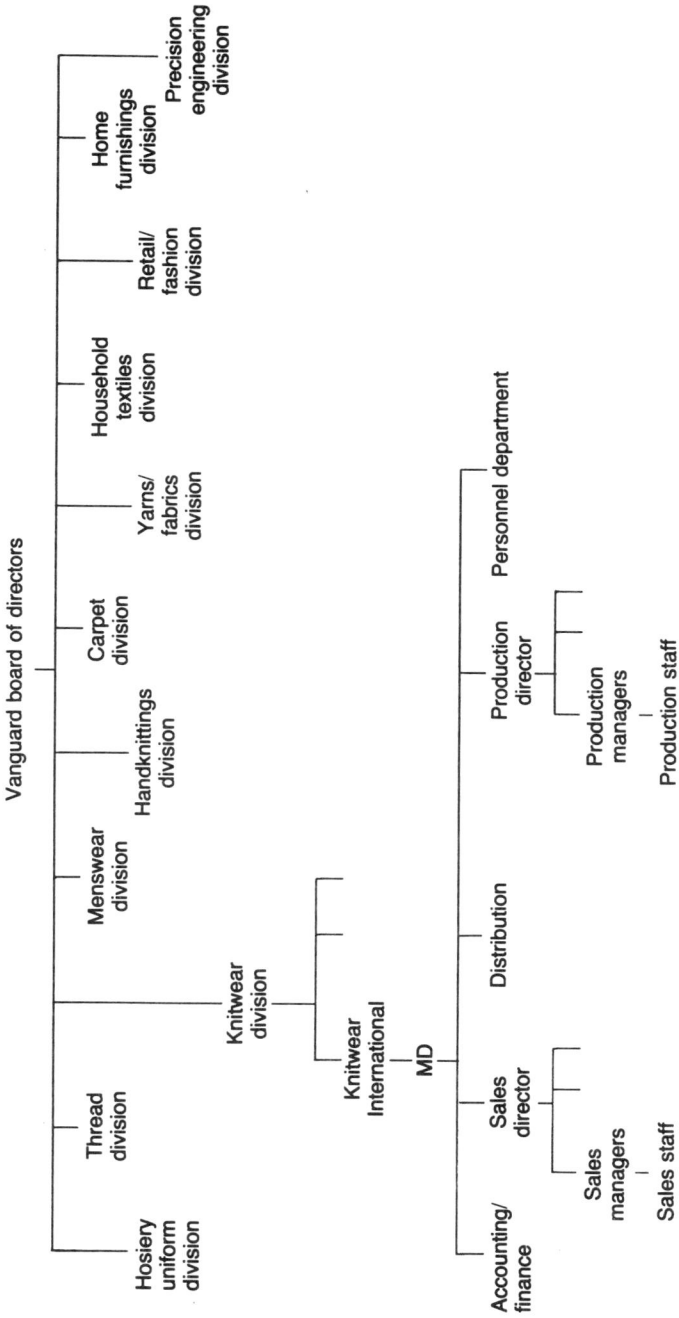

Figure 16.1 Vanguard organizational chart

Although he was familiar with most of the background history of the company he had just not anticipated the reactions he got.

The first discussion Keith had was with Neil Smith (the personnel officer). Keith had hoped for some support and help in setting up the team briefing sessions as he saw the personnel department as playing a central role in the initiation and maintenance of these. However, Neil commented:

'Mr Right [the previous MD for fifteen years] had a very patriarchal management style – he believed that employees were better off not being told anything about the company – he saw himself as a father figure – you know, protecting them from themselves really. But just before he retired we had to lay off fifty people. This was the worst slump we have ever had here – and he decided that he really couldn't keep it quiet – so we had a couple of briefing sessions to let everybody know what was happening. I don't get involved much on that side of things – my role is really to look after the pay roll and such like.'

In his meeting, Mike Adams (a production manager) told Keith he was equally disillusioned:

'You will probably get a pretty adverse reaction to your team briefing idea. Well, I am relatively new here too and I have found that communication never was a forte of Mr Right, so he never encouraged it . . . I can tell you it goes much deeper than you imagine. There is quite a poor relationship between production and sales here. I have had real trouble with the friction – the sales people see production as the back room boys who don't keep up with demand. People in production get very disillusioned as sales people seem to have most of the perks – new offices and cars while in production the working conditions haven't changed for over twenty years! Neither side seems to have any understanding of what the other actually does – we're never really working as a team.'

Keith outlined his ideas on the introduction of team briefing to Harry Bennett (a foreman and one of the local trade-union representatives). But he was met with a dry response:

'These briefings were used to go over the Union reps heads' last time – we were just told that 50 men were to be laid off. We know that management uses them as an excuse for giving out bad news – we all know times are hard – so does this mean more redundancies?'

His next meeting was with Geoff Murray (a machine foreman). Geoff commented:

'We have had these kinds of sessions before, but unfortunately it was to give details of the redundancies. As well as that, the people here are very used to having decisions made for them by Mr Right; they never had a lot of formal communication. Because of this we have a very powerful grapevine in the company. A lot of information is relayed by the grapevine and people rely on it.'

Geoff also provided some insight into feelings on the shop floor by relating some of the employees' reactions to Keith. Geoff had spoken to Margaret Knox (a machinist) who had said:

'Well, I feel that we don't really get told much, we never hear what is going to happen officially – notices are put on the board sometimes, but – of course, by the time something does happen, everybody in the factory has heard rumours – we just try to get on and do the job.'

Liz Jones (a packer) had agreed:

'I don't feel like I know what is going to happen in Knitwear International and I often hear news about our company from Jimmy [a delivery man who also visits a number of other sites]. It is usually bad news. But, I'm more bothered about what is going to happen here – is the company OK – are our jobs in danger?'

TASK

Having received this feedback on the current disposition of the workforce, you are Keith sitting in your office. Start by listing all the issues that are relevant to the current status of communications in your company. What implications do these issues have for your attempts to try to resolve the current situation?

17

THE EPICURUS LEISURE GROUP

Shaun Tyson

The case is set in 1982 when the Epicurus Leisure Group, a large British-owned group, seemed to be at the peak of its success. The group employed 9,000 people throughout the leisure and entertainment industries, including catering, leisure, and sports centres, bingo halls and a company which rented television receivers to over one million subscribers. As a group, its main period of growth had been from the mid-1960s to the late 1970s. The growth had slowed down between 1977 and 1982, when there had been no significant acquisitions. During this time, the group had come to rely on the television rental company for 60 per cent of its turnover.

EPICURUS RENTALS LIMITED

The main concern of the case is the television rental company, Epicurus Rentals Limited. The business in 1981 was simple, it started with the rental of TV sets when TV was a new phenomenon, and grew on the backs of successive technical and broadcasting innovations (ITV, BBC 2, colour TV, etc.) The original marketing idea proved durable up to 1981. By first selling the idea of cheap viewing and overcoming fears of unreliability by ensuring quick, competent service, with replacement sets wherever the need arose, customers were encouraged to rent. There were a number of reasons why people rented sets rather than purchased them:

1 The periodic advent of new developments encouraged customers to rent so they could have the latest set.
2 The high costs of TV sets when first produced helped form the renting habit, especially among low wage earners.
3 Given the low value of second-hand TV sets, customers were not interested in purchasing new receivers.
4 The 'drug' effect of TV – customers wanted assurance that they would never be without a TV receiver, even if there was a breakdown.
5 The product was seen as being technically 'sophisticated' – customers felt the need for advice, support over problems of reception/TV aerials, etc.

which they received from the continuing relationship with a rental company.

6 Government regulations on hire purchase made rental as attractive as purchase.

The rental business was highly competitive. In addition to the 'giants' many small retailers were also able to carve out a local corner of the market, but the advantage had stayed with the big battalions until recently.

In addition to rental, the major development was the home video recorder. The company forecast a large growth in demand for the rental of these and for video tapes, and made plans to exploit this. Among the marketing ideas being discussed at the time were the rental and servicing of home computers, and the rental of video films.

This company was represented throughout the UK with a network of 480 showrooms (mostly small, but on prime sites), 200 servicing depots and a total staff of 5,000 people. The turnover in 1981 was £113 million p.a.

COMPANY ORGANIZATION AND PEOPLE

1 The organization chart was as given in Figure 17.1. The company was reorganized into this form two years ago. The chairman of Epicurus Rentals was the chairman of the Epicurus group, and the managing director of the rental company was a member of the group's board.

2 Staff numbers and the labour turnover were as shown in Table 17.1

The *technicians'* jobs included the servicing of TV receivers, calling on customers to deal with technical complaints, helping in the installation of

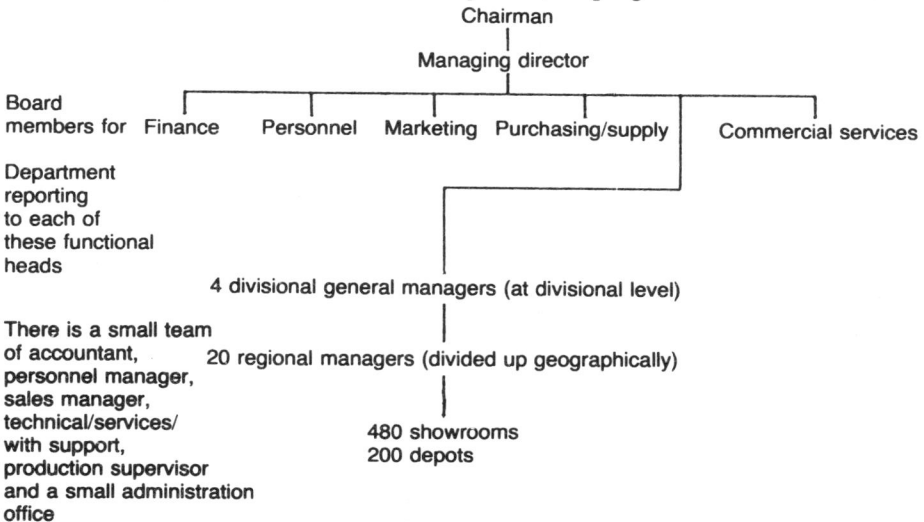

Figure 17.1 Epicurus Rentals Limited organization chart

125

Table 17.1 Epicurus Rentals: staff numbers and turnover

	Staff numbers	Labour % turnover p.a.
Technicians (almost all male)	1,935	10
Receptionists (almost all female)	506	20
Representatives	840	30
Showroom managers	450	18
District/regional management staff and senior technical staff	200	5
Cleaners (mainly part-time, female)	440	8
Drivers	100	10
Stores assistants/warehouse staff	130	10
HO staff	400	13
	5,001	

video equipment etc. Apart from about 150 apprentices all were trained to repair colour TV equipment. A small number had already been retrained to service home computers; and another group to service/repair video recorders.

Receptionists were based in the showrooms. Their work was to collect payment from customers, to sell the service to potential customers and to prepare the rental agreements.

Showroom managers were shop managers although they only had one receptionist working for them in some cases.

Representatives called on customers and potential customers in their homes, in order to sign agreements; they also installed and repossessed equipment, and collected bad debts.

Industrial relations

Eighty-five per cent of the technicians were members of the EPTU and 49 per cent of the remaining staff were members of other unions.

The relationships with management were very good. There were formal procedures for disputes, grievances and discipline to which both management and unions were committed.

There was one strike over pay about ten years ago, but since then the technicians in particular were satisfied with their pay and conditions. There was an annual pay awared, negotiated to take effect on 1 July each year.

There were common conditions of service across the Epicurus group for pensions, life assurance and senior management conditions.

THE CORPORATE PLAN, AS AT AUGUST 1981 FOR EPICURUS RENTALS LIMITED

The corporate plan proposed that the company would remain and develop within the home entertainment field – TV, video, video games, cassettes

Table 17.2 Net profit forecast

1981–2	1982–3	1983–4	1984–5	1986–7
£25m	£20m	£18m	£24m	£47m

rental; and would simultaneously develop the renting and servicing of home computers.

The company forecast that changes in the marketing environment such as greater reliability and easier servicing of the later models would gradually make inroads into the subscriber list, as more and more people decided to purchase television receivers, rather than to rent them.

The proposed net profit figure in the five year plan were as shown in Table 17.2. These forecasts were founded on the assumption that the rental of TVs would fall steadily until 1983–4, even with the marketing initiatives (e.g. capturing more of the contract rental market in hotels, encouraging rental of second TVs etc.), but that there would be a steady increase in the rental of video equipment to take up the shortfall. The figures also represented a modest growth in the field of home computers but assumed that they would remain a minor contributor for the next five years.

THE 'NEW REALITY' OF 1982

Due to a number of factors, the outcome was rather different from the plan. At the normal profit forecast at the end of first quarter of 1982 a number of disturbing factors were noted:

1 The trend towards owning rather than renting had accelerated.
2 The recession had forced more terminations of rental agreements in areas of high unemployment.
3 The video 'boom' in rental was projected at a time when supplies were difficult, and demand was growing. Demand had not increased as projected, and a number of Japanese manufacturers had started dumping cheaper videos on the market, thus encouraging purchase.
4 Costs had been rising sharply, for example the rates on premises, staff costs and distribution costs.

As a result, the projection for 1982–3 was now zero net profit.

QUESTION

Take the role of Epicurus Rentals Limited's board of directors and consider what alternatives there are (e.g. new products, new initiatives) and the implications for the human resources of the company in each case. In particular you should undertake to examine these questions:

1 Look at the possible impact of the human resource strengths/weaknesses on the alternatives considered above.

2 What personnel policy outcomes should derive from these changes in corporate plan?

PART III

HUMAN RESOURCE MANAGEMENT

The case studies contained in this section are concerned with how to turn corporate plans and management strategies into actions. They are about policies and systems which will make strategic changes of direction actually happen, and as such they describe situations where the original plan ran into difficulties, they show that often there are a number of policy options available, and they indicate with varying degrees of detail what those options are. In the following cases, it is possible to see how the interventions of human resource specialists or consultants can influence the options available. The cases cover the key human resource management areas: manpower, planning, reward structures, training and management development, recruitment and selection, as well as the personnel role.

Further, we have incorporated what used to be called industrial relations, then latterly employee relations, in this section. In our opinion, the study of the institutions, trade unions, employers and state bodies which control the structures, agreements, procedures and processes which in turn influence the behaviour of people at work, is an intrinsic part of human resource management. By dividing personnel practice from employee relations, an artificial distinction has been drawn between those who are management and those who represent staff interests. For any enterprise to attain and then maintain success, long term, the totality of people concerns need to be addressed under the same conceptual umbrella. In this way, a comprehensive understanding of what people do and need to do and feel in order to collectively attain high levels of organizational performance, is achieved.

The *Global Industries and European works councils* case takes a broad view of the social and economic environment in Europe, and examines whether a more integrated approach shaping the behaviour of employers and trade unions is likely and desired. The *Pallas Electronics* case focuses on manpower planning in a situation where the original plan has not been

129

achieved. This case study underlines the need to recognize the true nature of the interrelationships between the different personnel policy areas.

Archon Engineering looks at the problems of establishing a personnel role in an organization at a time of rapid change. While allowing the reader to address the organization structure issues of establishing a new role, the case also highlights the ambiguity so often associated with personnel specialists, who experience a disjunction between power and authority. *Lysander Products* puts the reader in the position of a new personnel manager, being asked to help create a new reward structure in a company where most personnel systems have fallen into disuse. For the old established firm of *Thomas Nestor* there is a more favourable climate for the personnel specialist's intervention. However, this is a crucial time for decisions to be made about the company's future management development policies.

Continuing with the theme of management development is an examination of job competencies in the *Competencies in the Public Collection Agency* case. It is worth noting that although management development is addressed in both parts II and III of this case book, a distinction is drawn between management development as an element of strategy development and the more 'nuts and bolts' human resource concerns in effective development practice.

The *Recruitment* case illustrates the significance of ensuring for an effective recruitment policy, as it provides an opportunity to explore a range of questions which must be addressed when undertaking personnel selection.

The other side to influencing people's performance at work significantly is that of job design. The *Clerical Medical Investment Group* case provides for an investigation of job design, in keeping with the company's strategy and as a mechanism for inducing high levels of performance from the job holders.

In the *Alcan Plate Limited* case, there is an opportunity to examine employee involvement. The emphasis on quality has led many large organizations to try and build a concern for quality into jobs and working practices through such devices as quality circles, which are discussed here.

The impact of new technology, and the growth of white-collar unionism, are two of the trends which are addressed in the *BIFU* case, where the reader has the opportunity to reflect on the direction of trade unionism as the century draws to a close.

As with the start of this section, a European-wide perspective is adopted in the *Trade Unions and European Pattern Bargaining* case. The point being made is that trade unions have traditionally emphasized a national outlook in both their economics and politics. 'Will the trade unions adopt a broader European perspective'? is the question posed.

18

GLOBAL INDUSTRIES AND EUROPEAN WORKS COUNCILS

Paul Teague

Global Industries is a large multinational enterprise with its head office in the UK. Operating in seventy-five different countries, it employs over three hundred thousand people and its commercial concerns span a large range of product markets. In Europe, the company is known as Global Europe and has plants in twelve different countries, including countries from the European Community, Scandinavia and the former east European bloc. A more limited range of goods are produced in the region, and as a result, most of the European plants are 'stand-alone' concerns producing specialized goods for niche markets. Only in one or two instances does a plant represent a part of an integrated pan-European production system. There is a strong trade-union presence in all of Global Industries European operations. Traditionally, the company has pursued decentralized 'polycentric' human resource management strategies whereby the plant adopts the mainstream industrial-relations practices of the country in which it is situated. Thus Global Germany has a system of works councils which are widespread in industry there and also partakes in sector-level wage determination agreements. Global UK on the other hand mirrors the British free collective bargaining tradition in which terms and conditions, including wages, results from local negotiations between trade unions and management.

As a result of moves toward deeper economic and political integration within the European Community, the company faced pressures to add to its existing human resource management arrangements by creating a pan-European works council. The objective of such a council would be to create Europe-wide information and consultation arrangements between the workforce and management. Pressures to establish such a forum came in two forms. One was the institutional pressures from the European Commission, the civil service of the European Community. As part of its efforts to create a social dimension to the EC, the Commission produced a draft law[1] (directive), which if passed would give the workforces in multinational companies operating inside the Community an opportunity to decide whether or not they wanted the enterprise to establish a European works council. In its proposal the Commission envisaged that the minimum functions of such a body would be an exchange of information and consultation about the company's European investment, employment and commercial strategies. With elected worker representatives (not necessarily drawn from the trade unions) from each subsidiary and plant, the Commission thought that such a body should meet at least once a year.

The second new pressure faced by the company was more societal in character. The distinction drawn by the German sociologist Tonnies in the last century between *Gemeinschaft* and *Gesellschaft* can be usefully deployed to throw light on the functioning of the EC as a community. For Tönnies, *Gemeinschaft* represents a society where instrumentalism and self-interest are the dominant norms and where transactions are normally based on contract. *Gesellschaft* on the other hand is about a community where values of kinship, common loyalties and values prevail, producing a harmonious and shared culture. Until now the EC operated mostly as a *Gemeinschaft* arrangement in which the member states bargained with each other in specific areas to obtain package deals through which everyone in some way benefited. However, with the upsurge in integration, the EC may for the first time be developing a *Gesellschaft* dimension in which European values and loyalties are emerging amongst the citizens of the member states. As a result, the EC may be developing all-important socio-psychological foundations. From *Gesellschaft*, European citizens may feel that their economy, polity and society should be governed in more common ways. Such expectations are manifesting themselves in ideas such as European citizenship which encapsulates the demand for individual and social rights to be underscored at Community level. The commercial world has not remained unaffected by these attitudinal innovations encouraging firms to examine whether amongst other things they should develop pan-European human resource management strategies.

In response to these institutional and societal pressures a debate emerged inside Global Industries about whether or not it should set up a European works council. Two strongly contrasting views were voiced on the issue. On the one hand, some managers opposed the setting up of such an arrangement. Numerous arguments were put forward justifying this opposition. One was that the way the company organizes its production operation in Global Europe did not warrant such a procedure. The argument was that if the company had an integrated chain of production or produced the same goods in different European countries then the case for a European works council would have some justification.

In such a situation, the company would clearly have pan-European corporate strategies, with strong human resource implications. Since such strategies would have been developed outside the nation state, a European works council which facilitated an exchange of views with employee representatives from different countries at European level on future employment and investment plans may actually improve policy making. If nothing else, such a procedure could build up the consensus, legitimacy and acceptance of company plans. But since Global Europe consisted of stand-alone production facilities this case was considered not to apply. As Global Germany was producing for different markets from Global France, Global UK and so on, they would be guided by quite separate commercial strategies. Thus there was little point in workers from various plants coming together at a European level since they would have little in common to discuss. In other words, a European works council was inappropriate because the multinational mainly operated stand-alone concerns in Europe.

A second argument was that the idea of a European works council would be highly incongruent with the company's strong decentralized approach to human resource management. Throughout the 1980s across Europe the company had pursued a rigorous campaign of hollowing out national corporate centres and decentralizing as many managerial tasks as possible to the local level. This effort was so far reaching that workers in local plants in some countries had not even an official forum or mechanism to discuss or exchange views at the *national* level within management. Thus when Global UK decided to close down a local plant it was local management that conveyed the decision and it was regarded as a local management action, instigated by the group. Trade-union protests that they wanted to discuss the issue at national level came to nothing since there was no procedure to facilitate such a dialogue. Now the argument was that it would be meaningless to establish a European works council without similar national mechanisms being in place. Thus it was argued that a European works council would trigger an entire new hierarchy of consultation arrangements which would undermine the decentralization gains made in the 1980s. As a result such an arrangement was regarded to be fundamentally at odds with the company's human resource management strategy.

Concern was also expressed that by creating a European works council, management may be giving a hostage to fortune since the arrangement may get out of control in one way or another. One view was that the trade unions would not be content with the council being a purely consultative institution and would campaign for it to be transformed into a genuine collective-bargaining arrangement. In other words, a European works council would become a contested terrain triggering unnecessary and avoidable battles between management and unions. A further worry was that such an arrangement would encourage the transfer of certain consultation practices followed by the company in one country to another country. A particular worry was mentioned that a European works council could lead to the spread of the German co-determination system across the company's entire European operation. Yet another point stressed was the potential 'spillover' effect of such an arrangement. If a European works council was established, then employees in Latin America or the Pacific Rim may demand a similar body for their region. Some managers envisaged calls for an international works council spanning the world-wide operations of the company. In other words, establishing a European works council was seen as likely to produce large scale and unwelcome changes across the organization and thus had to be opposed.

Question marks were raised about the practical usefulness of such an arrangement. It was estimated that an elaborate conference centre would be required to host a meeting of a European works council. To include all plants in Europe about two hundred and fifty worker representatives would have to attend such a meeting. In addition, interpretation facilities would have to be at hand since most of the workers would be mono-lingual. With representatives from the management side swelling the numbers to over three hundred, the chances of this group having a positive and constructive dialogue were considered to be fairly remote. In particular it was argued that it would be impossible to develop the ambience of trust and mutuality which make consultative exercises worthwhile and productive. Put bluntly, the feeling of some managers was that a European works council would be a costly failure having more to do with the political motivation of Community institutions than with any pressing commercial or human resource needs.

Indeed, many managers expressed the view that since a good deal of the pressure for the company to create a European works council was coming from the Community's institutional framework, the company was confronted with a key question of principle. The principle was whether the company should regard the Community as a legitimate industrial-relations sector with the capacity to oblige companies to adopt policies and arrangements which otherwise it might not do. The argument was that if the company adopted a European works council then the Commission would view it as a victory for their initiative on the subject and be encouraged to develop further proposals. By not establishing such an arrangement the company would be signalling to the Commission that it limit its interference in the employee-relations area. It would also signal that decisions about establishing a European works council should be based on commercial and business considerations alone.

The majority of managers opposed the establishment of a European works council. However, there was a minority who came out in favour of such an arrangement. They put forward two main arguments. One was that by not establishing such a consultative body the company was only postponing the inevitable. Their view was that the EC was moving rapidly towards a genuinely open economic space like that which existed in the United States. As a result of the formation of such a regional economic bloc, the company would be obliged to take more decisions at the European level, even in relation to stand-alone national plants. In the short term, the claim was that the company may be able to pursue extra-national corporate strategies without consulting the workforce. But sooner or later ground-level resentment would build up against such a form of decision making. Once that resentment emerged, management would have to appease the workforce by offering something like a European works council. However, by that stage a purely information and consultation arrangement may not be strong enough to satisfy worker demands which may be for some type of European collective-bargaining forum. Basically, the argument of the minority was that good management practice involved thinking ahead and averting difficulties by taking preventive action. Their view was that if the management set up a European works council, then it would be able to structure and organize the arrangement in a way that blended with the company's human resource strategies.

Another argument in favour of a European works council recognized the new significance of societal pressures on the company as a result of deeper European integration. According to this view, although the company had implemented a decentralized managerial structure, workers when formulating their collective bargaining demands used external comparisons. In particular, when judging what would be a fair pay rise they take note of the going rate in other (national) plants within the group and in their respective local labour markets. In other words, certain informal norms or conventions of perceived fairness underpin annual collective bargaining demands. Now as a result of deeper societal integration inside the Community, workers in a plant in one country may begin to demand the terms and conditions enjoyed by a worker in the group in another country irrespective of possible productivity or standard-of-living differences. Deeper European integration may encourage workers to pursue collective-bargaining demands in the absence of norms of equity or fairness. As a result, conflicts may very quickly emerge inside the company whereby unrealistic demands with regard to pay and conditions emerge. The argument put forward was that the only effective way to prevent such problems from arising was to establish an institution like a European works council which would establish rules limiting the possibilities of cross-national comparisons. In particular, the works council by making transparent the huge differences in productivity levels as well as wages could discourage collective bargaining demands which were not equitable.

Most of the managers did not find these arguments convincing. In particular, they thought that societal integration inside the EC would only impinge marginally on the collective-bargaining behaviour of workers in the different European countries. Thus it was decided that the company would not establish a European works council. However, it was also decided that the company's existing consultation arrangements be audited to see if they could in any way be improved. The purpose of this action was to signal to the European Commission that most multinational companies had already high-grade consultation arrangements and, as a result, no EC legislative intervention in the area was necessary.

NOTE

1 The title of the draft law is the amended proposal for a Council Directive in the establishment of a European Works Council in community-scale undertaking or groups of undertaking for the purposes of informing and consulting employees (*Official Journal of the European Communities*, no. C3367 31.12.92).

QUESTIONS

1 If you were a senior human resource manager in a company which had similar production plants across a number of EC countries would you recommend the establishment of a European works council?
2 Can an arrangement like a European works council be made compatible with a decentralized human resource management approach where a good number of decisions are taken at plant level?
3 Should the European Community have the capacity to oblige companies to adopt a particular type of human resource management practice?
4 Is the European works council proposal only of symbolic importance or could it be used as an effective consultation arrangement to build up trust and mutuality inside an organization?
5 Do you think that the upsurge in Europeanization requires companies to establish pan-European institutions?
6 In what circumstances do you think that a European works council might be necessary?

19

PALLAS ELECTRONICS

John Beresford and Shaun Tyson

Pallas Electronics was a manufacturer of electronic equipment for the telecommunications industry. Components were manufactured and assembled at five large factories in the UK. The company was organized in a traditional way, with a large production function, research and development, marketing, and finance departments (see Figure 19.1).

Attention is focused on the Bristol factory of Pallas. Each factory was run by a small team, which included the personnel manager, production control, transport manager and accountant. The organization chart is given in Figure 19.2.

The factory had been established for three years, and in addition to the supervisory staff, employed 200 female operatives.

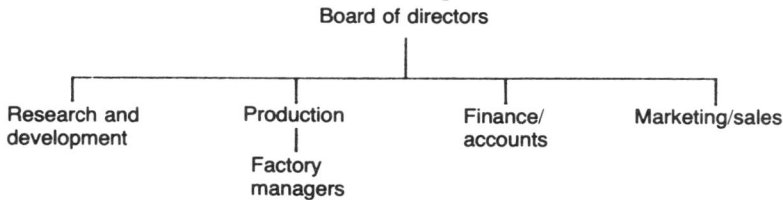

Figure 19.1 Pallas Electronics organization chart

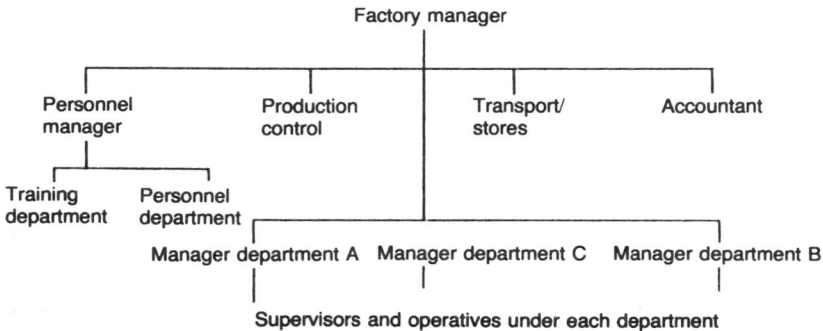

Figure 19.2 Bristol factory organization chart

137

The national marketing manager was able to negotiate a substantial order, which could only be met by a large increase in production. All the factory managers were called in to discuss how this could be achieved, and it was agreed that the Bristol factory would play an important part in the achievement of increased production, since there was room for expansion on the site and a good supply of labour was available.

The decision was made to build up the labour force to 300 operatives. Production was to be maximized as soon as possible, so the recruitment plan was an intake of 100 new operatives over the next 6 months. The plan, and its expected results are shown in Table 19.1.

Table 19.1 Six-month recruitment plan and expected results

Month	Planned recruits	Expected numbers	Expected utilization
0		200	40
1	25	221	43
2	25	240	46
3	25	259	50
4	25	277	54
5	15	290	57
6	12	300	60

The labour turnover was around 20 per cent per annum, and was expected to increase during the build up of labour. The utilization of labour at 40 per cent was rather low at the outset, compared with the four other factories, where some of the older established plants achieved 75 per cent utilization. During the first six months layout improvements were prepared, together with altered production methods, and a new pay and productivity incentive scheme was introduced. These changes were expected to improve utilization to 60 per cent at the end of six months, and to over 70 per cent by the end of twelve months. The term 'utilization' is used here as a rough measure of productivity – the number of units actually produced compared with the expert view of production management of the capacity of the factory for any given number of workers.

Table 19.2 Position at end of six-month period

Month	Recruits	Actual numbers	Utilization %	Units of output expected	achieved
1	25	216	40.3	950	870
2	25	231	42.0	1100	970
3	25	245	45.3	1300	1110
4	25	258	48.9	1500	1260
5	15	261	51.0	1680	1330
6	12	263	52.3	1800	1380

At the end of the six month period, the position was as shown in Table 19.2.

The recruits had been engaged as planned, and the quality of the applicants was good. They seemed to be attracted to the pay and the working conditions were good for the area. However, both the build up of numbers, and the utilization of the factory fell seriously below target. Converted into output units, the running rate at the sixth month was seriously below target and there was considerable management concern at a senior level. A running rate of 2,100 units of output per month had been expected by the end of a year, and the order intake to the company and thus to the Bristol factory depended on a good delivery performance. Production could not easily be switched to the other factories without disrupting their operations. Cumulative output was already so much in arrears that a month of output needed to be recovered as soon as possible, therefore making the problem worse over the next six months.

There was some concern about the ability of the training department to cope with a larger intake of people. The personnel department was under strong criticism in general, and various, excessively high, turnover rates were being quoted, some of the estimates being in excess of 40 per cent. The board gave a directive to the Bristol factory management team to produce a report on what had happened, and an action plan which should show how and when the optimum labour force of 300 would be reached.

QUESTIONS

1 You are in the position of the factory management team. Now that the first six months has passed, comment on the original plan in the light of the results, explaining in your answer the likely reasons for the variation between the planned and the actual results.
2 Produce a plan and a monitoring procedure for the next six months.

20

ARCHON ENGINEERING

Shaun Tyson

BACKGROUND

Archon Engineering was founded in the mid-1930s as an engineering company which manufactured a range of small components used in the automotive and aircraft industries. The Second World War saw a diversification of the company's activities, and after the war the company expanded to take over a number of smaller businesses in the fields of chemical and consumer products, valve manufacture and pipe manufacture.

The general style of management had been paternalistic. The original entrepreneur who had formed the company, Arthur Cohen (hence the 'Archon' name) had been succeeded by one of his sons, and his other son was also on the board. For many years the Archon group had been based in a suburb west of London. The head office was in the converted old house of the founder, and the close proximity of the rest of the companies in the group strengthened the paternalistic style. However, growth and diversification brought formality into relationships. The need to expand their capital base had resulted in the group becoming a public company in the early 1950s.

As the 1960s drew to a close, Archon was changing its style and organization structure dramatically. This case history concerns the events and the people who were involved in this period of growth and change. There was a growing requirement for more capital in 1969, which resulted in the group floating a rights issue. In order to impress the City of London, Sir Horace Scott was appointed chairman of the Archon board. Sir Horace had many friends in the city and was already a non-executive director of several well known companies. He had been seen as an ideal figurehead, aged in his late fifties, it was thought his presence would add 'weight' to the board, without upsetting the balance of power. In practice, he was much more vigorous than expected. By a series of deft political manoeuvres over a period of a year he was able to bring in several of his friends as directors. As a consequence of one year's bad results he was able to exploit differences among the members of the board, so that the managing director, John Cohen, 'retired' with a handsome settlement.

THE ARCHON GROUP IN 1971

By 1971, when this case is set, the group employed around four thousand people, had a turnover of £500 million created from about twenty small companies in the UK and abroad. Sir Horace and his board decided that a more formal, professional and consciously organized approach was necessary. The decision was made to 'divisionalize' the group into four divisions, and to give greater autonomy to the divisional general managers, who were directors of the group, and who would be accountable to the board as a whole for the profitability of their divisions. The new organization structure is given in Figure 20.1.

THE DIVISIONAL STRUCTURE

Each division of the group employed a management team which acted as the functional specialists for the operating companies. There were divisional marketing, finance and personnel managers, whose role was to provide expert advice to the operating company managing directors, and to produce a divisional strategy for acceptance at group level. Apart from the directors, at head office, there were only administrative departments covering for example the group pension scheme, and a secretariat which dealt with legal and insurance matters for the group. When the divisional strategy was formulated, therefore, it was the directors who evaluated the plans put forward.

The consumer products division

The consumer products division consisted of three companies: each operating company had its own products, style and traditions. The products

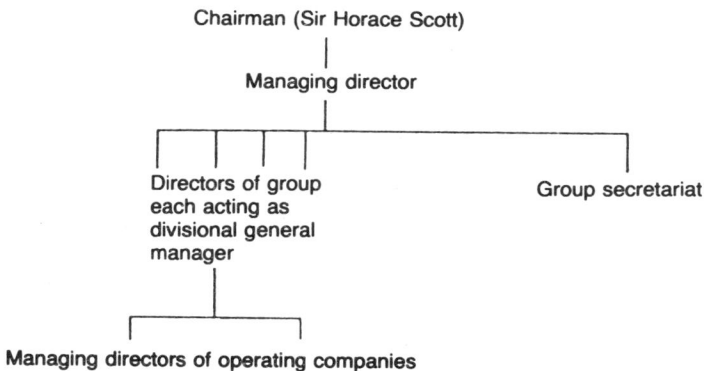

Chairman (Sir Horace Scott)

Managing director

Directors of group
each acting as
divisional general
manager

Group secretariat

Managing directors of operating companies

Figure 20.1 Archon Group organization chart

Divisional general manager (Robertson)

Divisional personnel manager

Divisional finance manager

Divisional marketing manager

Managing directors of operating companies

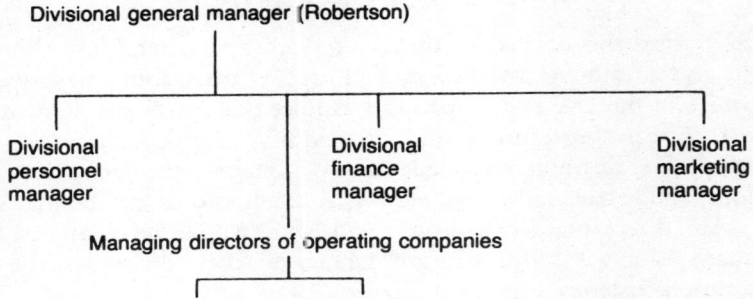

Figure 20.2 Consumer products division organization chart

were paints and chemicals, domestic products (window furnishings, blinds etc.) and radiators. The divisional general manager of the consumer products division was Alexander Robertson, one of the new directors brought in by Sir Horace. The divisional personnel manager was Neil Jones who was regarded as the most professional personnel manager in the group, where he had been the personnel manager in the engineering company. Personnel departments were well established in the radiator company, which was fully unionized with a closed shop, and in the paint company, an old-established company dating back to the eighteenth century which the group bought in 1958. The other two companies merely kept personnel records and left all personnel decisions to line managers, and ultimately to their managing directors.

The organization structure of the consumer products division is given in Figure 20.2. The division employed 1,200 people in small factories and offices throughout the UK. The total divisional turnover was £30 million.

When the new structure was announced, it was made clear that personnel managers reported to their operating company managing directors, but had a 'dotted line' functional relationship with the divisional personnel manager. The divisional offices were located on the largest site in the division where the paint company's manufacturing facilities were.

THE DIVISIONAL PERSONNEL MANAGER'S POSITION

The divisional personnel manager arranged to meet Robertson when taking up his appointment. Jones was keen to discover how he should perform this new role.

The interview with Robertson

Robertson had a strong view of the personnel role. Putting his views simply, Robertson viewed the personnel function as an arm of his own policy. In particular, he wanted to rid the division of a number of managers whom he disliked; he regarded them as 'useless', unable to cope with new conditions and not sufficiently in tune with his divisional philosophy.

Among the specific proposals discussed was Robertson's opinion that all the companies in the division should offer the same conditions of service. These, he felt, should be based on those pertaining in the paint company. Jones said he would investigate but managed to avoid committing himself. Robertson was prepared to appoint further executives to the divisional personnel function, but there was a strong feeling in the meeting that Robertson did not want to build a personnel function on a separate power base from his own. He wished to take all the major decisions on personnel, and to see the personnel department as a source of data for him about people in the division.

Neil Jones reflected on his meeting. He decided to discover what the managing directors of the operating companies thought before setting out his own position on the role of personnel specialists within the division.

Interview with the paint company's managing director

Geoff Wayne was the managing director of the paint and chemical company. Employing six hundred people, a substantial number of whom were hourly rated, the paint company faced more problems than Wayne was prepared to admit at first. The paint company was desperately in need of new products and of a marketing image which would distinguish the brands of colour paints from other manufacturers. The factory was as old as the company, and there were many breakdowns due to the old machinery. Wayne regarded his managers as loyal and hardworking, but untrained. The personnel department consisted of an ageing ex-naval officer who spent most of his time on recruitment, and attending to the personnel records, and a welfare officer who also had responsibility for the canteen. Industrial relations was handled by line management who negotiated with the Transport and General Workers Union, and the General and Municipal Union who represented most of the hourly rated personnel. There was a strong rumour that ASTMS were recruiting among the supervisors, and managers, many of whom expressed their dissatisfaction with their pay and conditions. There were no fixed pay scales for management, and salary administration was rudimentary.

By contrast, the separate chemical plant which manufactured degreasers and chemical cleaning fluids only employed around thirty people, most of whom were in sales. This was a highly profitable plant with modern automated equipment and was often held up by Wayne as an example of how the paint company should operate.

Interview with the consumer products company's managing director

This company employed around four hundred people and was regarded by its Danish managing director, Per Nielson, as a part of the 'home fashion' industry. He could see no logic in associating it with the other companies in the division. Indeed he was openly hostile to Jones, whom he saw as Robertson's stooge.

Although the company only had a small financial turnover it was highly profitable, with a record of steady growth and reliability in performance. The managers who worked there were loyal to the consumer company, rather than to Archon. There was no trade-union membership, and no personnel department. Personnel records were kept by the chief accountant who made whatever personnel decisions were necessary in conjunction with Per Nielson. The majority of the employees were female, and worked in small factories spread all over the UK on subassembly work. Most employees were only trained to a semiskilled level, and there was a growing trend towards the employment of part-time staff and subcontract when orders justified this, instead of extra permanent employees.

Interview with the radiator company's managing director

This company employed around two hundred people, mostly male. Manufacturing was in a West Country factory which was highly mechanized. All employees were trade-union members, except the senior management group, and a post-entry closed shop was operated by the AUEW. The managing director, Arthur Wilson, was a gloomy individual – he was aware his company was making losses, but considered this to be the fault of an incorrect pricing policy imposed by Archon. He was complacent about his own organization, and pointed to the small numbers employed already when questioned about the efficiency of his operation.

There was a small personnel department. The personnel officer was largely concerned with the maintenance of existing agreements with the unions, and leant heavily upon the Engineering Employers Federation for advice. Conditions of service and pay were well above the minimum, however, and there were some especially generous sick pay and holiday benefits. Jones's impressions when he left were of a cosy atmosphere, where the greatest sin was to suggest change.

Jones had promised he would go back and talk with Robertson about the role personnel should play.

QUESTIONS

1 From the perspective of Jones, how do you believe the role of the personnel function should be structured at divisional level?
2 What priorities would you suggest to Robertson?

21

LYSANDER PRODUCTS

Shaun Tyson

BACKGROUND

This case concentrates on the problems of job evaluation and salary administration in a company where the personnel systems had fallen into disuse. Lysander Products was the UK subsidiary of Lysander Incorporated, a multinational pharmaceutical company, with manufacturing plants in Europe, Africa, Australasia and in Canada, where its head office was located. The UK company was part of the European Division and European headquarters were in Geneva. The general manager for the UK was a member of the European division board, and was accountable for the profitability of the UK company, within the European corporate plan.

A new general manager had recently been appointed to the UK from the French company, with a brief to improve the profitability of the UK company, to slim down its operations and to enliven its marketing effort.

Lysander had been trading on the reputation it had gained for forty years from the success of a pain-reliever, which had been a market leader, but which was now showing signs of a downturn in its lifecycle as a product.

There had been attempts to improve the product range in prescribed drugs (ethical pharmaceuticals), where there was an active research base. However, it was mainly in the over-the-counter products that most of the growth had come (for example, indigestion tablets, throat lozenges etc.). Some new product ideas had failed miserably – notably a special chewing gum, and a brand of boiled sweets. There was anticipated to be a growth of only 1–2 per cent in sales turnover in the next three years.

LOCATION AND ORGANIZATION

The UK company had its offices and factory on one site twenty-five miles west of London. The organization's charts which follow (see Figures 21.1–21.7) show the detailed structure. The research centre was about three miles away, and there were several small distribution depots throughout the UK. There were about 160 managers employed, together with approximately 300 clerical and other monthly staff and 900 hourly rated personnel.

The hourly rated personnel were mostly members of trade unions. There were thought to be around 20 per cent of managerial and other monthly staff with membership of ASTMS

PERSONNEL DEPARTMENT

A new personnel manager was appointed. He was a 32-year-old recently graduated MBA, with three years' experience of personnel. The new French general manager appointed him from a well-known British business school. He found himself facing a number of run-down 'systems' with rather a weak personnel department to support him (weak in skills and weak in positive ideas). There were three separate grading systems for each of the groupings mentioned above (managerial, monthly/clerical and hourly rated). There were a number of problems with the managerial group.

PROBLEM AREAS

1 In the past managers had been appointed outside the salary bands. The reasons had long since been forgotten but the consequences were that anomalies had arisen, and this was a source of constant grumbles.
2 Managers complained that there was no incentive because increments were arbitrary, not based on understood criteria, or within scales that were realistic.
3 A number of managers (the younger ones) were threatening to leave because they said they were underpaid.
4 According to some senior managers, there were a number of managers who were overpaid.
5 There was constant pressure from 'grade F' managers for regrading to 'E' where they would automatically receive a company car.
6 No one seemed to understand the current grading scheme – it had lost face validity. Some higher-grade managers were reporting to managers of equivalent grades, for example, due to reorganizations which had taken place.

The job-evaluation scheme

The existing job-evaluation scheme was of a type known as a classification or grading system. It was an in-house scheme, which required the examination of jobs in the light of predetermined definitions of grades, where the level of work was described in terms of responsibility. New jobs were compared with the predefined grade description to indicate the placing of the job in a relationship with other graded jobs.

The grade of managers is shown in brackets on the organization charts (Figures 21.1–21.7), and a list of grade definitions is attached (Appendix 21.1).

Salary administration

There was no salary administration guide, but there were written rules concerning the benefits which applied at each grade. The actual salary scales were not published, however, although the grade definitions were. Pay for all grades (monthly and hourly rates) were reviewed on 1 July each year when new salary brackets were agreed by the UK company board and for the grades B and above by the European division. Managers could make recommendations for increments, at the time of the review. Strictly according to the rules, these increments were supposed to be within the scale; however, there were many occasions when due to pressure from managers threatening to leave, increments beyond the grade scale had been granted.

ACTIONS REQUIRED

The personnel manager examined the existing salaries by grade (see Table 21.1), and discussed the problems with the general manager. His response was that he wanted the problems solved quickly, within the next six months (i.e., before the next pay review), but he was anxious not to raise expectations for more money at the review. He was proposing only a modest rise (possibly even zero for some people!). The general manager indicated his intention to reduce the number of people employed by Lysander Products over the next two years, as part of his drive for greater efficiency. He asked the personnel manager to try to include in his plan for salary administration provision for a reduced head count. The personnel manager took this to mean that there would be some flexibility in the salary budget, but also realized that the existing jobs would be changing. In the past, a number of one-off attempts had been made to improve the job-evaluation scheme, without long-term success. The time and effort management had expended on these had led to a degree of scepticism about job evaluation, which may be one of the reasons the old scheme fell into disuse, and the problems abounded.

QUESTION

What actions should the new personnel manager take, and what should he recommend to the general manager and the UK board?

APPENDIX 21.1: GRADE DEFINITIONS

Grade A: Chief executive of the major units in the group.
Grade B: Those people reporting to the chief executive, who have a corporate responsibility beyond the function of which they are head. In common with the chief executive they are also responsible for planning the corporate growth and policy of the unit.

Grade C: Those people who do not report directly to the chief executive but who head up a function or a large, significant subfunction. They may *advise* on policy formation.

Grade D: These people will report to those in grade B or C; they will head up a subfunction and/or possess specialized knowledge and expertise. They may be specialists (e.g., sales manager) or generalists (e.g., general manager). They will have clear responsibilities for the implementation of policy at the operational level, and may advise on policy formation also.

Grade E: This is the bottom level of manager who is expected to be accountable for improving the profitability of the company. They will either be budget controllers, managing others who may also be budget controllers, or top specialists, where the emphasis is on individual contribution rather than the control of others. They will be closely involved in the day-to-day running of a division or function.

Grade F: This is the most senior level of manager whose job it is to manage a department or unit without necessarily being regarded as accountable for taking profit-effective initiatives. This level of supporting management may include specialists as well as managers with some years of experience and/or seniority.

Grade G: Junior managers and senior supervisors: in the former case they will be starting up the management ladder, in the latter they will be experienced, senior or less able than those in grade F. This grade also includes the secretary to the chief executive. All are engaged in *supportive* roles.

Grade H: Supervisors and others whose responsibilities place them in this lowest management grade. They may or may not have responsibility for others. Secretaries working full-time for those who report to the chief executive are on this grade also.

Table 21.1 Existing salaries by grade

Grades	Number in post	Average salary	Comparative ratio	Minimum/ maximum of range of scale	Actual range of salaries paid
B	2	£54,000	104.8	£49,000–54,000	£53,000–55,000
C	9	£43,017	102.6	£38,900–44,875	£40,000–50,000
D	10	£33,470	99.3	£31,200–36,150	£30,500–36,000
E	27	£26,527	96.4	£25,325–29,675	£25,000–29,500
F	28	£23,523	99.4	£22,100–25,200	£21,300–27,700
G	45	£19,500	97.8	£18,550–21,315	£18,300–21,600
H	34	£15,814	97.5	£14,975–17,450	£14,700–17,500

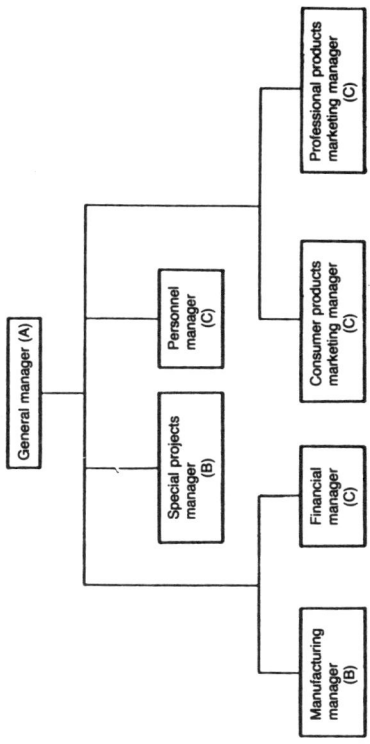

Figure 21.1 Senior management organization structure

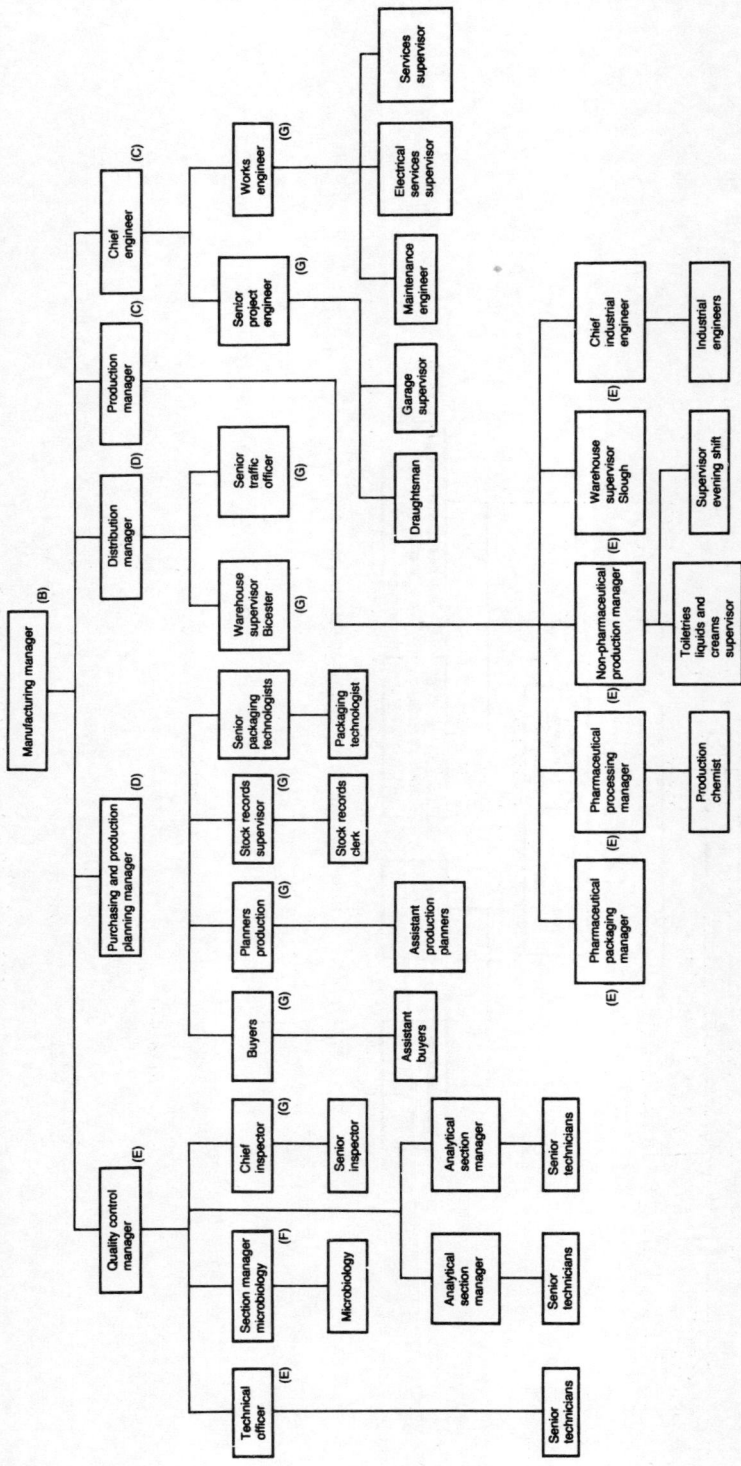

Figure 21.2 Organization structure: manufacturing

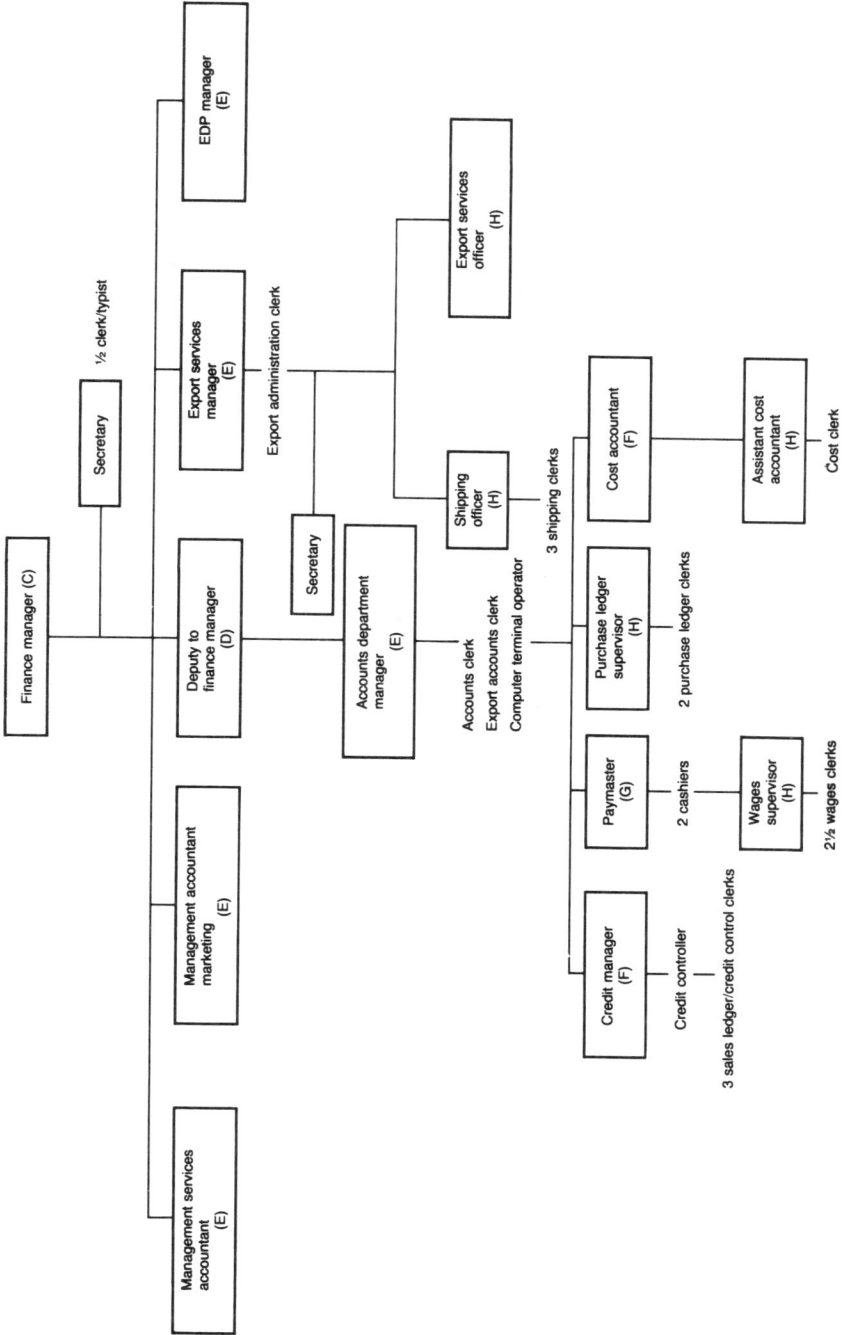

Figure 21.3 Organization structure: finance

The chart shows the following positions:

- Finance manager (C)
  - Secretary — ½ clerk/typist
  - Management services accountant (E)
  - Management accountant marketing (E)
  - Export services manager (E)
  - EDP manager (E)
  - Deputy to finance manager (D)
    - Secretary
    - Export administration clerk
      - Export services officer (H)
    - Accounts department manager (E)
      - Accounts clerk
      - Export accounts clerk
      - Computer terminal operator
      - Shipping officer (H) — 3 shipping clerks
      - Credit manager (F) — Credit controller — 3 sales ledger/credit control clerks
      - Paymaster (G) — 2 cashiers
        - Wages supervisor (H) — 2½ wages clerks
      - Purchase ledger supervisor (H) — 2 purchase ledger clerks
      - Cost accountant (F)
        - Assistant cost accountant (H) — Cost clerk

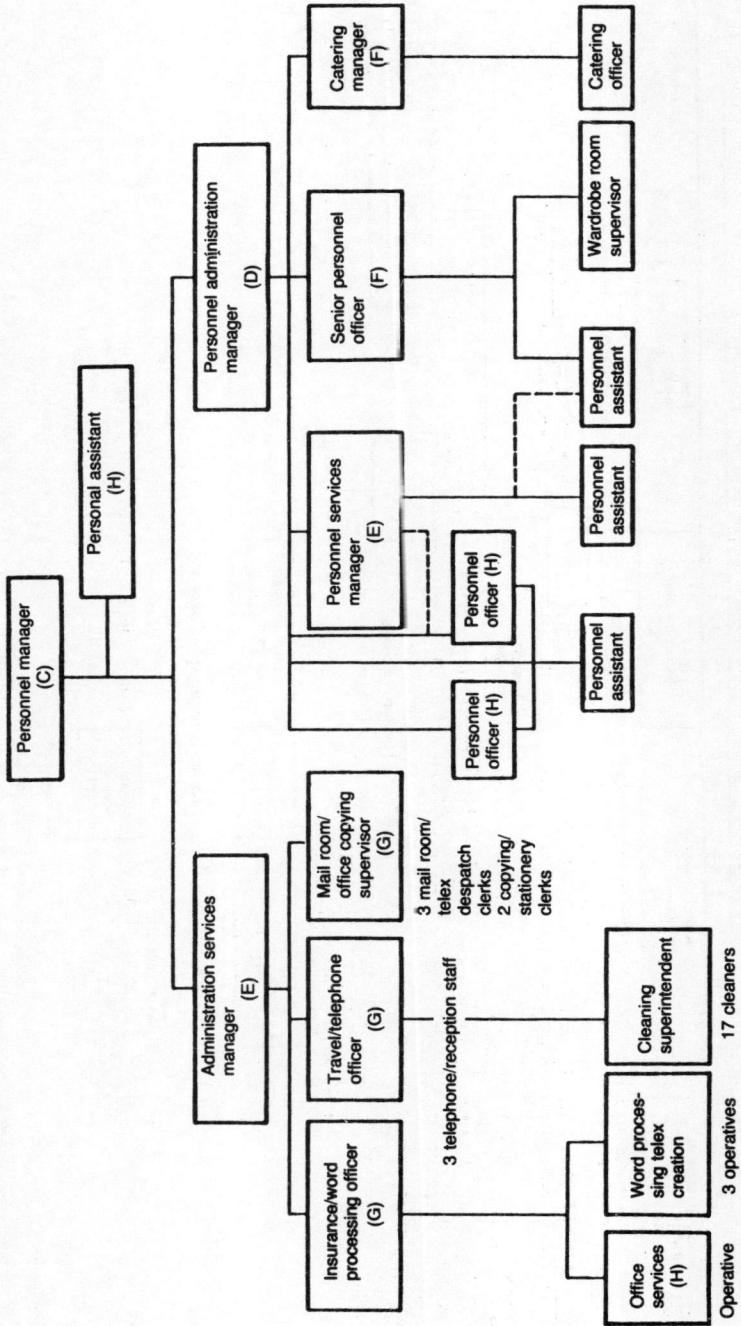

Figure 21.4 Organization structure: personnel

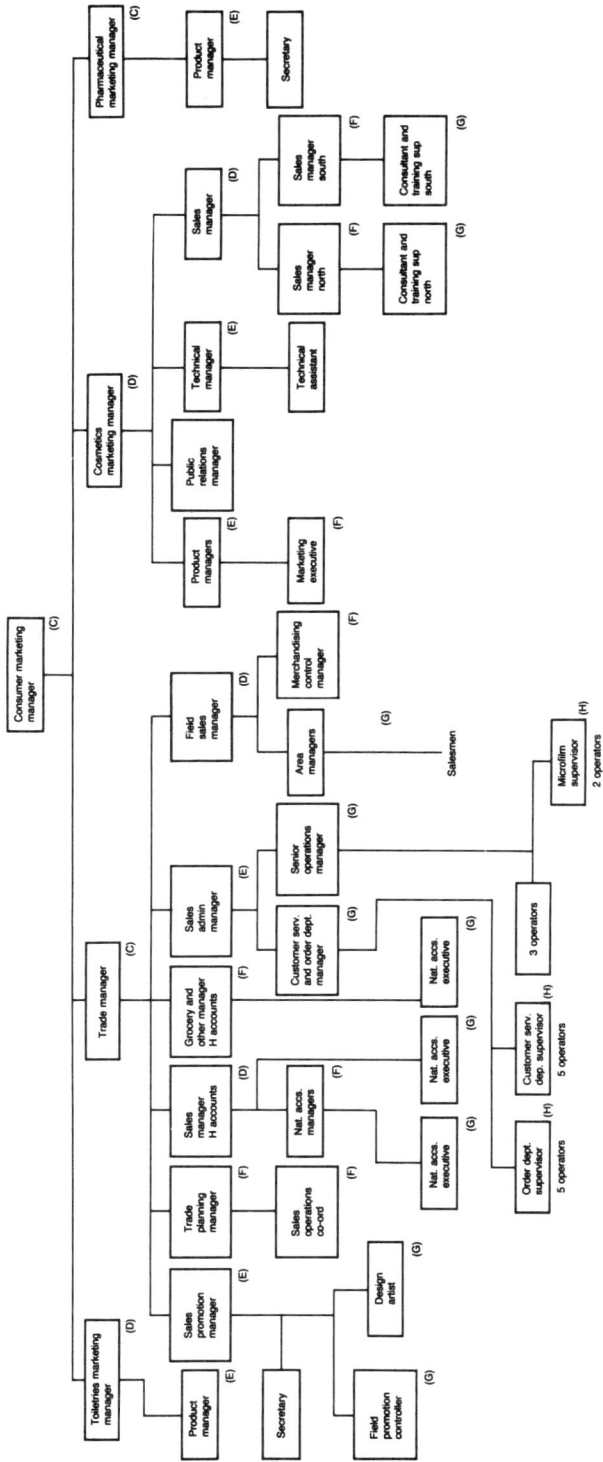

Figure 21.5 Organization structure: consumer marketing

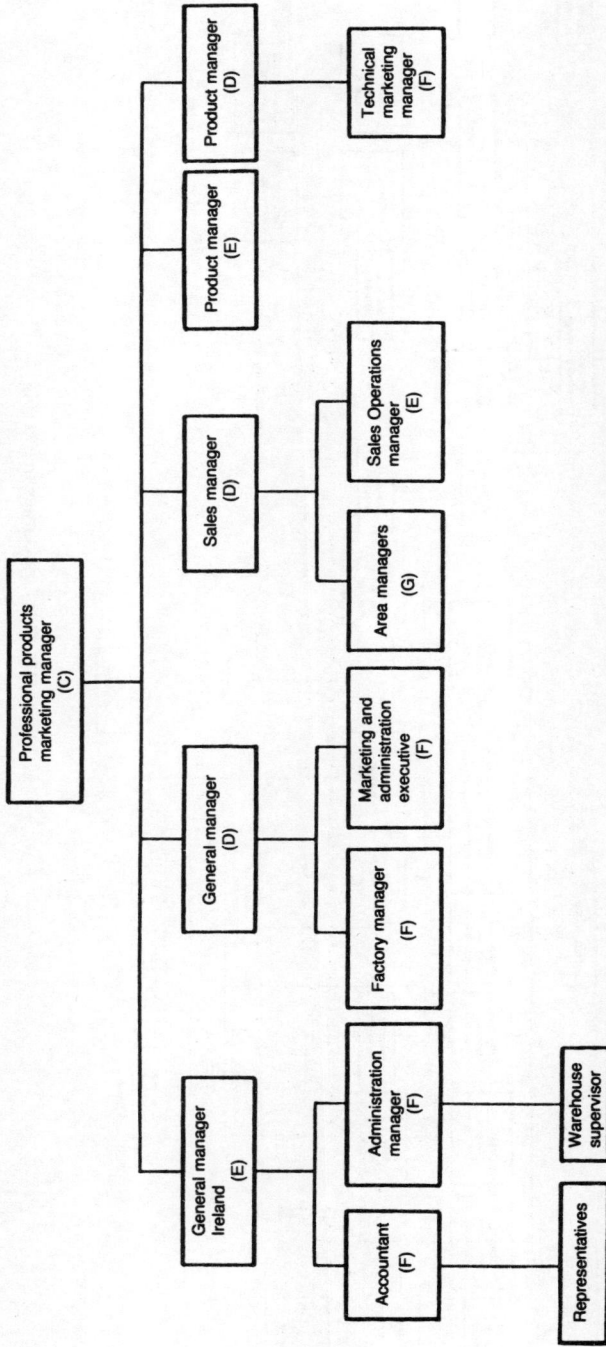

Figure 21.6 Organization structure: marketing professional products

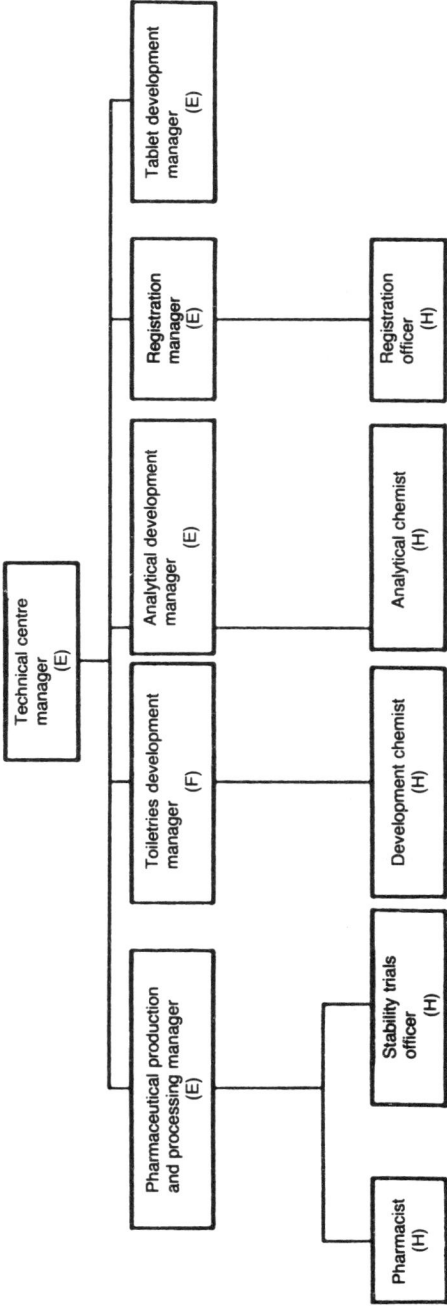

Figure 21.7 Organization structure: technical centre

22

THOMAS NESTOR LIMITED

Shaun Tyson

Thomas Nestor Limited was an old established book printing business, originally founded by members of the Nestor family in the early nineteenth century, and carried on as a family business by successive generations. The business started in the east end of London, but after the printing works were bombed during the Second World War, the company moved into the countryside, near to a coastal market town.

'Nestors' as it became known was soon the major employer in the area, with a large printing works, offices and warehousing. In the expansion of the business the local connections were enhanced by family ties, and it was not unusual for husbands, wives and fathers to be working alongside each other. The company grew, and began to diversify its interests. By the late 1970s, there were a number of subsidiaries, including a printing works in Singapore, a colour printing works in a satellite factory which produced coffee-table books, bookbinding and paperback printing. The Nestor family still up to this time occupied most of the seats on the board.

The recession of the late 1970s came before the business into which the company had expanded could be made profitable. Competition from home and abroad became fierce, and the costs of production in Nestor's organizations were too high.

The technology in use had hardly changed since the war, and at the same time, high wages and a large staff with the costs of maintaining the sprawling premises combined to put Nestors in a difficult position. The original intention of the board had been to diversify its business as a response to growing demand. The company was overstretched, with inadequate returns coming from its investments, and with managers devoting much of their time to businesses which were becoming smaller instead of gaining new customers.

The problems reached a crisis in 1981 when a loss of £1 million was announced. This change in fortunes led to a drastic shift in the board's approach to the business. The older members of the board, including several members of the Nestor family retired. A younger board of directors was appointed, retaining only one of the Nestor family. A corporate plan was formed. The subsidiaries were sold or closed (and the work transferred to the main plant), and new techniques were introduced for the production of paperback books on long runs. The working arrangements had to be altered to make this possible, and new computer-based printing methods had to be introduced, in place of the old hot metal methods. The production facility became more flexible, and soft-cover books began to be produced at competitive prices.

The changes resulted in redundancy for 600 people, reducing the headcount to around 120. The redundancies had included managers, and the remaining managers were made accountable for their own units which were regarded as profit centres, the costs and transfer pricing being controlled through a new system of computerized management accounts.

These far-reaching measures were negotiated with the trade unions. The workforce was totally unionized (NGA, Sogat 82, etc.), and although the unions were not prepared to give management carte blanche, the degree of cooperation achieved between the two sides was remarkable. The credit for the agreement to change was due to both the personnel director, and the dynamic young managing director.

THE PERSONNEL FUNCTION OF MANAGEMENT

Up to the time of the crisis, the role of personnel management had been defined as a support function, with no capacity to advise senior management or to instigate new policies. The policies that did exist were drawn from the industrial relations traditions of the printing industry, and were only amended marginally to meet changing conditions. The members of the department were a personnel officer, and a training officer. Apart from running a routine administrative function, their activities centred on health and safety, and the organization of the apprenticeship scheme. Both men were close to retirement.

During the reorganization of the board, a personnel director was appointed, who redefined the role of the personnel department as a major player in the management of change. The training officer was retired early, and the remaining personnel officer was retained to carry out all the routine administration of personnel. This left the personnel director free to work with the managing director on the development of a change strategy.

Gradually, a personnel change 'philosophy' emerged, agreed between the personnel director, the managing director and the board. Essential elements in the personnel philosophy were a high level of trust between work people and management, a cooperative but firm approach to the trade unions, employee involvement in the management of their own working practices, and strong leadership from front-line supervisors and middle managers. From their long history, Nestors had acquired a style of management at once paternalistic and respectful of their union representatives. The

Table 22.1 Data on managers

Age range in years		Number of managers
Over 25 under 30		2
Over 30 under 35		4
Over 35 under 40		8
Over 40 under 45		14
Over 45 under 50		7
Over 50 under 55		4
Over 55 under 60		2
Over 60 under 65		3
	Total	44
Managers' length of service (in years)		
Under 5 years		2
Over 5 under 10		3
Over 10 under 15		17
Over 15 under 20		7
Over 20 under 25		8
Over 25 under 30		3
Over 30 under 35		2
Over 35 under 40		–
Over 40 under 45		1
Over 45 under 50		1
	Total	44
Managerial split by function		
Personnel	4	
Finance	8	
Production	21	
Sales/marketing	8	
Technical	3	

management of change at Nestors built on this tradition. Trust could not have been created where management or unions had acted deceitfully before. The fathers of the chapel (employee representatives) were persuaded to give their support to a plan in which cooperation at the introduction of new technology, and more redundancies of their fellow members were essential parts.

There was a need to do more than just negotiate the changes, management action was needed in order to support and sustain the new approach. Employee involvement was institutionalized, through a parallel communication route, with briefing groups and large-scale meetings which were regularly addressed by the directors. Each accountable profit centre was reported on to the employees by the responsible manager.

With the new structure, came new roles, and new challenges for management. It was the managing director's intention that there should be a new open style. During discussions between the managing director and the personnel director, the question of how the management team could be supported and developed was raised.

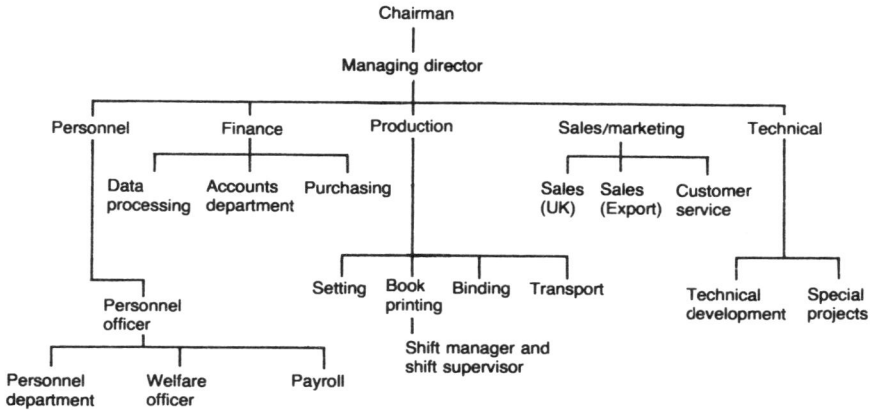

Figure 22.1 Thomas Nestor Limited organization chart

THE MANAGEMENT

There were forty-four managers other than directors in the company, the majority being employed in production functions. The organization chart (Figure 22.1) shows the main areas of accountability.

Educational background and previous training

Apart from the more senior members of the management team, most of the managers at Thomas Nestor's were not graduates. They were untrained in management. They relied on their knowledge of the products, and of the processes. The prevailing management style at the time was a form of benevolent paternalism. The general impression gained by the personnel director was of scepticism about the idea of 'learning' management. There had been a short course on communication run by the Industrial Society, which had been well attended at the time the new briefing system was introduced.

No data was available on the managers' training needs. There was no formal appraisal scheme. Following the reorganization, some managers had been promoted to new positions, and there were few established facts about managerial performance. It was clear, however, that managerial behaviour was going to be regarded as one of the keys to success for the company in the future.

THE FINANCIAL POSITION

The previous year (1981) the company produced poor financial results because it was overcoming its difficulties. A statement was sent to employees showing what happened to the revenue, and showing some of the costs of the reorganization. Sales for 1981 were up, at £18.9 million, as compared to £18.2 million in 1980; however, the extra costs of wage increases, interest charges and redundancy pay, plus the cost of new equipment led to a loss of £1.7 million.

However, 1982 has proved to be a good year. The order book is full – and costs have now been brought under control. The new book press is being utilized to maximum efficiency on long runs of paperbacks, and the profit forecast for 1982 shows prospects of nearly £1m net profit.

QUESTION

As the personnel director, you are asked to prepare a management development strategy.

In your answer, give precise details of what steps you would take, and of the development activities you would arrange, including particular training objectives.

23

COMPETENCIES IN THE PUBLIC COLLECTION AGENCY

Shaun Tyson

INTRODUCTION

During the 1980s the British Civil Service created a new approach to management development based on 'competencies' – the knowledge, skills and attitudes necessary for successful job performance. Staff were to be asked to assess themselves against a range of competencies. Training needs would be derived from the gap between competencies required and possessed. The appraisal process ensured a discussion between the official and senior management, in order to agree the development needs, and to match succession plans, and to monitor standards. From this brief introduction, one can see that the descriptions of the competencies were vitally important for the management development programme. How to establish and to describe competencies in one large public agency is the subject of this case.

THE PUBLIC COLLECTION AGENCY

The agency was a large department, with around ten thousand employees who worked all over the UK, in a regional structure, the head office being in London. It was responsible for collecting taxes of various kinds, and its remit entailed officials entering premises, questioning members of the public and preventing wrongful actions. The agency had clear and published personnel policies, which were under constant review. These policies covered: recruitment, probationary periods, career development, appraisal, training, promotion as well as industrial-relations policies in the areas of efficiency, discipline, health, safety and negotiation procedures.

Staff were appointed to grades – general working levels – at which a number of different jobs could be performed. Lateral transfers were therefore quite common in the development of an individual's career. As the policy guidelines put it: 'Career development is not just about promotion. It is just as much about gaining the necessary knowledge and experience to do the work of your present grade better. You are encouraged to take an active part in planning and developing your own career.'

One of the chief elements within career development was the appraisal policy. Appraisals were used to assess performance, to indicate suitability for other posts, to provide information on development needs, to be one input to the promotion decisions and to provide information on potential.

Promotion was competitive, requiring suitable candidates to attend formal 'boards' for senior managers to interview them, and here the track record, from the appraisal reports, would be influential. A brief outline of the competencies at each grade therefore existed, although the descriptions were only in the broadest terms. For example, the promotion criteria for those applying to become 'senior officers' emphasized 'positive leadership qualities, full acceptance of responsibility, and the ability to assimilate quickly the essential aspects of a situation', as well as technical competence in the agency's work.

Mindful that 'competencies' were a cornerstone in the new management development programme the central Civil Service personnel function in the cabinet office issued a 'competency list'. These were broad headings which came from a small research project in which interviews were held with top civil servants in all the main departments. These interviews were not able to establish specific competencies covering all aspects of each department's work, and remained therefore as general guidance. A list specific to the work in each department or agency was required – which would be comprehensive, and draw on the particular attributes needed for success in that department.

THE CONSULTANCY PROJECT

A consultancy project was undertaken, to discover the competencies amongst the agency's senior staff. The central cabinet office's competency list had to be used as a basis for the agency project, since this would ensure consistency across all government departments – but within this rather loose framework there were to be detailed definitions of each competence, together with examples. The terms of reference of the project were:

1 The competencies would be those of principal, senior principal and assistant secretary level staff, in both headquarters and the outfield establishments of the department.
2 The research was to use the existing headings of 'core' and 'important' competencies as a basis for the attributes sought.
3 The research had to be completed within three months.
4 It was understood that the competencies listed would require further refinement, following inputs from the training division and as a consequence of the first year's senior management development programme.

THE APPROACH TO BE TAKEN

The requirements of the work for each level are clearly defined, but this still leaves room for discretion, in how the work is done, and because of the variety of activities within the public sector no blanket job description of grades can be accurate. The work has a high profile with the public, and the senior management jobs are subject to stress, and to continuous change.

The approach recommended was one which drew on the perceptions of the job holders, this being in accord with the agency's philosophy. Only four people could be used to gather the data (two from within the agency) and the time scale posed limitations on how much research could be done.

There were approximately forty Assistant Secretaries, seventy Senior Principals, and five hundred principals in the agency, spread over all the regions and HO. The specialist roles at head office were excluded from the study which reduced the numbers above by about half. One of the most important roles was that of assistant secretary responsible for a region (there were around fifteen of these jobs). An example of a job description is shown in Appendix 23.1, and organization chart in Figure 23.1. The competency headings agreed by the Civil Service personnel function are shown in Appendix 23.2.

QUESTIONS

1 What strategy would you adopt to provide detailed descriptions of competencies – at assistant secretary level?
2 What techniques would you use to discover the competencies?
3 How would you check the validity of your findings?

APPENDIX 23.1: JOB DESCRIPTION OF ASSISTANT SECRETARY

Purpose and objectives

1   To ensure that all matters assigned to the agency are administered efficiently within the region, that government, and EEC laws are administered effectively and impartially, and that the revenue is collected in the most economic and efficient manner.

2   To act as the agency's principal representative in the area, to see that good public relations with trade and other local organizations are established and maintained, and to ensure that headquarters is provided with local views and advice on matters relating to current and future policies and procedures.

3   To ensure that a satisfactory system for monitoring activities, levels of performance and deployment of resources is established and maintained and to account to the director for the overall performance of the region.

4   To plan for the future and to encourage and initiate change where necessary.

Main activities

Management

(a) Works with area management (AM) to develop an effective regional management team and to formulate area policy and through them directs and controls the activities of the region. In the execution of this he/she:
  - has periodic meetings with the AMs and assistant AMs to inform himself/herself about, and to discuss, the more important matters arising from the region's activities, to agree objectives and priorities and to plan for the future;
  - has periodic meetings with staff to discuss management problems and to inform them about activities;
  - agrees with area managers a system of local inspections and monitors the effectiveness of these during regular visits to offices and districts;
  - sees work performance targets and achievements and collects management information;
  - discusses with AMs the deployment of their resources;
  - resolves management matters which cannot be resolved by, or between, individual AMs;
  - meets trade-union side as necessary.

(b) Personally deals with personnel management matters which cannot be delegated to AMs. This involves:
  - making himself/herself aware of strengths and weaknesses of his/her AMs and their work;
  - monitoring regional staff reporting standards;
  - getting to know staff and their performance in order to discharge his head of office responsibilities;
  - dealing with personnel management matters concerning AMs and others;
  - taking decisions to proceed with disciplinary, health and inefficiency cases;
  - approving proposals for changes in complement;
  - dealing with health, safety, complementing and other personnel matters with trade unions on which disagreement remains;
  - controlling all matters relating to industrial action in the region.

(c) Chairs local consultative committee.

(d) Replies to ministerial and MPs' correspondence concerning the region.

(e) Visits staff in situ to keep in touch with local problems, to monitor performance, to exchange views, to get to know staff and their capabilities and to be seen by the staff.

(f) Sits on HQ promotion boards as required.

Technical

(a) Keeps himself informed of policy/procedural changes which are likely to affect the operation of the areas or their relationship with outside bodies and organizations, whether originating from HQ or from within the region.
(b) Deals with technical casework assigned to the post of region which cannot be delegated.
(c) Acts as member of HQ technical committees or other reviews as required.

Representational

(a) Attends functions and visits outside bodies and organizations where it is necessary for the agency to be represented at this level.
(b) Meets senior representatives of local government/trade organizations etc. where issues significant to the operation of the region as a whole or to regional relationships with these bodies, are to be discussed.

Advisory

(a) Advises the director and/or the head of the appropriate technical division of any significant developments or any other matters likely to affect departmental policy or have a major impact upon the staffing or management of the region.
(b) Sees advice offered to HQ divisions by his staff and contributes his/her own views where necessary.

APPENDIX 23.2 GENERALIZED COMPETENCIES: ASSISTANT SECRETARY

1 *Management of resources: organizations.* This covers the managerial role concerned with planning, organizing, coordinating and controlling.
2 *Management of staff.* This competency covers management style, 'team building', staff motivation, appraisal, personnel administration, management development communications, morale and discipline.
3 *Knowledge/understanding of the context of the work.* This competency covers the economic, political and social context in which the Agency operates, and also includes the intra departmental context – the whole range of its activities with which a senior member of staff should be familiar.
4 *Managing own work.* How to plan, and organise time so that a high degree of personal effectiveness is achieved: how to apply logic and reasoning to the analysis of problems and to the development of policies. How to make decisions.

Regional controller (assistant secretary)

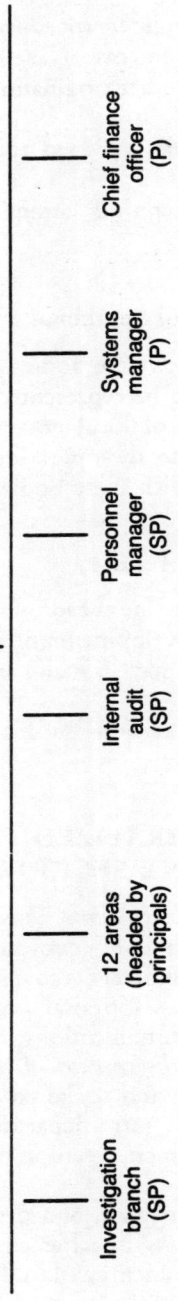

| Investigation branch (SP) | 12 areas (headed by principals) | Internal audit (SP) | Personnel manager (SP) | Systems manager (P) | Chief finance officer (P) |

Figure 23.1 Regional organization
Notes: SP: Senior principal; P: Principal.

5 *Information technology*. How to make use of information technology in conducting the work of the Agency, and understanding how information technology is used by others.

6 *Specialized knowledge*. Knowledge of the regulations, laws, control systems of the Agency.

7 *Representational/presentation skills*. How to represent the department to external bodies successfully, and how to represent one's own unit externally.

8 *Written (administrative skills)*. How to write briefs, prepare cases, to draft regulations and to supervize this work in others.

9 *Policy management*. How to research, review policies, to initiate new policies or amend existing policies, and how to gain acceptance of policies.

10 *Accounting and finance*. How to manage division, regions, projects within agreed budget limits.

24

RECRUITING A NATIONAL SALES FORCE

Fergus Panton

BACKGROUND

The case is concerned with the entry into the UK market of a giant international company which dealt mainly in fast-moving consumer goods (FMCG). Students of 'business policy' might find the historical and legal circumstances which led up to the situation, of absorbing interest, but they do not materially affect the issues involved and they will, therefore, be dealt with in a summary fashion. Suffice it to say, the company concerned, which we will call International Consumer Goods (ICG) had been prohibited from trading in the UK since 1902, owing to the terms of an agreement reached with a major competitor who is a household name in the UK. Both companies in fact flourished as a result of this agreement. ICG particularly so, as it was given freedom to trade anywhere in the world, provided it kept out of Great Britain and Ireland. The world became a very profitable oyster for ICG.

The requirements of the Treaty of Rome 1972, in anticipation of the UK joining the Common Market, led to the cancellation of the agreement by mutual consent. This left ICG free to enter the UK market, if it so wished.

In the seventy intervening years, 1902–72, several other companies, not circumscribed in the same way, also became established in the same industrial field. Understandably, therefore, ICG, in the face of well-established competition approached the whole question of entry into the UK market with considerable circumspection; but there were quite clearly commercial opportunities in the offing. Britain's entry into the EEC heralded a range of taxation changes, the principal effect of which was to cause a dramatic shift in consumer demand for the products made and sold by ICG.

In a classically 'good' marketing approach, ICG researched the market thoroughly, initiated test markets successfully in 1976 and 1977, and as a result decided to go full steam ahead and make a total company entry into the UK.

THE TASK

Complex and critical decisions on investment, production and marketing had been made, but the success of the initial operation was clearly going to be greatly dependent on whether the 'people' resources could be procured on time, at the right quality and in the numbers required. Virtually a whole sales force had to be recruited, together with marketing staff and support services. Some 250 bodies had to be found and be operative within 7 or 8 months.

A number of factors combined to complicate the issue. ICG was not well known in the UK, apart from two locations, one in the south and one in the north, where it had factories which manufactured for export. It had a high blue-chip rating in the city but it was jokingly known as the 'whispering giant'. Its products and brands were not known to the UK consumer and it had no established reputation for marketing expertise in the UK and little knowledge of local conditions.

On the credit side, there was a wealth of experience on tap of recruiting and training sales staff all over the world. It was an opportunity to put this knowledge to the test and one of the first illustrations was the decision to recruit the sales force from the UK, it being a commonly held belief in ICG circles that it was sound practice to employ nationals of the country in which one was operating.

Other considerable potential advantages were freedom to choose their own organizational structure, freedom to offer attractive salaries and conditions at a time of pay restraint and substantial financial support for the whole project.

Reputations both collectively and individually were at stake and much hinged on the acquisition of talent to do the job. The need for commercial security was paramount and conflicted with the need for 'selling' the company to establish a PR image and to attract applicants. Everyone was working under considerable pressure, time was in short supply and the need to devise a recruitment system which was economic of effort yet thorough in application was critical.

The main job of the sales force was to sell, promote and merchandise the company's products in order to achieve agreed sales volume and distribution targets. This entailed the establishment of a widespread distribution network through which the company's products would flow from the factory to wholesalers, agents or distributors down to a mass of retail outlets varying in size from supermarkets to corner shops and encompassing pubs, wine stores, newsagents and confectioners.

The overall plan envisaged a phased recruitment programme, but by far the largest number had to be taken on in the first phase so as to obtain comprehensive distribution and coverage of urban outlets. Significant differences in organization structure from those adopted by the competitors were in higher ratios of managers to sales representatives, with a view to developing small, compact work teams. Untypically, the area manager was to have 3 to 4 reps in his team and he was himself to make calls, estimates varying from 20 per cent to 30 per cent of his time. Equally, the next level of manager, called regional, was to have no more than 4 area managers reporting to him and in some cases initially only 3 or 2.

The first phase saw an expansion of the existing sales force of 18 (3 managers and 15 reps) to 150. This figure comprised an establishment under the national sales manager of 2 divisional managers, 9 regional managers, 28 area managers and 114 sales reps. In addition, there was to be a central sales training department.

In numbers alone, this was going to entail a sizeable problem of sequencing through the principal elements of the recruitment and selection process – planning, specifying requirements, advertising, screening/shortlisting, interviewing, selecting and appointing. How many people might apply was anybody's guess – one estimate was as high as 50 per post which would have meant 7,500 applicants and interviewing perhaps 1,500 applicants!

Obviously, additional resources were going to be required if the recruitment task was to be achieved in seven months. Both the marketing and personnel departments were deeply involved and there was a need for coordination so that any systems that were designed by either function were compatible. The sheer volume of work meant extra pairs of hands would be needed.

A senior marketing manager was appointed project coordinator, an experienced sales training manager was seconded from another part of ICG group, personnel staff were reallocated to special duties and a recruitment consultant employed on a short-term (six months) contract. A key figure in the project was the national sales manager who had run the test markets in the UK and been appointed as a result of his success.

THE PROBLEM

At the first meeting of the project team in September, some immediate decisions were made. Target dates for the recruitment of the three principal levels; regional managers, area managers and sales representatives, were set as follows: 9 regional managers to join by mid-December; 28 area managers by mid-January and 114 sales reps by the end of March. This was to be the first phase.

The consultant pointed out that this was an uncomfortably tight schedule, allowing only half the time normally budgeted for management selection. He felt it was a pity that when the financial and commercial decisions were being made, the short- and long-term manpower implications had not been considered. The answer he received was that these were the requirements of the business plan and they had to be met.

The other significant decision made was to make use of recruitment agencies for the preliminary screening of area managers and sales representatives. Two were appointed, one based in Manchester for coverage of the north; the other in Guildford to cover the south. But personnel was none too happy about the way the agents had been selected, partly because they had not been involved. It was evident that there was friction between the sales and personnel managers: both functions saw themselves as having prime responsibility for the successful implementation of the project.

QUESTIONS

1 The conventional route of job analysis–job description–person specification was required for most of the thirty different jobs. How accurate a specification could be produced in the time available?

2 No survey had been carried out of the employment market, which contrasted interestingly with all the money and effort expended on the test market. Where were these bodies going to come from? What was going to attract them to apply – and join? Competitive companies? Similar industries? Others?

3 If the company was, virtually simultaneously, recruiting three levels of management, what career prospects could they offer to applicants?

4 The twenty-eight 'areas' were determined geographically. How important was it that managers/reps should 'know' the area and/or be identified with it?

5 What about product knowledge? Should people be wooed from the competition, or was sales expertise more important?

6 Was there an equal opportunity policy? How would this work in practice?

7 What should the remuneration policy be? Same as the competition or better?

8 How important were status of car, allowances etc.?

9 How important was it that people should have managerial experience if they were to be recruited for managerial jobs? Would eight years as a senior representative in a competitive company be worth more or less than four years as a manager in non FMCG?

10 What differences should there be between the person specifications at different levels?

11 Was there a requirement for a balanced force and if so should people be selected because they had *different* qualities?

12 Experience was vital, but so was motivation and people skill. Should tests be used? If so, what? What about using an assessment centre approach? If so, what and for whom?

13 If you were a recruiter, how would you react to the attached person specification? Are any elements within the specification potentially discriminatory, in terms of sex, or race? Prepare a person specification for sales representative, regional and area managers.

Table 24.1 Person specification, sales representative

Profile	Essential	Desirable
Physique, health, appearance		
Height	Slightly above average for region	5ft 8in to 6ft
Build	In proportion to height	Well proportioned
Hearing	Normal	Perfect
Eyesight	Normal	Perfect
General health	Good	Excellent, physically active
Looks	Presentable	Acceptable to all levels
Grooming	Smart	Acceptable to all levels
Dress	Business-like, presentable	Takes care in appearance
Voice	Clear, concise	Interesting and commanding manner; acceptable accent
Attainments		
General education	O-level English language, Maths and 1 other O-level or equivalent	HND or equivalent
Job training		Courses in selling and appreciation of business methods
Job experience	Two years' direct sales fast-moving consumer goods with major UK company	Two years' experience first line sales management
Special aptitudes		
Verbal	Communicates well in all media	Communicates well in all media
Numerical	Capable of calculating using simple arithmetic.	Read and interpret management accounts, apply statistical techniques and use software
Interests		
Physically active		Participates in active pastimes
Aesthetic		Appreciates design tastes as applied to packaging, advertising etc.

Table 24.1 Continued

Profile	Essential	Desirable
Disposition		
Acceptability/Leadership	Ambassador of company	Can influence others to accept his/her recommendations
Stability	Self-control under normal circumstances	
Self reliance	Working without supervision and handling company's and customers' money	
Circumstances		
Age	22–35	
Mobility	Car driver – valid licence – no pending charges	No more than one endorsement
Domicile	Controls own movements during working week Prepared to work in any location Ready to work irregular hours	
Others	Takes pride in professional selling	
Notice	Not more than one calendar month from offer	

25

CLERICAL MEDICAL INVESTMENT GROUP

Glenys Emam

INTRODUCTION

The company

CMIG's parent company is a mutual life assurance office employing around 2,000 staff, of whom 1,200 are based in its Bristol head office. There are also around 150 staff (mainly specialists, such as the Investment function) in a London head office. The remainder, sales and sales support staff, operate from 27 branches and 10 sub-offices throughout the UK. The company markets a range of life, pensions and other investment products, and is one of a minority which chose not to 'tie' after the Financial Services Act. Its sales force operates through Independent Financial Advisors (IFAs) and a high proportion of its clients are in the AB category. CMIG includes a number of subsidiary companies, of which the most important are Clerical Medical Managed Funds Ltd, Clerical Medical Unit Trust Managers Ltd, and Clerical Medical International. The company is not unionized but has a staff association with a high level of membership.

The project

The job design project was set up in the spring of 1990 and involved two of the policy servicing divisions within the parent company – the new business and records division, dealing with traditional individual business (TIB), and the unit-linked division. Together they employ over 400 staff, one-third of the Bristol head office population. The project was initially targeted at the clerical and supervisory levels, and had the following objective:

> To examine the organization of tasks, working methods and job relationships to achieve the most effective *match* between the requirements of the business and its technology and the needs and capabilities of jobholders. The project will have implications for organizational structure, manpower planning, and training, and will be viewed as part of the business strategy to improve customer service.

174

BACKGROUND

The business strategy

Late in 1989 a decision was taken to reorganize two of the policy-servicing divisions, dealing with TIB and unit-linked products. This was partly reactive to market forces; TIB products (including the endowment market) had suffered a downturn, whereas unit-linked products had experienced an enormous surge in business. These trends were expected to be sustained long term, creating a need to redeploy resources. There was, however, a strong proactive element in that CMIG's ability to maintain its competitive edge in service standards – in this case by introducing a unified service to IFAs and policy holders for both product ranges – was seen as critical. This view was reinforced by a marketing strategy aimed at higher-earning 'professionals' (in the broadest sense of the word), who clearly expected an excellent level of service in return for their investment.

There were also questions of staff morale and motivation within the two divisions; one division had over-capacity whilst the other was drowning in sheer volume of work, aggravated by a computer system which was not meeting expectations. The first priority of the organization at the time was to ensure that all aspects of the unit-linked operation (financial, systems, human resources and training) were optimized. It was within this context that the two division managers approached the personnel function for help in job design.

The personnel viewpoint

CMIG had been undergoing a major job evaluation exercise; the results were to be implemented with a new pay and grading structure later in the year. The process had highlighted a number of job and organizational design problems, and the opportunity to tackle some of them was welcomed. In addition, Bristol is a city dominated by financial services companies competing for staff, and it was hoped that, in the longer term, improved job design would increase CMIG's ability to recruit and retain quality staff by offering more motivating jobs. One complication was the development of an additional site in Clevedon, fifteen miles south of Bristol, to relieve pressure on head office accommodation and enable expansion. A number of departments which were to be involved in the Job Design Project were due to relocate in eighteen months' time. There were therefore manpower planning issues in ensuring availability of a solid core of managers, super-visors and clerical staff ready and willing to work in Clevedon. (Many staff already commuted into Bristol from the Clevedon area but were not necessarily employed in the relocating departments, so considerable internal movement and re-training was expected.) It was intended to recruit additional staff from the Clevedon area, some of whom would be attracted from other financial-services companies. However, at the clerical level, many were expected to be 'mature' women without relevant experience (Clevedon had recently lost many manufacturing jobs) and the expectations and capabilities of these recruits were an unknown factor. The type of recruits and training implications were an important consideration if the objectives of the project were to be fulfilled.

INFLUENCES ON JOB DESIGN

Company culture

CMIG had experienced continuing growth in the 1970s and 1980s, and its product range had diversified from traditional life assurance to a broad spectrum of financial services products. Cultural change, as is often the case, had lagged behind; the organization was very status conscious, and it was only recently that efforts to move away from traditional, paternalistic attitudes to performance and a service-oriented approach had begun to impact.

The advent of the Financial Services Act had forced CMIG critically to consider its future business strategy and this led to the decision to remain independent, in the belief that an excellent track record combined with innovative market-led products would provide a sound business base. This was supported by a marketing strategy targeting the upper end of the market, with a clear message to staff that if the company was to serve 'professionals' it would have to *be* professional. A customer care programme had been initiated to emphasize the importance of service standards, a performance pay scheme introduced for all administrative staff, and the appraisal system revamped.

The division managers involved in the job design project were two of CMIG's more forward-thinking managers, and were convinced that well-designed jobs could actually bolster service standards, whereas the existing haphazard groupings of tasks which had evolved over the years were probably detrimental.

The technology

The policy servicing areas were highly computerized and this appeared to limit the scope for job design. In the past, the response to new technology had been to break down processing activities into small chunks with short training lead times. In many ways, the operation resembled a production line, with fragmented jobs and several layers of supervision to coordinate them. This had also led to a dichotomy between the 'doers', inputting data and checking and distributing output, and specialist staff or problem solvers. Procedures were normally highly standardized with little opportunity for discretion, and this had been further strengthened by the need to comply with statutory requirements in the handling of other people's money, particularly since the Financial Services Act.

On the other hand, an increasing proportion of the data input, quotations, basic underwriting and provision of output was being done on-line at the branches, where staff were very much in the front line of customer contact. Eventually all IFAs would have their own on-line computers, pushing much of the routine work even further back to the customer. This ultimately meant that head office staff would spend a greater proportion of their time problem solving and dealing with unusual cases. It would be some time before this stage was reached, but from the job design viewpoint the need to develop more technically competent staff at the clerical level to prevent frequent referral of problems, offered some opportunities for job enrichment.

In addition, the need to provide an integrated customer service for both TIB and Unit Linked products (e.g. the handling of new business for both product ranges; or the issue of one, rather than two, separate commission payments to IFAs) could lead to increased product, accounting or systems knowledge requirements.

Organizational structure and implications for service

Structures were hierarchical and typical of a bureaucracy. The job evaluation exercise was having some impact on this, but results were not due to be implemented for some time. A major difficulty was that the company had always viewed promotion in terms of climbing the supervisory tree and failed to recognize increased technical expertise as being equally valid in developmental terms. For example, senior clerks had been promoted to unit leaders, in charge of a small group of clerks; in practice they continued to operate as they had done in the senior clerk role, creating a conflict of interests. Problems perpetuated by this hierarchy included:

1 Small spans of control, with too many supervisors in relation to 'doers'.
2 Creaming off of the more interesting work by each layer above, and imposition of (often) unnecessary control, a further symptom of the status conscious nature of the organization.
3 Overlapping or unclear accountabilities, confusing to both staff and customers.
4 Fragmentation of clerical jobs into discrete tasks, rather than identifiable pieces of work, leading to low variety of skills and activities, restriction of learning/growth opportunities, lack of flexibility, and difficulty in providing meaningful feedback on performance.

The organizational hierarchy from department manager level down was:

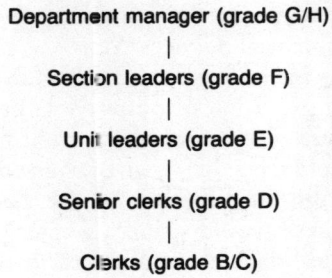

Department manager (grade G/H)
|
Section leaders (grade F)
|
Unit leaders (grade E)
|
Senior clerks (grade D)
|
Clerks (grade B/C)

Within this typical structure were any combination of:

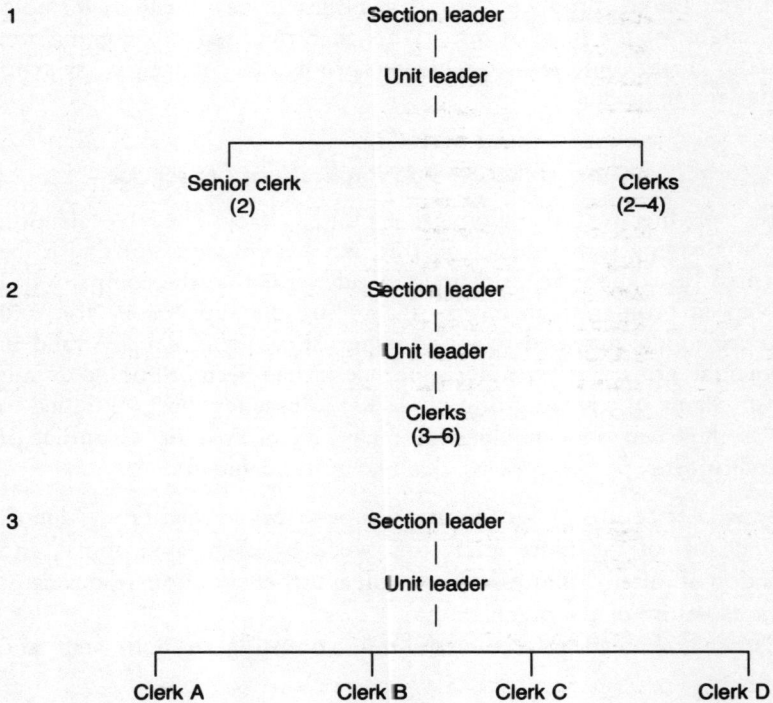

1

Section leader
|
Unit leader
|

Senior clerk   Clerks
(2)   (2–4)

2

Section leader
|
Unit leader
|
Clerks
(3–6)

3

Section leader
|
Unit leader
|

Clerk A   Clerk B   Clerk C   Clerk D

Figure 25.1 Organizational hierarchy

178

5 Low awareness of how jobs fitted into the overall picture, and of their impact on others (i.e. customers).

6 Strong vertical communication systems at the expense of horizontal communication; problems passed up the chain of command, providing little opportunity for initiative but endless opportunities to 'pass the buck'.

From the customer service viewpoint the structure clearly had many undesirable features; the overall result was that the clerks who initially received queries were able to deal with only the most routine of problems without referral, either through lack of technical knowledge or because of the layers of control from above. Clearly, introducing the concept of job enrichment/enlargement by the broadening and deepening of technical expertise was critical to service improvements. This was not to say that the organization should cease to develop competent supervisors, but that better appraisal of staff potential should open up other lines of development. Higher levels of technical competence in the 'rank and file' would also free managers and supervisors to concentrate on managing and supervising (which was not currently the case).

The people

There was a perception (at this stage untested) that whilst many staff were content with their jobs, there were others who were capable of doing far more demanding jobs if these could be made available (along with the necessary tools, training and confidence), and that these people were being under utilized because of poor job design.

Improving job design to allow for enriched/enlarged jobs at the clerical level would inevitably remove at least one layer from the hierarchy and increase spans of control. This was potentially threatening to unit leaders and section leaders. It was essential to sell the advantages of job design to these people, and to ensure that, for those removed from the line, genuinely developmental work could be provided. In an organization requiring constant adaptation of systems, procedures and products to cope with a competitive market and frequent changes in legislation, there was, in fact, no shortage of interesting and demanding project work and 'trouble shooting' to occupy these staff meaningfully.

Questions

1 As personnel advisor, prepare a presentation for the department managers within the two divisions to introduce the concept and principles of job design within the context of current events, with the aim of gaining understanding and commitment to setting up a job design project.

2 At the end of the presentation, suggest and achieve agreement on the way forward in terms of implementing the project, assuming a consultative approach between management and employees.
Consider:
(a) participation;
(b) control;
(c) resource;
(d) timescale;
(e) on-going review/evaluation.

26

SUSPENDING QUALITY CIRCLES
Alcan Plate Limited
John Bank

Preparing for a £11.5 million expansion, while many other firms in the Midlands were contracting, put Alcan Metal in an enviable position in the spring of 1981. It seemed a very good time to launch quality circles.

BACKGROUND

Alcan Plate Limited is a subsidiary of British Alcan Aluminium. Alcan is the short name for Alcan Aluminium Limited of Canada, a multinational based in Montreal, whose main business is aluminium, from the mining of ore to the production and sales of numerous finished products. It has gross assets of over $US6.4 billion. British Alcan Aluminium employs over 7,000 people in Britain and operates one of the only two major aluminium smelters left in the UK.

Alcan Plate Limited's works and offices are in Kitts Green (Birmingham). It now employs about 700 people, who are engaged in the manufacture and sales of plate products and the rolling of special sheet products. At the time of the quality circle launch the workforce numbered 1,000.

Production of aluminium has continued at Alcan Plate since 1938, when the company operated the plant to meet the needs of aircraft production during the Second World War. Throughout the years, the works have been continually modernized and the company has invested many millions of pounds in major plant and equipment since the late 1950s and early 1960s. Alcan Plate is the only source of aluminium plate in Britain and one of three large plants in Europe.

The works receive aluminium ingot and coil from other companies and convert this into a variety of semi-finished products by rolling and other methods. In recent years the company has been associated with, and supplied the metal for, a number of prestige products.

Almost all the major British aircraft – including the Anglo-French Concorde – have incorporated Alcan metal in their structure. The company currently provides material for the Trident, European Airbus, RAF Nimrod, the multirole combat aircraft Tornado, the Jaguar and the Harrier, as well as many others. The Scorpion aluminium tank uses plate from Alcan. The European spacelab also required Alcan's aluminium plate.

A wide variety of high-technology plate produced by Alcan is also utilized in the shipbuilding industries. Ironically, Alcan aluminium plate was used both in HMS *Coventry* and HMS *Sheffield* and in the Exocet missiles that sank both ships during the Falklands war. Alcan produces coated strip aluminium for engineering markets and for cladding mobile homes and for use as architectural building sheets. For the domestic market, Alcan supplies circles from which saucepans and kettles can be pressed and spun. This domestic side of the business and the market for coated strip aluminium was very depressed in the spring of 1981. The backbone of Alcan Plate, the military and aircraft market, was buoyant but becoming more fiercely competitive.

CONVERGENCES

The thrust to set up quality circles came from two separate sources. On the technical side, both Graham Johnson, quality supervisor, and his immediate superior, Brian Simons, quality manager, had read about quality circles and Johnson attended a half-day conference about them. They were keen to start pilot circles.

Quite independently, Colin Siddle, training manager, and David Gregson, personnel manager, had initiated a training intervention for middle managers which dealt primarily with superintendents. The management development programme was undertaken in parallel with the extensive investment programme coming on stream. One of the concerns of senior management on site was to ensure that managers at all levels operated fully and consistently with their positions. It was observed that managers tended to drift to tasks and roles below their levels. A modular course was designed at the Cranfield School of Management to re-focus the superintendents and to counter the downward drift of managerial activity. Projects undertaken at the plant were linked to the learning modules at the business school. One of these projects was for the superintendents to help Graham Johnson launch a pilot programme of quality circles.

The decision to launch the quality circles was taken at board level just before Easter in 1981. Early in April, the superintendents attended a five-day management development module at Cranfield. Quality circles was one of the topics discussed. At the end of the module the men selected the introduction of quality circles at Alcan Plate as their project to be effected between 9 April and their next module at Cranfield on 20 September. The quality circles project seemed a perfect choice, as it encompassed many ideas of effective employee participation and good industrial relations.

By late June the preparation for the launch of quality circles was well under way. The superintendents working with Graham Johnson had selected a strategy for introducing the concept of quality circles. They used the 'portakabin' communication centre, affectionately called 'the Wendy house' to reach the workforce in small groups with a showing of a film on quality circles from British Leyland. No outside quality circle consultancies were employed. No formal training in quality circles was given to either foreman or circle members. The company was intent on growing its own circles using only its own resources, and this later proved to be a weakness in the programme.

AVOIDING A CRISIS

Although it is desirable to 'grow your own' quality circles, there are certain core principles that emerge from the data on successful circles programmes, for example, voluntariness and the *training* of circle members, which are ignored at a company's peril. Alcan kept the programme voluntary, but the superintendents were on the verge of violating several other key principles.

The superintendents had no expert input, nor had they been to visit quality circles in other companies. Not surprisingly, the plan the superintendents produced contained three fundamental errors.

1 They wanted to hand down the initial problems for the circles to solve, rather than let the circles select the problems themselves. This would affect the 'ownership' of the problems. It also affected the level of trust in the circle members, particularly when linked with the desire of superintendents to attend circle meetings happening on their 'patch'.
2 They had decided to give some 'chairmanship' training to the foreman, and *no* quality circles training to the foreman or to circle members.
3 They were over-reacting to an initial rebuff from the craft trade unions.

The trade union issue was by far the most immediate. At short notice, the superintendents had invited six representatives from the craft trade unions to an introductory session on quality circles at the plant communications centre. The short session was to consist of the showing of a film on quality circle introduction at British Leyland. The initial response of the trade unionists to the face-to-face invitations was positive. They all said they would be there. But at the appointed time, not one trade-union leader came. 'Well, they've had their bite of the cherry,' one superintendent said, 'they'll not get another. We'll do it without them.' Fortunately, cooler heads prevailed and the trade-union representatives were approached again.

Industrial relations at Alcan Plate were running smoothly in 1981. The main unions on site were the Transport and General Workers Union with two-fifths of the blue-collar workforce, and the balance divided among the Amalgamated Union of Engineering Workers, the Electrical, Electronic,

Telecommunications and Plumbing Union and the National Union of Sheet Metal Workers, Coppersmiths, Heating and Domestic Engineers. Staff belonged to the Association of Scientific, Technical, Managerial and Supervisory Staffs or the Association of Clerical, Technical and Supervisory Staffs.

The introduction of continuous shiftworking (the continental shift) had earlier met trade-union opposition, but management had prevailed without building up a legacy of hostility. A renegotiation of the bonus system in the winter of 1981 to bring it into line with the company's profits rather than tonnage of production went surprisingly well. The main union involved in the quality circle installation was the T&GWU.

START-UP

The two pilot quality circles were begun in the Plate Finishing Department and in the paint line section in late August. Because Alcan Plate works a continuous shift system, the meetings were held every twelve days at the start of the day shift for the circle members.

Ken Smith, general foreman in the plate finishing department, became the first QC leader. He summed up the launch: 'Initial reactions were the same as in the past: "Well it's another meeting and it will die a death." We got volunteers which included the shop steward who came to only one meeting but continued to give his support.' The QC in the plate finishing department decided, as its first problem, to improve the surface quality of magnesium (non-heat-treatable) plate. Alcan had a bad reputation for surface quality in the marketplace for customers looking for scratch-free, decorative finish on magnesium plate. The company's plate tended to be pitted and scratched, which was all right for machining or forming, but unsatisfactory if the customer planned to leave it as it came from the factory.

The QC produced a dozen solutions to the problem of surface scratches. These included using vacuum beans to handle the large wide plates, the use of foil to protect overlaps at annealing, and the use of card as protection when getting shoes across plate. The QC instigated the use of 2 ft × 2 ft wooden spacers (offcuts from cases that are used in another department) between the large sheets of metal at the stacking on the stretcher and did other practical things such as putting felt on rest plates and fitting more air wipes to blow swarf more successfully off the plate; all in an attempt to eliminate or reduce surface scratches. The basketful of ideas produced a 25 per cent lower rejection rate for surface defects as compared to the preceding six months, saving 3.36 tonnes of plate. In a period when customers were driving up inspection standards, this produced a direct saving (in six months) of $1,200 and an unquantifiable advantage in the market as the quality of Alcan magnesium plate began to rival that of its competitors.

Graham Johnson credits the QC with a 'dramatic improvement' in the surface quality of the magnesium plate. 'We went from horrible surfaces for non-heat treatable magnesium to quite presentable surfaces as good as any in Europe and our salesmen felt the improvement immediately. This was directly attributable to the quality circle.' He explained, 'the circles enabled us to get closer to the guys, to feed them information about the problems and the implication. They came up with ideas and ways of solving the problems. They asked for more information and this increased their overall interest in the job.'

The second pilot quality circle was started in the paint line with K. Rider as leader. Its first project was to improve the tannoy system to effect speedier line communications. This proved to be an important project because a five-minute delay can cost up to 400 kg of scrap. During its first meeting the circle also decided to improve on line viewing facilities which helped to spot paint defects.

Two further circles were started: another in plate finishing and one in the foundry. The foundry circle was the most dramatic first project. It registered savings of £15,000 per year.

The project was aimed at reducing melt loss. In the foundry casting furnaces, process scrap, raw ingots of aluminium and the necessary alloying elements are combined together and melted in one of three large casting furnaces. After the molten metal has been fluxed and cleansed it is cast into slabs or ingots by the semi-continuous direct chill method. At all stages in the process, samples are taken for quality control purposes to ensure that the metal is of the correct alloy composition and of the highest quality.

During the melting process the dross rises to the top and is dragged off with rakes. Alcan Plate used to pay an outside firm to take away the dross, reclaim good aluminium metal and then sell the metal back to Alcan. The quality circle in the foundry took on this problem of melt loss, solved it, and was able to dispense with the services of the outside firm. The circle then began to look at ways of improving draining and preserving spillage scrap as a usable commodity. The suggestions they came up with and implemented included:

1 Designing small dross pans with holes to drain holder dross after fixing it with a flux. (The flux makes the dross cling to it, and when the flux is raked into an atmosphere with more oxygen it flares up again, releasing the aluminium.)
2 Developing spillage pans for scrap.
3 Using serrated rakes (instead of straight-edge ones) to reduce the amount of metal being skimmed off along with the dross.
4 New procedures for charging pellets.

The use of the small pans alone is saving about 28 kg of metal every time a furnace is charged. This is worth over £15,000 per annum.

185

FIGHTING FOR SURVIVAL

Despite the initial success, circumstances at Alcan Plate conspired against QCs. There were the problems of installing the new furnace and computer systems. Furthermore, a sharp downturn in the market forced about 300 redundancies on the already small workforce. The redundancies took away the attention of management which was necessary for quality circles to thrive. As Graham Johnson explained in the autumn of 1983, 'When you go through a large redundancy programme you tend not to adjust immediately. You don't gear straight away, you try to carry on providing the information and services you did before. We now must learn to adjust. During the last nine months, we've not had the time for circles, so they've been suspended. But we are now planning a relaunch. We want one in each department on each shift.' The excessive dependency of the circles on the two managers, Graham Johnson and Ken Smith, meant they could not operate without the men in attendance.

QUESTIONS

1 Should Alcan reinstate quality circles? Provide reasons for your answer.
2 If you consider that quality circles should be reinstated in Alcan how should they be structured so as to function effectively?
3 What are the advantages of introducing quality circles into an organization?
4 Identify the possible reasons for quality circles' failure in an organization.

27

THE BANKING, INSURANCE AND FINANCE UNION
Trade Union Structure and Growth[1]
Paul Willman

BACKGROUND

The Banking, Insurance and Finance Union (BIFU) is a large TUC-affiliated union organizing manual, clerical and managerial staff in the financial sector. It had approximately 170,000 members in 1990 and, unlike many UK unions, it has continued to grow since 1979, on average by about 3 per cent per year (Figure 27.1). This reflects the continued expansion of employment in the financial services sector, rather than an increase in union density. Much of the sector remains unorganized; moreover BIFU is not the only representative body. Other TUC affiliates, such as Manufacturing, Science and Finance (MSF), and in-house staff associations both in banking, insurance and building societies, organize in the sector.

The union is recognized for the purposes of collective bargaining in banks, building societies, insurance companies and finance houses, but its main strength remains where the union began – in retail banking. It is recognized by all of the major English and Scottish banks. However, the growth areas for membership have been insurance, finance houses and foreign banks. This is a consequence of the growth strategy pursued by the union since 1971.

HISTORY

BIFU, (formerly NUBE: the National Union of Bank Employees) was founded in 1918. From the outset, NUBE waged a long struggle for recognition by the clearing banks which was to last until 1969. Throughout the period the banks were reluctant to accept trade unionism, and after 1921 they relied on in-house domestic staff associations to channel discussion on pay and conditions with staff. Despite NUBE's growth, the banks chose to recognize their staff associations for collective bargaining in the early 1950s when staff discontent over pay increased. NUBE's membership continued

187

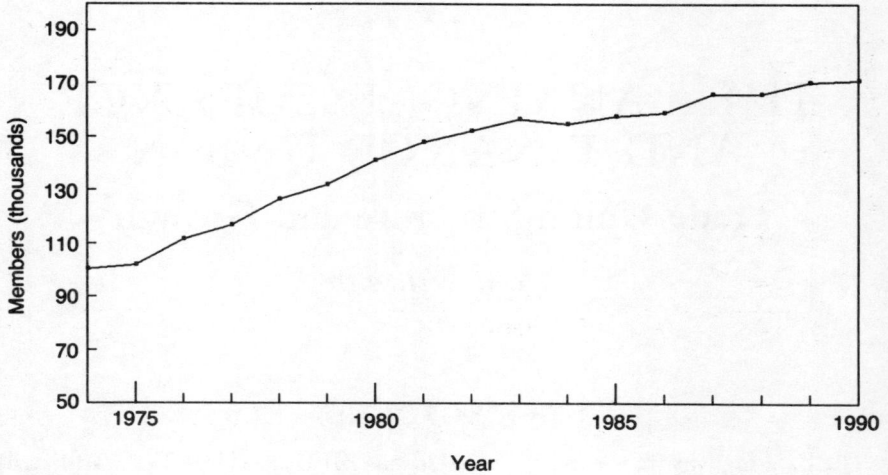

Figure 27.1 BIFU membership, 1974–90

to grow throughout the 1950s and 1960s since staff discontent over pay was a continuing problem, even souring relations between the banks and the staff associations. In 1967, the issues of pay and hours of work came to a head. NUBE began 'Action 67', an organizing campaign which added 30 per cent to its membership in the year. Unprecedentedly, it also mobilized strike action. The banks called their – reluctant – associations and NUBE to the bargaining table, and in 1968 negotiations began on pay and principal conditions of employment. Domestic negotiating rights were offered *jointly* to NUBE and the association in 1968–9, and by 1970 NUBE achieved bargaining rights for non-clerical as well as clerical workers.

However, the joint staff side covered very different organizations. The associations emphasized 'internalism', stressing the common interests of bank and employees, objecting to TUC membership and opposing strike activity. NUBE, by contrast, stressed the importance of national and regional organizations, independence from particular banks and a reliance on collective bargaining backed up by the threat of strike action. Frequent conflicts occurred between the staff representatives side on the negotiating machinery, but NUBE was generally outvoted by the combined associates since voting strength was based on membership numbers. Throughout the period since recognition, NUBE/BIFU was outnumbered by the combined staff associations. Eventually, in 1977, NUBE formally withdrew from the joint staff side in protest.

The failure to outgrow the associations was a substantial problem for NUBE. The associations were financially independent of their banks, but gained commission from the sale of insurance business which enabled them

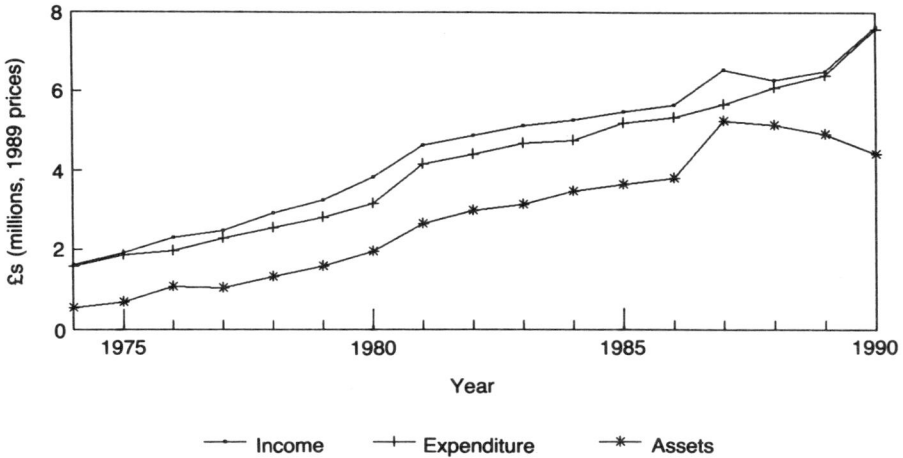

Figure 27.2 BIFU income, expenditure and assets

to charge low subscriptions. NUBE was to keep its own subscriptions low in order to compete, and had a precarious financial position as a consequence (Figure 27.2). It possessed few assets, and had little excess of income over expenditure. Because of bank hostility to union organization historically, it relied on full-time officials rather than office representatives, and its fixed costs were consequently high. Membership growth was an economic as well as political imperative.

DIVERSIFICATION

In the face of these problems, NUBE chose to diversify out of banking, in 1971, seeking members in building societies and insurance. It also sought to organize foreign banks in the City of London. It used the recently passed legislation to assist this process. The 1971 Industrial Relations Act (s. 45) allowed unions to apply to the Commission on Industrial Relations for recognition rights in establishments where the union had substantial membership but where collective bargaining did not already take place. Although the Act was repealed in 1974, this clause was re-enacted by the incoming Labour government as s. 11 of the 1975 Employment Protection Act, so for much of the period 1974–9 NUBE had the opportunity to use a statutory route to recognition.

However, membership actually *fell* from 1972 to 1975. Because it had chosen to register under the Industrial Relations Act, as had the clearing bank staff associations, NUBE was expelled from the TUC. It thus had two problems. On the one hand, it was open to competition from TUC unions who were no longer bound to respect NUBE's membership and bargaining

189

rights, and ASTMS took the opportunity to move into the retail banking area, taking over the Midland Bank Staff Association which NUBE had long sought to absorb. On the other, it was less differentiated from the associations as far as prospective members were concerned, no longer being part of the TUC, yet its subscriptions were higher. The result was net membership *loss* in the clearers, which was not offset by the relatively small gains made elsewhere.

The process of gaining members by recruitment outside the clearers was relatively costly, and although membership increased after 1975, the union's finances did not materially improve until 1978, when it began to pursue growth by merger in the insurance sector. Beginning with Guardian Royal Exchange Association in 1978, NUBE began to acquire associations by negotiating membership transfers rather than seeking members through costly organizing drives. NUBE expanded its membership in insurance from 1 per cent of the total in 1976 to 11.5 per cent in 1984. The transfers brought in subscription income and assets at a relatively low cost compared with that of organizing new areas. However, the price of success had included deterioration in its relationship with MSF (then ASTMS), which has a large insurance membership, and increasing competition for merger candidates by the TUC affiliates in the financial sector.

As a result of successful diversification, the proportion of the union employed in the English clearers has fallen sharply. NUBE was still a clearing bank union in 1972, with 73 per cent of members employed there, but BIFU in 1984 had only 48 per cent clearing bank membership.

CONSEQUENCES

The strategy of diversification has secured steady growth for the last fifteen years. The union is still relatively small compared to several of its TUC competitors, and has few assets in comparison with its larger competitors, so the generation of new subscription income is vital (Figure 27.2). Growth is also important for the union's status and political influence within the TUC; the general secretary has recently become a member of the TUC general council, following a rule change which automatically grants seats to unions over 100,000, on the basis of membership. However, growth has presented several problems. They are as follows.

The clearing bank staff associations

BIFU has wavered between the pursuit of mergers with the clearing bank staff associations on the one hand, and the pursuit of separate negotiations aiming at dissolution of the associations, on the other. Both would result in sole representation of staff by a single representative body, thus removing inter-union competition which BIFU argues, has undermined effective representation.

The expansion of membership outside the clearers makes it more difficult to negotiate a merger. The associations stress the distinctiveness of their own institutions and the importance of in-house organization. They fear loss of identity in a merger. The wider the span of BIFU membership, the more difficult the exercise of convincing them of the benefits of merger becomes. Since the clearers remain the biggest employment concentrations in the sector and the associations are still the larger body in retail banking, these mergers are crucial for BIFU's growth.

Separate negotiations on an industry-wide basis seem unlikely. In some banks, BIFU is out-competing the relevant association, and where there is no competition, it has done very well. But in Barclays and Natwest, the two biggest banks, it remains the minority union. In any event, industry-wide bargaining in retail banking has disappeared.

Competition

BIFU has grown outside the banking area primarily by absorbing staff associations in mergers ('transfer of engagements'). This had caused conflict between the union and MSF in the insurance sector, which MSF had previously regarded as its own. The two unions now compete to offer the best terms to likely staff associations, one consequence of which has been discontent among the union's own employees about the pay levels offered to staff association heads on merger. Another consequence has been the involvement of the TUC in membership disputes between the two affiliates.

Structure and democracy

Pressures have arisen over the accommodation of members in new sectors. Traditionally, BIFU was organized regionally, branches electing to area councils and thus to the executive committee. However, minorities in the union, such as in foreign banks, find their votes swamped by clearing bank members who still predominate in most areas. The union has created 'sections' based on institutions to cope with this; so, for example, there is a foreign banks section council with some independent, decision-making power (Figure 27.3). But the executive committee is still elected on a regional basis and is clearer dominated; it is the central decision-making body and controls finances and the right to call strikes.

The clearer membership will resist further 'sectionalization'. But there are two powerful pressures for its continued development. The first is that it makes it easier to attract staff associations outside the clearing banks into membership: staff in insurance and building societies do not want to be ruled by the clearing bank membership. The second is that the full-time officials of the union, who are appointed by the general secretary rather than elected by the membership are very much in favour of sections, since it

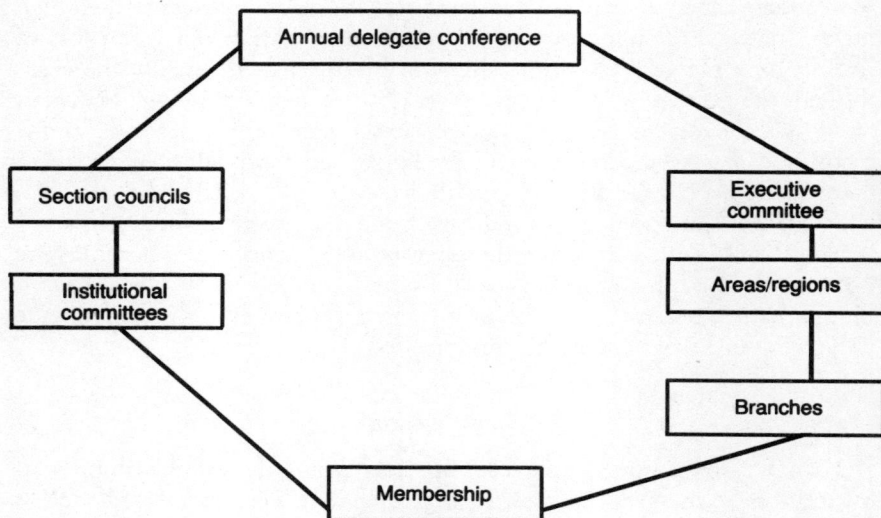

Figure 27.3 Organization and structure

organizes the union along the lines on which collective bargaining actually occurs. The major obstacle remains the current electoral system, which allows clearing bank membership to block change through their area councils and the annual delegate conference. In practice, some sections such as technical and services which control maintenance work in the bank computer centres are sufficiently powerful to go their own way.

Ownership and control

BIFU would probably have had to organize outside the clearing banks sooner or later in order to retain control over employment in a substantial proportion of the financial services market. Increased levels of competition, particularly between banks and building societies, would have required extension of the membership base to preserve bargaining power. But the present sectional structure does not map that of firm ownership. The clearers actually own most of the finance houses and a number of other employing institutions outside the clearing bank section. The union may be diversifying at the wrong time. In any event, mergers and reorganizations have been frequent in recent years, and structures of collective bargaining have also had to change. Deregulation of financial markets further complicated the ownership picture.

Technical change

The use of computer technology has affected BIFU in several ways. On the one hand it has led to the growth of computer and technical staff members. Such staff are highly unionized and BIFU has used the threat of strike action in computer centres as a way of levering the banks into better pay settlements. More recently, however, it has led to cutbacks in branch networks, increases in the numbers of part-time and female staff (which BIFU finds difficult to organize) and threats to jobs. Moreover, the distinctiveness of bank work is eroded when technical changes such as counter automation and point-of-sale terminals cloud the distinction between banking and, for example, retailing, where terms and conditions of employment are generally much poorer and union membership lower. There have been widespread job losses within the branch networks in recent years. The union's membership is good in 'new technology' areas, but the banks generally will not discuss their future plans for the application of technology. Much of the union's membership remains in the retail bank branch network; most banks are considering further rationalizations of branch structures and cutbacks in employment in such networks.

NOTE

1 This case was prepared by Dr Paul Willman of London Business School as the basis for class discussion rather than to illustrate effective or ineffective handling of an administrative situation.

QUESTIONS

1 What are the major immediate problems facing the general secretary of the union?
2 How should he reform the structure and organization of the union in the next five years?

28

TRADE UNIONS AND EUROPEAN PATTERN BARGAINING

Paul Teague

LMU is a large British-based trade union. It has a membership in excess of one million drawn from a range of industrial sectors. Reflecting the diverse nature of its membership, the union is organized more or less on confederal lines. Thus although an annual conference and an executive committee decides overall policy, the union has some nine separate industrial groups which have considerable autonomy in determining union policy for that industry. In addition to these industrial groups, the union has a strong regional structure which also has the scope to launch independent activities provided they do not conflict with the overall policy of the union. Of course the union has also got a strong central team providing research, education and bargaining support. Thus the union has a dense internal structure which is reflected with it having more full-time officials and staff than any other union in Britain.

Traditionally, like so many other British trade unions, the union had an anti-EC policy. This position was largely based on the view that economic prosperity could only be genuinely secured and the interests of workers advanced by *national* economic planning and intervention. Since the EC was seen as promoting open markets and competition as well as constraining the ability of individual member states to take independent action, it was an institution that needed to be opposed. Thus the union was against British entry into the EC and when Britain became a member it adopted the position that a future Labour government should withdraw the country from that entity. In line with this policy outlook, the union did not get actively involved in EC-related matters for most of the 1970s and 1980s. If it wanted to object to a proposed EC initiative it would lobby the government at Westminster in an effort to get it to block the initiative rather than get involved directly at Community level. It did participate in the various European trade-union bodies which were closely connected to the EC, but only symbolic importance was attached to these organizations. Thus the vast bulk of the union's activity was confined to domestic British concerns. The union was involved in international trade-union politics through various international trade secretariats and the umbrella world body for western trade unions, ICFTU. In addition, it did partake in international combine committees which unofficially organized different national trade unions employed by the same multinational. But these activities only represented a small fraction of the union's overall work and did not dent its national orientation to industrial and labour matters.

However from the late 1980s the union has gradually moved away from its long-standing anti-EC position. At first the motivation was purely political. As part of the root-and-branch efforts to remodel itself, the British Labour Party abandoned its anti-EC stance and became firm supporters of the Community. However, it was something of an Achilles' heel for its major financial backers – the trade unions – to remain hostile to European integration. Thus to remove this inconsistency many trade unions, including LMU, were put under pressure to soften their stance on the EC. In addition, Jacques Delors, the head of the European Commission along with other senior Community figures started announcing that the 1992 programme required a social dimension involving legislation on workers' rights and conditions. After a decade of Conservative governments in Britain during which the trade unions experienced a sharp decline in influence the prospects of the EC establishing some type of European plinth of workers' rights proved irresistibly attractive. But it would have been completely opportunistic and probably counter-productive for the union to support the idea of a social dimension to the 1992 programme whilst at the same time opposing British membership of the EC. Thus in 1988 the union abandoned its policy of opposition to the EC and declared that in future its energies would focus on building a workers' Europe.

At the outset, this pro-European conversion impinged little on the union's mainstream industrial and collective bargaining activities. These remained largely domestic concerns. But as the revival of European integration continued unabated with moves towards monetary union, increased commercial activity across the member states and so on, the union leadership began to realize that it was not enough to have a paper policy in support of the EC and a social dimension to the 1992 project. Rather they came to the view that only through the active and concerted efforts of trade unions would safeguards with regard to workers' rights be built into the new Europe. Thus LMU introduced a series of internal reorganizations which led to the streamlining of the research, international and education departments and the creation of a European department. This new team was given the responsibility of developing a European dimension to the union's mainly national activities.

Very quickly the new department started to launch initiatives with a strong pan-European flavour. A number of education courses were organized to give shop stewards more information and a better understanding of the likely political and economic changes resulting from the 1992 programme. With the help of EC funding, several of the regional offices started to make contact with trade-union organizations from other Community regions to exchange experiences on industrial restructuring and so on and to lay the basis for collaborative action. Perhaps the most interesting innovation involved the European department meeting with officials connected with a number of the union's national industrial groups to assess whether a European dimension could be developed to their collective bargaining activities. Several initiatives got off the ground from these people getting together.

One important scheme involved the European unit and the union's national officials covering the chemical industry deciding to try to reorientate, or at least add a new dimension to, the activities of the official European trade-union sector committee. Within the union, and indeed in other unions, this sector committee was seen as being too embroiled in extra-national institutions like the EC, OECD and ILO. As a result, the body was regarded as being too bureaucratic and reactive in character, simply responding to whatever initiative or agenda came out of these various institutions. LMU thought that the committee's institutional focus resulted in a lack of corporate-level trade-union action across Europe. It was precisely in this 'horizontal' arena that the union thought that more activity was required. Thus at a meeting of the sector committee, LMU with the help of other unions succeeded in getting a policy adopted which argued for greater corporate-level European trade-union action. Subsequently, a seminar was organized to discuss possible forms of European 'horizontal' collective bargaining in the chemical industry. At this gathering, the unanimous view was that any European trade-union strategies launched must be credible and have a realistic chance of succeeding. Excessive and unrealistic strategies were seen as being potentially counter-productive since they may cause trade unions to remain cocooned within national bargaining arrangements and reinforce the deep reluctance of managers in multinational companies to engage in any type of European employee-relations dialogue.

Thus the unions ruled out any form of European bargaining involving pay. Productivity and cost of living differences, divergent 'social wage' levels as well as uneven welfare and pension benefits were regarded as being too great across Europe to launch a concerted campaign for uniform pay rates. With the hardcore bargaining issue removed from the agenda, the discussion focused on subtler and more workable forms of collaborate trade-union action. From this discussion the seminar decided that the unions should adopt a two-pronged strategy. One strategy was to try to get established some formalized procedure within multinationals for managers and trade unions to exchange views on the company's investment and employment plans. In other words, the unions decided to push for the setting up of European Works Councils so much promoted by European level trade-union leaders and Commission officials. Secondly, the unions agreed informally to synchronize collective bargaining demands across national frontiers on specific topics. Through this strategy, unions employed by the same multinational would prioritize their collective-bargaining demands – other than pay – and simultaneously present them to the company. From this activity, it was hoped that broadly similar policies with regard to certain working conditions would be in place across Europe.

At the same time as attempting to redirect the activities of the official European trade-union sector committee, LMU officials had also been busy reactivating a number of dormant combine committees – unofficial bodies that organize trade union shop stewards in the same multinational. One of these committees was chosen to pioneer the implementation of the informal strategy of synchronizing collective bargaining demands. Several meetings of this committee were convened at which a host of formal agreements that were operable in separate plants of the multinational on issues such as equal opportunities, health and safety and the introduction of new technology were examined for comparability. After careful reflection, it was decided to target equal opportunities as the area for concerted action. Specifically, national unions selected those items in agreements operating in other countries which would enhance their own agreement and together they decided to push across Europe for the provision that a father could have a two-day leave of absence when a child was born over and above existing maternity leave provision. Not to trigger management opposition simply on the basis that it was a Euro-initiative, no publicity was attached to the plan.

The outcome of this initiative was generally satisfactory for the union. In 4 of the 5 plants concerned, the unions were able to get specific amendments made to existing equal opportunities policies. In 3 out of the 5 plants they were able to push through the special two-day leave provision for fathers. However, in 2 of these 3 cases the unions had to make some concessions. With regard to the two cases where the union demand failed, local management in one plant committed themselves to a review of the issue whereas in the other plant management flatly rejected the proposal. Overall the union was happy with the situation and almost immediately the combined committee agreed to target health and safety and working time arrangements as the next area for synchronized European collective bargaining.

For its part, management only realized after the agreements had been signed that the unions had launched a coordinated pan-European collective-bargaining initiative. Beyond being annoyed about being hoodwinked, management was divided on what its response should be to this development. The hardline response was that any subsequent efforts by the unions to synchronize collective bargaining issues should be met with strong resistance. The softline approach was that whilst the company should not get involved in pan-European bargaining, it should undermine this development by identifying the areas where more approximation could be made to employee-relations practices across Europe. After some deliberation the hardline approach has been adopted by the management. Unions were undeterred with this stance and remained committed to pursuing a synchronized collective-bargaining strategy. It is too early to communicate what happened next, but certainly the European dimension has taken hold inside this company.

Whilst the union's involvement in the synchronized collective-bargaining venture went relatively smoothly, its involvement in the scheme to get a European works council adopted proved more problematic. In pursuit of the policy objective of achieving formalized pan-European information and consultation procedures within multinational companies in the chemical industry, the unions identified three possible sympathetic organizations to be approached. In one instance the union received a firm rejection and in another a commitment to review the situation in two years' time. However, one organization gave the unions a positive response and signalled that they would be prepared to discuss the establishment of a European works council. Since the organization in question had a plant in the UK, LMU officials were invited to take part in the discussions on the issue. The company suggested that the model European works council constitution produced by the Commission as part of its European Company Statute should be the basis of the company's information and consultation body. Importantly, this constitution refers to employees and not trade unions and lays down that elections to the council should be by all employees and not simply by trade-union members. For the German, French and Dutch unions also involved in the discussions with the company, such issues caused no problems since they merely reflected their national experiences.

However, the matter was not so straightforward for LMU. In Britain arrangements such as information and consultation procedures, works councils, worker directors and the like have traditionally been treated with deep suspicion by trade unions. The prevalent view amongst the unions, and LMU is no exception, is that such bodies are anti-union manoeuvres designed to undermine the collective voice of employees. Domestically, where companies attempted to introduce a works council or something similar the consistent line adopted by LMU has been that trade-union representatives and not individual employees should sit on such bodies. Quietly, LMU had reservations about the European trade-union sector committee adopting as its number one priority the setting up of European works councils. But it believed that little would come of this initiative as it assumed that European management would fiercely oppose the establishment of any such body. However, with a European multinational prepared to set up a European works council, LMU was firmly put on the spot. To get around the problem of non-trade-union employees being the British representatives on the council, LMU proposed that in relation to the UK only, the representatives should be elected from the trade unions.

This suggestion was rejected by the company and also received little sympathy from the other trade unions. Thus LMU faced a dilemma: should it abandon a long-standing policy in favour of its new found European commitment or should it stay with tradition thereby placing strict limits to its European activity. In the end, the union decided to give way and accept that the work councils would be an arrangement to promote employee rather than trade-union information and consultation. Of course, union members were not necessarily excluded from being a representative. Indeed as it turned out 2 out of 3 representatives from Britain on the company's European works council were LMU members.

Inside the union, officials thought that this episode had far-reaching implications for its long-term European strategy. At the outset, the union thought that building a European dimension to national collective bargaining would strengthen and reinforce trade-union demands. What was not considered was that getting involved in pan-European industrial-relations activities may have 'spillback' consequences in terms of modifying and changing traditional national union perspectives and behaviour. In other words, whilst Europe may hold out certain opportunities it may also entail certain costs. Currently the union is debating how far it should be prepared to compromise traditional policies and practices to get involved in European industrial and labour affairs. No conclusion has been reached to this debate but since it would have been extremely unlikely for the union to have such a discussion five years ago, LMU appears to have taken large steps towards building a European dimension to its activities.

QUESTIONS

1 If you were a human resource manager what significance would you place on the development of synchronized collective-bargaining strategies by trade unions?
2 If you had to formulate a company response to such a development what would be your view?
3 Do you think that trade unions will be able to build an effective European dimension to their national industrial-relations activities?

INDEX

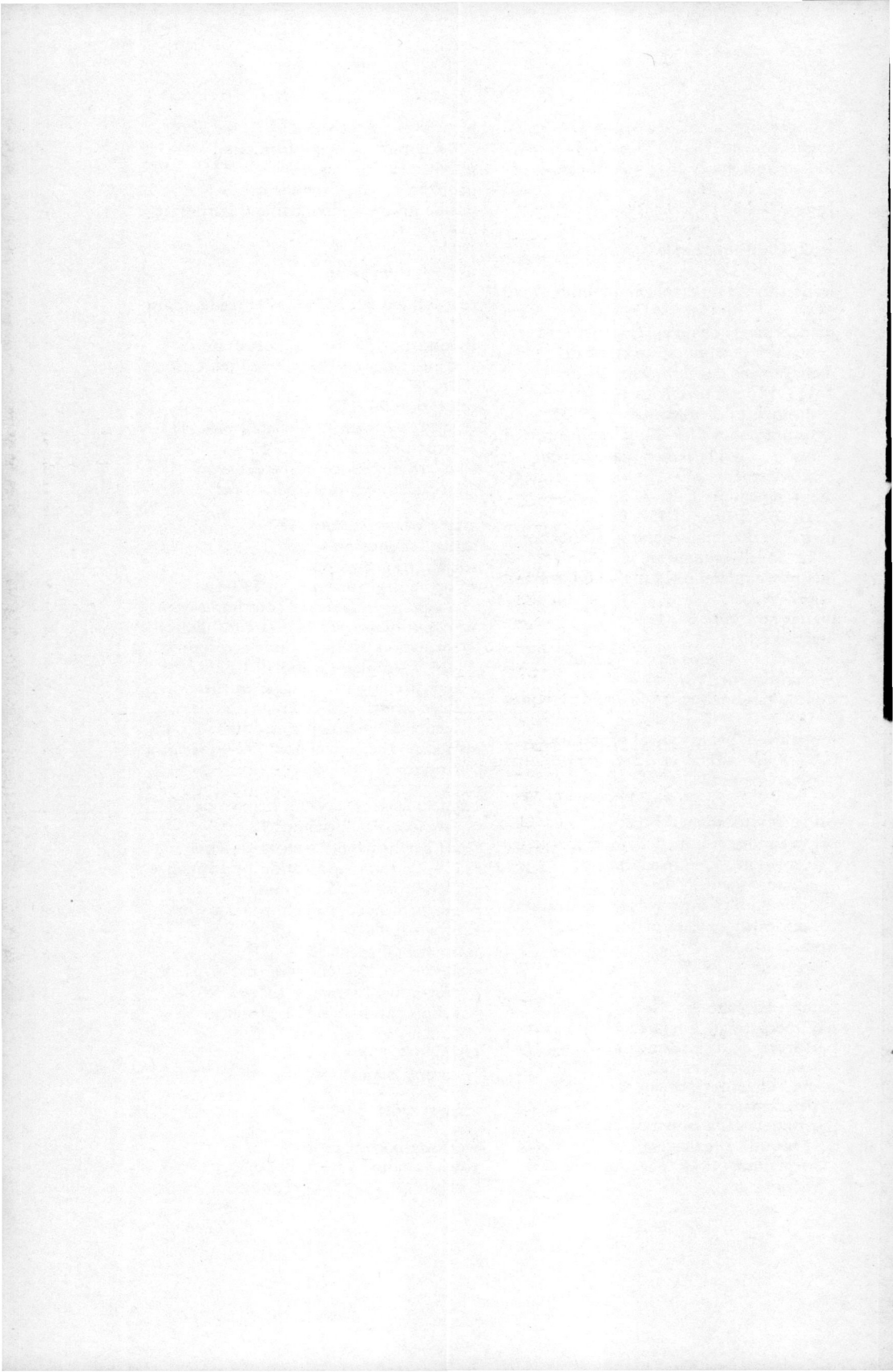